Perspectives

Debates in World Civilization

Edited by
Joseph T. Stuart

Perspectives: Debates in World Civilization

© 2019 Schlager Group Inc.

For Schlager Group:

Vice President, Editorial: Sarah Robertson
Vice President, Operations and Strategy: Benjamin Painter
Publisher: Neil Schlager

ISBN: 9781935306702

eISBN: 9781935306436

All rights reserved. No part of this book may be reproduced or utilized in any form or by any means, electronic or mechanical, including photocopying, recording, or downloading, without permission in writing from the publisher. For more information, contact:

Schlager Group Inc.
1111 W. Mockingbird Lane, Suite 735
Dallas, TX 75247
(888-416-5727)

Contents

About the Editor	p. vi
Acknowledgments	p. vii
Introduction	p. viii
Debate Rubric	p. x
Debate Activities	p. xi
Debate 1: "The Chinese Emperor resolves to close the Silk Road to Buddhist pilgrims."	p. 1
Debate 2: "Emperor Diocletian resolves that the Christians are a threat to the Roman Empire and should be persecuted."	p. 4
Debate 3: "King John should sign the Magna Carta."	p. 7
Debate 4: "Thomas More is guilty of treason."	p. 10
Debate 5: "The Second Continental Congress resolves that the American colonies should be independent."	p. 13
Debate 6: "Globalization is good."	p. 16
Noble Eightfold Path	p. 19
Rock and Pillar Edicts of Asoka	p. 32
Analects of Confucius	p. 45
Mandate of Heaven	p. 75
Canon of Filial Piety	p. 77
Han Feizi	p. 85
Huan Kuan: Discourses on Salt and Iron	p. 90
Han Yu: "Memorial on the Buddha's Bones"	p. 95
Twelve Tables of Roman Law	p. 98

Marcus Cato (the Elder): On Agriculture — p. 115

Marcus Aurelius: Meditations — p. 119

Pliny the Younger and Emperor Trajan: Letters on Treatment of the Christians — p. 130

Letter of the Smyrnaeans on the Martyrdom of Polycarp — p. 132

Epistle to Diognetus — p. 139

Laws Ending Persecution of Christians in the Roman Empire — p. 146

Julian the Apostate: Letter to Arsacius — p. 150

Pope Gelasius I: Letter to Emperor Anastasius — p. 152

Bernard Atton, Viscount of Carcassonne: Charter of Homage and Fealty — p. 153

Henry IV of Germany and Pope Gregory VII: Letter and Ban — p. 155

Magna Carta — p. 157

Martin Luther: Address to the Christian Nobility of the German Nation — p. 164

Act of Supremacy — p. 167

First Act of Succession — p. 168

Second Act of Succession — p. 175

Treasons Act — p. 177

The Trial of Thomas More — p. 180

James Otis: The Rights of the British Colonies Asserted and Proved — p. 191

Patrick Henry: Resolutions in Opposition to the Stamp Act — p. 194

John Dickinson: Letters from a Farmer in Pennsylvania — p. 196

Proclamation of 1763 — p. 203

Samuel Seabury (as "A. W. Farmer"): A View of the Controversy between Great Britain and Her Colonies — p. 208

Olive Branch Petition — p. 216

Proclamation by the King for Suppressing Rebellion and Sedition — p. 220

The Second Continental Congress Responds to King George III's Proclamation of Rebellion — p. 222

Nzinga Mbemba: Appeal to the King of Portugal — p. 225

Andrew Ure: The Philosophy of Manufactures — p. 228

Yukichi Fukuzawa: "Good-bye Asia" — p. 233

Yukichi Fukuzawa: Western Civilization as Our Goal — p. 236

Feng Guifen: "On the Adoption of Western Learning" — p. 239

Hu Shi: "Our Attitude toward Modern Western Civilization" — p. 240

Osama bin Laden: Declaration of Jihad against Americans — p. 241

About the Editor

Joseph T. Stuart (PhD, University of Edinburgh, 2010) is Associate Professor of History at the University of Mary. His research examines the relation between religion in culture during the Enlightenment and around the time of World War I. Stuart won the 2017-2018 Regents' Award for Teaching Faculty at the University of Mary. He teaches surveys of world history and Western civilization as well as advanced courses in his research areas: historiography, political religion, and the history of science and medicine. He recently co-produced the original theatrical production *North Dakota Voices from the Great War* and served on the North Dakota Department of Public Instruction Social Studies Content Standards Development Committee.

Acknowledgments

Han Feizi: Reprinted from *Sources of Chinese Tradition,* Volume 1, 2nd edition, edited by Wm. Theodore de Bary and Irene Bloom. Copyright 1999 Columbia University Press. Reprinted with permission of the publisher.

Huan Kuan: Discourses on Salt and Iron: Reprinted from Kuan Huan, *Discourses on Salt and Iron: A Debate on State Control of Commerce and Industry in Ancient China,* by Kuan Huan, translated by Esson McDowell Gale. Leyden: E. J. Brill Ltd., 1931. Reprinted with permission.

Han Yu: "Memorial on the Buddha's Bones": Reprinted from Victor Mair, Nancy Steinhardt, and Paul Goldin, eds., *Hawaii Reader in Traditional Chinese Culture,* University of Hawaii Press, 2004. Reprinted by permission of the publisher.

Yukichi Fukuzawa: Western Civilization as Our Goal: Reprinted from *An Outline of a Theory of Civilization,* by Yukichi Fukuzawa, translated by David A. Dilworth and G. Cameron Hurst III. Copyright 2009 Columbia University Press. Reprinted with permission of Columbia University Press.

Feng Guifen: "On the Adoption of Western Learning": Reprinted with permission from *Changing China: Readings in the History of China from the Opium War to the Present,* by J. Mason Gentzler. New York: Praeger Publishers, 1977.

Hu Shi: "Our Attitude toward Modern Western Civilization": Reprinted from *Sources of Chinese Tradition,* Vol. 2, by Wm. Theodore de Bary and Richard Lufrano. Copyright 2000 Columbia University Press. Reprinted with permission from the publisher.

Osama bin Laden: Declaration of Jihad against Americans: Reprinted from *Messages to the World,* by Osama bin Laden. Verso, pp. 23–30. Reprinted by permission of the publisher.

Introduction

The general goal of these debates is to create an entry point for students into the interpretation and application of historical material. Talking with former students over the years, I have found that these events are usually the most memorable part of the class. They are high energy and fun, with students preparing research for presentation while acting (and sometimes dressing, if they want to!) in historical character. These debates are imaginary in that they never actually took place, although they are based on real historical topics and primary sources. Students pretend they are characters who lived during the time of the topic in question. Students may not use evidence that would not have been known to their characters in the debate. They may use any information that would have been reasonably available to their characters. Each student gives a prepared, two-minute opening statement, after which they participate in a cross-examination period. This is generally the most creative and entertaining part of the debate. At the end, each team concludes its argument with a two-minute closing statement.

I stage three debates per semester during class periods—enough for all students to participate on one team, but not so many as to interfere unduly with lecture time. I announce the debates at the beginning of the semester but do not talk much about them until within two weeks or so of debate #1. Then I send around a sign-up sheet: everyone in the class must choose to take either a positive or negative position in a debate. The "positive" team argues in favor of the proposition, the "negative" team against. In a class of 35, this makes for around 5 to 6 students per team. This means that only 10 to 12 students of the 35 will actually debate at any one time. Two tables face each other in front of the class, and there the two teams sit and make their cases.

The rest of the class serves as the audience and the judge of which team wins. I do not decide the winner. I simply moderate and keep notes for grading during the debate. After the event, the teams and I leave the room. The rest of the class informally discusses who won the debate—which team creatively engaged with the evidence and worked together best to stay in character. While waiting outside the classroom, the participants and I debrief and discuss how we feel the debate went overall. After these deliberations, the participants are called back into the classroom and take their seats. Two designated students then stand up before the debaters and talk about what both teams did well before announcing the winner. Each member of the winning team receives fifty extra bonus points on their last quiz.

The key to a solid debate is to motivate students to work hard both individually and collectively as a team. The bonus points serve as motivation for the entire team; as for the individual student, I grade each participant for oral and written performance.

Lectures start to introduce material for the debate about two weeks in advance. Students learn about feudalism, church-state relations, and medieval culture before they debate the Magna Carta, for example. I meet with each team right after class during the week before the event and go over the rules and expectations for the coming debate. At that time, each team chooses a team leader whose responsibility is simply to organize communication between all members, introduce the team members during the debate, and deliver two-minute opening and closing statements. I encourage students to think through the best counterarguments to their position and prepare extra material in case they need it. I also encourage them to bring printouts of relevant primary sources to the debate, to take notes, and to work together during the debate. Each student must dress semi-formally or in character.

As moderator, I rigorously enforce time for each student during opening and closing statements. I may let the cross-examination section of the debate run long if it is going well and clearly generating interest in the rest of the class. If cross-examination is not going well, I may insert myself by asking a question to try to jump-start interaction between the teams. I am careful, however, to avoid giving any indication of which team I favor during the debate.

Organizing these debates and integrating them into the syllabus takes some effort on the part of the instructor, but it is well worth it. After the students see one debate, they know what to expect for the second and third, so these usually go more smoothly.

Debates have proven to be among the most successful tools in my experience as a teacher to encourage students to work with primary sources. By uniting the art and science of history, debates have worked so well for me that once we even staged a public debate so the rest of the university could enjoy the fruits of our labors! I encourage you to try them. Please contact me if I can be of any assistance in getting started with student debates, or to make any suggestions for improving the ones I have provided. (jtstuart@umary.edu)

Joseph T. Stuart, PhD

Debate Rubric

Procedure:　　　　　　　　　　　　　　　　　　　　　　Time allotted:

Opening statements of main arguments　　　　　　　　　　2 mins./student

Cross-examination and questions from audience　　　　　　10 mins. (total)

Closing remarks　　　　　　　　　　　　　　　　　　　　2 mins./team

Classroom discussion to decide winner　　　　　　　　　　10 mins.

Directions:

Each team member prepares a written essay defending the team's position with footnotes for use as an opening statement and during cross-examination and/or closing remarks. Try to anticipate counterarguments and prepare some research to refute them. What evidence from primary sources and historical events do you have to support your position? Each debater's grade depends on the written essay and presentation performance during the debate; by demonstrating knowledge of the sources, creativity, and reasoning, a student can obtain an excellent grade even if the team as a whole loses.

The rest of the class pays close attention to the debate, takes notes to turn into a debate summary, and decides which team wins the debate based on who had the best evidence and historical thinking.

Debate Activities

Post-debate Questions

1. After debating the topic, where do you stand on the issue?

2. What arguments were effective and what arguments were not effective?

3. Did components of the other team's argument change your mind? Explain.

4. Were there components of your team's argument that you disagreed with? Explain.

5. What other questions arose as you debated the topic?

6. Why are primary sources important to debating the issue?

7. If this problem arose today, how might the issues and the outcome be different?

Essay Topic

Develop your own perspective on the problem. Strengthen your argument with sources from the debate as well as sources you discover from additional research.

Post-debate Activity

Choose one of the protagonists from the debate and write a journal entry from his or her perspective. How do you feel about the issue? What circumstances led to the problem? How will the outcome affect you?

Debate 1: "The Chinese Emperor resolves to close the Silk Road to Buddhist pilgrims."

This imaginary debate takes place in the Chinese capital in front of Emperor Taizong of Tang of the Tang Dynasty. It is an official deliberation with representatives from different groups present to make their case. This debate allows for creativity because it links India, China, and the rising Islamic civilization by way of the Silk Road. (Muslim armies reached Central Asia by 642.) In 645 CE, Xuanzang, the famous Chinese Buddhist pilgrim and scholar who brought back Buddhist documents from India to China along the Silk Road, returned to his homeland. He was welcomed by many, but this debate imagines a controversy over Buddhist influence arising with his return. Should the Silk Road remain open to people like him? What effects does Buddhism have within China? Can it be reconciled with Chinese identity?

This debate anticipates the Great Buddhist Persecution of 845, and reviewing documents connected to that era, such as the "Memorial on the Buddha's Bones," may help students think through why some may have opposed Buddhism in China. Students may not quote any sources from later than 645 in the debate itself.

Place: Chang'an, capital of the Tang Dynasty

Time: 645 CE

Documents:

- Noble Eightfold Path (ca. 528 BCE)

- Rock and Pillar Edicts of Asoka (257–240 BCE)

- Analects of Confucius (ca. 479–249 BCE)

- Mandate of Heaven (ca. 475–221 BCE)

- Canon of Filial Piety (ca. 300–239 BCE)

Positive Team:

Yes, the Chinese Emperor should close the Silk Road to Buddhist pilgrims.

Possible Reasons:

- Buddhism is a threat to the Chinese state because it is foreign

- Buddhism undermines filial piety

- Buddhism's morality is irrelevtant to strong government

- Buddhism's monasteries lower tax revenue

- The Silk Road introduces foreign and dangerous influences into China

- The Silk Road is too dangerous for Buddhists to travel due to increasing numbers of Islamic warriors in the area

Possible Protagonists:

- Legalists

- Confucians

- Ex-monk

- Tax collector worried about the economic effects of Buddhist monasteries

- a Muslim representative

Negative Team:

No, the Chinese Emperor should not close the Silk Road to Buddhist pilgrims.

Possible Reasons:

• Buddhism is not a threat to the Chinese state because it shares common ideas with Confucianism

• Buddhism inspires great leaders like Asoka

• Buddhism teaches personal discipline

• The Silk Road introduces new and helpful ideas into China

Possible Protagonists:

• Confucians

• Buddhist monks

• Buddhist nuns

• Loyal monastery serfs

• Local merchants selling monastery goods

• Xuanzang, a Chinese pilgrim to India via the Silk Road

Debate 2: "Emperor Diocletian resolves that the Christians are a threat to the Roman Empire and should be persecuted."

When Christianity first arose within the Roman Empire, it appeared to be a minor annoyance. Soon after its founding, however, it had spread so quickly that by the late third century, emperors had begun to worry about its overall effects upon Roman civilization. Desiring to restore Rome to its former glory, Emperors Diocletian, Maximian, Galerius, and Constantius issued edicts taking away Christians' legal rights and demanding they comply with traditional religious practices. This imaginary debate takes place at the beginning of the Great Persecution, the first to target the entire Roman Empire.

Place: The Roman Senate, Rome

Date: 303 CE

Documents:

- Twelve Tables of Roman Law (451 BCE)

- Marcus Cato (the Elder): On Agriculture (ca. 160 BCE)

- Marcus Aurelius: Meditations (ca. 170–180 CE)

- Pliny the Younger and Emperor Trajan: Letters on Treatment of the Christians (112 CE)

- Letter of the Smyrnaeans on the Martyrdom of Polycarp (156 CE)

- Epistle to Diognetus (ca. 200 CE)

- Students may use ideas from the following documents but may not cite them directly in the debate, as their inclusion would be anachronistic: Laws Ending Persecution of Christians in the Roman Empire (311 and 313 CE); Julian the Apostate: Letter to Arsacius (ca. 362 CE)

Positive Team:

Yes, the Christians are a threat to the Roman Empire and should be persecuted.

Possible Reasons:

• Christianity is a private cult that threatens the Roman way of life because it undermines ritual and the Pontifex Maximus

• Christians are atheists because they refuse to worship the emperor

• The Oracle at Delphi commands the persecution

• Christianity undermines local economies and the military

• Christians reject public festivals, refuse to take part in the imperial cult, avoid public office, and publicly criticize ancient traditions

• Christianity tears families apart

• Christianity is a frivolous novelty

Possible Protagonists:

• Senators

• Roman priests

• Shop owners near the depopulating temples

• Military commanders

• Unhappy parents of a daughter who converted to Christianity

Negative Team:

No, the Christians are not a threat to the Roman Empire and should not be persecuted.

Possible Protagonists:

- Senators

- Christian soldiers, women, bishops, and intellectuals

- Poor pagans helped by Christian health care and welfare

Possible Reasons:

- Christianity teaches profound respect for political authority

- Christians swear oaths not to commit sin or hurt anyone

- Christians take care of the sick and poor

- General persecution is unwise because it can corrupt the justice system as people try to accuse their enemies of being Christian

- Christianity is true. Examples include martyrs such as Polycarp

- Christianity is far older than the Romans themselves

- Christianity uplifts the dignity of women and children

- Christianity strengthens the Roman army

Debate 3: "King John should sign the Magna Carta."

The Middle Ages witnessed titanic struggles between church and state to determine the proper limits of ecclesiastical and political authority. Ecclesiastics and kings asserted their rights against the other, and the ideas and policies that emerged from these struggles helped lay the basis for limited government, individual rights, and freedom of religion in England. These "rights of Englishmen" later inspired the American Revolution and the U.S. Constitution.

The medieval English people could not have known this future. Their leaders faced the question of whether the English king should sign away some of his claims to power, risking social and political chaos. While we know that King John was forced to do this, people at the time still had to think through the implications. This imaginary debate will help students understand the issues at stake.

Place: Runnymede, England

Date: 1215 CE

Documents:

- Pope Gelasius I: Letter to Emperor Anastasius (494 CE)

- Bernard Atton, Viscount of Carcassonne: Charter of Homage and Fealty (1110 CE)

- Henry IV of Germany and Pope Gregory VII: Letter and Ban (1076 CE)

- Magna Carta (1215 CE)

Positive Team:

King John should sign the Magna Carta.

Possible Reasons:

- King John holds limited power from God through natural law and the freemen of the realm (not from the pope or God directly)

- King John is a tyrant and broke the feudal oath of fealty with his barons

- King John inhibits business by taxation without representation

- King John infringes on the freedom of the Church and on the rights of freemen

Possible Protagonists:

- Stephen Langton, Archbishop of Canterbury (a chief negotiator, inspired by the earlier example of resistance to an English king by St. Thomas Becket)

- Robert Fitzwalter (a leader of the opposition to King John)

- Lord Mayor of the City of London

- English Baron angry at King John's actions

- Isabella, Countess of Gloucester (ex-wife of King John)

- Freeman 1

- English Lord angry at King John's actions

Negative Team:

King John should not sign the Magna Carta.

Possible Reasons:

- John is a good king who holds full power directly from God through the pope

- The barons have sworn fealty to King John

- Chaos threatens the realm and the rebellious barons are only concerned about their selfish interests

- The English Archbishop of Canterbury is trying to assert himself over the English state

- The papacy threatens to nullify the Magna Carta anyway because it is an illegal rupture of feudal relationships

Possible Protagonists:

- King John (in a feudal alliance with the papacy)

- William Marshall (Earl of Pembroke, King John's counsellor, a chief negotiator of the charter, and respected by Langton)

- Freeman 2

- Foreign Representative

- English Baron (supporter of King John)

- Papal Lawyer

- English general (supporter of King John's French campaigns)

Debate 4: "Thomas More is guilty of treason."

The Reformation in England was not an upwelling of popular social discontent, but was rather the consequence of top-down political action. King Henry VIII placed the English church under his authority, and as its supreme head, he required the country's elites to acknowledge his position with an oath. This created a crisis of conscience for Thomas More, whose refusal to comply with Henry's wishes prompted a crisis that ultimately served to centralize the power of the English monarchy as the modern state took shape.

Place: Westminster Hall, London

Time: July 1, 1535

Documents:

- Pope Gelasius I: Letter to Emperor Anastasius (494)

- Magna Carta (1215)

- Martin Luther: Address to the Christian Nobility of the German Nation (1520)

- Act of Supremacy (1534)

- First Act of Succession (1534)

- Second Act of Succession (1534)

- Treasons Act (1534)

- Trial of Thomas More (1535)

Positive Team:

Yes, Thomas More is guilty of treason.

Possible Reasons:

• Refusal of the Act of Succession (1533)

• Refusal to take the Oath of Supremacy

• Malicious conspiracy with Bishop Fisher

• Denial under examination of Parliament's authority to make King Henry VIII head of the Church of England

Possible Protagonists:

• King Henry VIII

• Thomas Cromwell, who is a lawyer, Protestant, and the king's chief minister

• Sir John Baldwin, Lord Chief Justice

• Richard Rich, lawyer and acquaintance of Thomas More since boyhood

• Thomas Audley, Lord Chancellor

• Thomas Boleyn, politician and father of Anne Boleyn

• Thomas Howard, Duke of Norfolk, politician and uncle of Anne Boleyn

Negative Team:

No, Thomas More is not guilty of treason.

Possible Reasons:

- Silence suggests consent

- Limited power of Parliament

- Untrustworthy testimony of Richard Rich

- Magna Carta

- Consensus of Christendom on the authority of the papacy to govern the Church

Possible Protagonists:

- Thomas More

- Margaret More, Thomas More's daughter

- William Roper, a lawyer married to Margaret More

- Barristers (lawyers) of the defense

Debate 5: "The Second Continental Congress resolves that the American colonies should be independent."

After the battles of Lexington and Concord in April 1775, tension mounted between the American colonies and England. Moderates such as John Dickinson argued the king would find a way to mediate between the two sides, but the Proclamation by the King for Suppressing Rebellion in August of the same year weakened that position. This imaginary debate over independence takes place in December, before Thomas Paine's *Common Sense,* which entirely shifted the terms of debate, appeared in January 1776. This December timing of the debate helps students appreciate all the arguments at play.

Place: Independence Hall, Philadelphia

Date: December 6, 1775

Documents:

- James Otis: The Rights of the British Colonies Asserted and Proved (1764)

- Patrick Henry: Resolutions in Opposition to the Stamp Act (1765)

- John Dickinson: Letters from a Farmer in Pennsylvania (1767–1768)

- Proclamation of 1763

- Samuel Seabury (as "A.W. Farmer"): A View of the Controversy between Great Britain and Her Colonies (1774)

- Olive Branch Petition (1775)

- Proclamation by the King for Suppressing Rebellion and Sedition (1775)

- The Second Continental Congress Responds to King George III's Proclamation of Rebellion (December 6, 1775)

Positive Team:

Yes, the American colonies should be independent.

Possible Reasons:

- No taxation without representation

- The tyranny of Parliament and the king

- Unjust laws, such as the Intolerable Acts

- Desire for land

- British freedom

- Presence of British troops

- Religious freedom and fear of Quebec Act

Possible Protagonists:

- Samuel Adams, a political writer who founded the Sons Of Liberty in Boston

- Patrick Henry of Virginia

- James Otis, lawyer from Massachusetts

- John Pownall, a British politician who wrote the Proclamation of 1763 but who supported the American cause up until the Revolution began

- Abigail Adams of Massachusetts

- John Dickinson, writer from Pennsylvania

- Lockeian theorist

Negative Team:

No, the American colonies should not be independent.

Possible Reasons:

- America's British culture

- Virtual representation

- The common good of the Empire as preserved in the Proclamation of 1763

- Protection of Americans against foreign enemies, Native American uprisings, and domestic terrorism by the Sons of Liberty and other groups

- The tyranny and illegality of the Continental Congress

- The legal regulation of American trade

Possible Protagonists:

- King George III (representatives)

- Representatives of Parliament

- Samuel Seabury, loyalist Episcopalian bishop living in New York

- General William Howe, Commander in Chief of British forces

- Flora MacDonald, a woman loyal to the king

Debate 6: "Globalization is good."

This debate allows for much creativity on the part of students. The instructor chooses a region or a continent (other than North America) in which the debate will take place. Each team then decides what country to represent from that region or continent. Teams will want to choose countries that will best support their position. Each team must reveal their chosen country to the other team for the sake of enabling them to prepare their counter arguments.

Since modern globalization started with Columbus, students are free to use any source from that time up to present. Several options are suggested below. Students will also find statistics and additional primary sources from the countries they choose to represent. Imagine the debate taking place virtually with representatives located in their countries communicating by online video conferencing with the audience in class.

Place: Chosen by the students within the region or continent determined by the teacher

Date: The present

Documents:

- Nzinga Mbemba: Appeal to the King of Portugal (1526)

- Andrew Ure: The Philosophy of Manufactures (1835)

- Yukichi Fukuzawa: Western Civilization as Our Goal (1875)

- Yukichi Fukuzawa: "Good-bye Asia" (1885)

- Feng Guifen: "On the Adoption of Western Learning" (ca. 1850)

- Hu Shi: "Our Attitude toward Modern Western Civilization" (1926)

- Osama bin Laden: Declaration of Jihad against Americans (1996)

- Other sources from chosen countries

Positive Team:

Yes, globalization is good.

Possible Reasons:

- Economic opportunity

- New ideas versus "old fashioned" ways of life

- Bicultural identities

- Cool technologies and global brands

- Spread of human rights

Possible Protagonists:

- Young person excited about global brands and new economic opportunities in factories and cities

- Local leader seeking allies to help protect human rights

- Retailer selling lots of new technologies and global brands

- University professor pushing new educational opportunities for people

- Business executive seeking global partnership

Negative Team:

No, globalization is not good.

Possible Reasons:

- Imperialism

- Economic exploitation

- Pollution

- Loss of cultural identity

- Secularism and demographic crisis

- Imposition of foreign ideas and morality

Possible Protagonists:

- Local business owner put out of business by humanitarian aid drop-offs

- Exploited worker in factory

- Family suffering from industrial water pollution and consumer debt

- Local leader in traditional clothing concerned about loss of cultural identity

- Young person with identity confusion and hatred of foreign powers

- Parent concerned about effects of global media

Noble Eightfold Path

ca. 528 BCE

Document Text

It is the Noble Eightfold Path, the way that leads to the extinction of suffering, namely:

1. Right Understanding.

2. Right Mindedness, which together are Wisdom.

3. Right Speech.

4. Right Action.

5. Right Living, which together are Morality.

6. Right Effort.

7. Right Attentiveness.

8. Right Concentration, which together are Concentration.

This is the Middle Path which the Perfect One has found out, which makes one both to see and to know, which leads to peace, to discernment, to enlightenment, to Nirvana. Free from pain and torture is this path, free from groaning and suffering; it is the perfect path. Truly, like this path there is no other path to the purity of insight. If you follow this path, you will put an end to suffering. But each one has to struggle for himself, the Perfect Ones have only pointed out the way. Give ear then, for the Immortal is found. I reveal, I set forth the Truth. As I reveal it to you, so act! And that supreme goal of the holy life, for the sake of which, sons of good families rightly go forth from home to the homeless state: this you will, in no long time, in this very life, make known to yourself, realize, and make your own.

First Step: Right Understanding

WHAT, now, is Right Understanding? It is understanding the Four Truths. To understand suffering; to understand the origin of suffering; to understand the extinction of suffering; to understand the path that leads to the extinction of suffering: This is called

Right Understanding Or, when the noble disciple understands what is karmically wholesome, and the root of wholesome karma; what is karmically unwholesome, and the root of unwholesome karma, then he has Right Understanding. ["Karmically unwholesome" is every volitional act of body, speech, or mind which is rooted in greed, hatred, or delusion, and produces evil and painful results in this or any future form of existence.] What, now, is "karmically unwholesome"? In Bodily Action it is destruction of living beings; stealing; and unlawful sexual intercourse. In Verbal Action it is lying; tale-bearing; harsh language; and frivolous talk. In Mental Action it is covetousness; ill-will; and wrong views.

And what is the root of unwholesome karma? Greed is a root of unwholesome karma; Anger is a root of unwholesome karma; Delusion is a root of unwholesome karma. [The state of greed, as well as that of anger, is always accompanied by delusion; and delusion, ignorance, is the primary root of all evil.] Therefore, I say, these demeritorious actions are of three kinds: either due to greed, or due to anger, or due to delusion. What, now, is "karmically wholesome"? In Bodily Action it is to abstain from killing; to abstain from stealing; and to abstain from unlawful sexual intercourse. In Verbal Action it is to abstain from lying; to abstain from tale-bearing; to abstain from harsh language; and to abstain from frivolous talk. In Mental Action it is absence of covetousness; absence of ill-will; and right understanding. And what is the root of wholesome karma? Absence of greed (unselfishness) is a root of wholesome karma; absence of anger (benevolence) is a root of wholesome karma; absence of delusion (wisdom) is a root of wholesome karma. Or, when one understands that corporeality, feeling, perception, mental formation, and consciousness, are transient [subject to suffering, and without an Ego], also in that case one possesses Right Understanding....

The Two Understandings

Therefore, I say, Right Understanding is of two kinds:

1. The view that alms and offerings are not useless; that there is fruit and result, both of good and bad actions; that there are such things as this life, and the next life; that father and mother as spontaneously born beings (in the heavenly worlds) are no mere words; that there are monks and priests who are spotless and perfect, who can explain this life and the next life, which they themselves have understood: this is called the "Mundane Right Understanding," which yields worldly fruits, and brings good results.

2. But whatsoever there is of wisdom, of penetration, of right understanding, conjoined with the Path—the mind being turned away from the world, and conjoined with the path, the holy path being turned away from the world, and conjoined with the path, the holy path being pursued;—this is called the "Ultramundane Right Understanding," which is not of the world, but is ultramundane, and conjoined with the Path. [Thus, there are two kinds of the Eightfold Path: the "mundane," practiced by the "worldling"; and the "ultramundane," practiced by the "Noble Ones."] Now, in under-

standing wrong understanding as wrong, and right understanding as right, one practices Right Understanding [1st step]; and in making efforts to overcome wrong understanding, and to arouse right understanding, one practices. Right Effort [6th step]; and in overcoming wrong understanding with attentive mind, and dwelling with attentive mind in the possession of right understanding, one practices Right-Attentiveness [7th step]. Hence, there are three things that accompany and follow upon right understanding, namely: right understanding, right effort, and right attentiveness....

Karma: Rebirth—Producing and Barren

Verily, because beings, obstructed by Delusion, and ensnared by Craving, now here now there seek ever fresh delight, therefore such action comes to ever fresh Rebirth. And the action that is done out of greed, anger and delusion, that springs from them, has its source and origin there: this action ripens wherever one is reborn; and wherever this action ripens, there one experiences the fruits of this action, be it in this life, or the next life, or in some future life. However, through the fading away of delusion through the arising of wisdom, through the extinction of craving, no future rebirth takes place again For the actions, which are not done out of greed, anger and delusion, which have not sprung from them, which have not their source and origin there—such actions are, through the absence of greed, anger and delusion, abandoned, rooted out, like a palm-tree torn out of the soil, destroyed, and not liable to spring up again.

In this respect one may rightly say of me: that I teach annihilation, that I propound my doctrine for the purpose of annihilation, and that I herein train my disciples; for, certainly, I do teach annihilation—the annihilation, namely, of greed, anger and delusion, as well as of the manifold evil and unwholesome things. ["Dependent Origination" is the teaching of the strict conformity to law of everything that happens, whether in the realm of the physical, or the psychical. It shows how the totality of phenomena, physical and mental, the entire phenomenal world that depends wholly upon the six senses, together with all its suffering—and this is the vital point of the teaching is not the mere play of blind chance, but has an existence that is dependent upon conditions; and that, precisely with the removal of these conditions, those things that have arisen in dependence upon them—thus also all suffering—must perforce disappear and cease to be.]

Second Step: Right Mindedness

WHAT, now, is Right Mindedness? It is thoughts free from lust; thoughts free from ill-will; thoughts free from cruelty. This is called right mindedness. Now, Right Mindedness, let me tell you, is of two kinds: 1. Thoughts free from lust, from ill-will, and from cruelty:—this is called the "Mundane Right Mindedness," which yields worldly fruits and brings good results. 2. But, whatsoever there is of thinking, considering, reasoning, thought, ratiocination, application—the mind being holy, being turned away from the world, and conjoined with the path, the holy path being pursued—: these "Verbal Operations" of the mind are called the "Ultramundane Right Mindedness" which is not of the world, but is ultramundane, and conjoined with the paths.

Now, in understanding wrong-mindedness as wrong, and right-mindedness as right, one practices Right Understanding [1st step]; and in making efforts to overcome evil-mindedness, and to arouse right-mindedness, one practices Right Effort [6th step]; and in overcoming evil-mindedness with attentive mind, and dwelling with attentive mind in possession of right-mindedness, one practices Right Attentiveness [7th step]. Hence, there are three things that accompany and follow upon right-mindedness, namely: right understanding, right effort, and right attentiveness.

Third Step: Right Speech

WHAT, now, is Right Speech? It is abstaining from lying; abstaining from tale-bearing; abstaining from harsh language; abstaining from vain talk. There, someone avoids lying, and abstains from it. He speaks the truth, is devoted to the truth, reliable, worthy of confidence, is not a deceiver of men. Being at a meeting, or amongst people, or in the midst of his relatives, or in a society, or in the king's court, and called upon and asked as witness, to tell what he knows, he answers, if he knows nothing: "I know nothing"; and if he knows, he answers: "I know"; if he has seen nothing, he answers: "I have seen nothing," and if he has seen, he answers: "I have seen." Thus, he never knowingly speaks a lie, neither for the sake of his own advantage, nor for the sake of another person's advantage, nor for the sake of any advantage whatsoever. He avoids tale-bearing, and abstains from it. What he has heard here, he does not repeat there, so as to cause dissension there; and what he heard there, he does not repeat here, so as to cause dissension here. Thus he unites those that are divided; and those that are united, he encourages. Concord gladdens him, he delights and rejoices in concord, and it is concord that he spreads by his words. He avoids harsh language, and abstains from it. He speaks such words as are gentle, soothing to the ear, loving, going to the heart, courteous and dear, and agreeable to many.

… He avoids vain talk, and abstains from it. He speaks at the right time, in accordance with facts, speaks what is useful, speaks about the law and the discipline; his speech is like a treasure, at the right moment accompanied by arguments, moderate and full of sense. This is called right speech.

Now, right speech, let me tell you, is of two kinds: 1. Abstaining from lying, from tale-bearing, from harsh language, and from vain talk; this is called the "Mundane Right Speech," which yields worldly fruits and brings good results. 2. But the abhorrence of the practice of this four-fold wrong speech, the abstaining, withholding, refraining therefrom—the mind being holy, being turned away from the world, and conjoined with the path, the holy path being pursued—: this is called the "Ultramundane Right Speech," which is not of the world, but is ultramundane, and conjoined with the paths. Now, in understanding wrong speech as wrong, and right speech aright, one practices Right Understanding [1st step]; and in making efforts to overcome evil speech and to arouse right speech, one practices Right Effort [6th step]; and in overcoming wrong speech with attentive mind, and dwelling with attentive mind in possession of right speech, one practices Right Attentiveness [7th step]. Hence, there are three things that accompany and follow upon right attentiveness.

Fourth Step: Right Action

WHAT, now, is Right Action? It is abstaining from killing; abstaining from stealing; abstaining from unlawful sexual intercourse. There, someone avoids the killing of living beings, and abstains from it. Without stick or sword, conscientious, full of sympathy, he is anxious for the welfare of all living beings. He avoids stealing, and abstains from it; what another person possesses of goods and chattels in the village or in the wood, that he does not take away with thievish intent. He avoids unlawful sexual intercourse, and abstains from it. He has no intercourse with such persons as are still under the protection of father, mother, brother, sister or relatives, nor with married women, nor female convicts, nor, lastly, with betrothed girls. This is called Right Action.

Now, Right Action, let me tell you, is of two kinds: 1. Abstaining from killing, from stealing, and from unlawful sexual intercourse—this is called the "Mundane Right Action, which yields worldly fruits and brings good results. But the abhorrence of the practice of this three-fold wrong action, the abstaining, withholding, refraining therefrom—the mind being holy, being turned away from the world, and conjoined with the path, the holy path being pursued—: this is called the "Ultramundane Right Action," which is not of the world, but is ultramundane, and conjoined with the paths. Now, in understanding wrong action as wrong, and right action as right, one practices Right Understanding [1st step]; and in making efforts to overcome wrong action, and to arouse right action, one practices Right Effort [6th step]; and in overcoming wrong action with attentive mind, and dwelling with attentive mind in possession of right action, one practices Right Attentiveness [7th step]. Hence, there are three things that accompany and follow upon right action, namely: right understanding, right effort, and right attentiveness.

Fifth Step: Right Living

WHAT, now, is Right Living? When the noble disciple, avoiding a wrong way of living, gets his livelihood by a right way of living, this is called Right Living. Now, right living, let me tell you, is of two kinds: 1.When the noble disciple, avoiding wrong living, gets his livelihood by a right way of living—this is called the "Mundane Right Living," which yields worldly fruits and brings good results. 2. But the abhorrence of wrong living, the abstaining, withholding, refraining therefrom—the mind being holy, being turned away from the world, and conjoined with the path, the holy path being pursued—: this is called the "Ultramundane Right Living," which is not of the world, but is ultramundane, and conjoined with the paths.

Now, in understanding wrong living as wrong, and right living as right, one practices Right Understanding [1st step]; and in making efforts to overcome wrong living, to arouse right living, one practices Right Effort [6th step]; and in overcoming wrong living with attentive mind, and dwelling with attentive mind in possession of right living, one practices Right Attentiveness [7th step]. Hence, there are three things that accompany and follow upon right living, namely: right understanding, right effort, and right attentiveness.

Sixth Step: Right Effort

WHAT, now, is Right Effort? There are Four Great Efforts: the effort to avoid, the effort to overcome, the effort to develop, and the effort to maintain. What, now, is the effort to avoid? There, the disciple incites his mind to avoid the arising of evil, demeritorious things that have not yet arisen; and he strives, puts forth his energy, strains his mind and struggles. Thus, when he perceives a form with the eye, a sound with the ear, an odor with the nose, a taste with the tongue, a contact with the body, or an object with the mind, he neither adheres to the whole, nor to its parts. And he strives to ward off that through which evil and demeritorious things, greed and sorrow, would arise, if he remained with unguarded senses; and he watches over his senses, restrains his senses. Possessed of this noble "Control over the Senses," he experiences inwardly a feeling of joy, into which no evil thing can enter. This is called the effort to avoid.

What, now, is the effort to Overcome? There, the disciple incites his mind to overcome the evil, demeritorious things that have already arisen; and he strives, puts forth his energy, strains his mind and struggles. He does not retain any thought of sensual lust, ill-will, or grief, or any other evil and demeritorious states that may have arisen; he abandons them, dispels them, destroys them, causes them to disappear. . . .

What, now, is the effort to Develop? There the disciple incites his will to arouse meritorious conditions that have not yet arisen; and he strives, puts forth his energy, strains his mind and struggles. Thus he develops the "Elements of Enlightenment," bent on solitude, on detachment, on extinction, and ending in deliverance, namely: Attentiveness, Investigation of the Law, Energy, Rapture, Tranquility, Concentration, and Equanimity. This is called the effort to develop.

What, now, is the effort to Maintain? There, the disciple incites his will to maintain the meritorious conditions that have already arisen, and not to let them disappear, but to bring them to growth, to maturity and to the full perfection of development; and he strives, puts forth his energy, strains his mind and struggles. Thus, for example, he keeps firmly in his mind a favorable object of concentration that has arisen, as the mental image of a skeleton, of a corpse infested by worms, of a corpse blue-black in color, of a festering corpse, of a corpse riddled with holes, of a corpse swollen up. This is called the effort to maintain. . . .

Seventh Step: Right Attentiveness

WHAT, now, is Right Attentiveness? The only way that leads to the attainment of purity, to the overcoming of sorrow and lamentation, to the end of pain and grief, to the entering upon the right path and the realization of Nirvana, is the "Four Fundamentals of Attentiveness." And which are these four? In them, the disciple dwells in contemplation of the Body, in contemplation of Feeling, in contemplation of the Mind, in contemplation of the Mind-objects, ardent, clearly conscious and attentive, after putting away worldly greed and grief.

Contemplation of the Body

But, how does the disciple dwell in contemplation of the body? There, the disciple retires to the forest, to the foot of a tree, or to a solitary place, sits himself down, with legs crossed, body erect, and with attentiveness fixed before him. With attentive mind he breathes in, with attentive mind he breathes out. When making a long inhalation, he knows: "I make a long inhalation"; when making a long exhalation, he knows: "I make a long exhalation." when making a short inhalation, he knows: "I make a short inhalation"; when making a short exhalation, he knows: "I make a short exhalation." "Clearly perceiving the entire [breath]-body, I will breathe in": thus he trains himself; "clearly perceiving the entire [breath]-body, I will breathe out": thus he trains himself. "Calming this bodily function, I will breathe n": thus he trains himself; "calming this bodily function, I will breathe out": thus he trains himself.

Thus he dwells in contemplation of the body, either with regard to his own person, or to other persons, or to both. He beholds how the body arises; beholds how it passes away; beholds the arising and passing away of the body. "A body is there— "A body is there, but no living being, no individual, no woman, no man, no self, and nothing that belongs to a self; neither a person, nor anything belonging to a person"—this clear consciousness is present in him, because of his knowledge and mindfulness, and he lives independent, unattached to anything in the world. Thus does the disciple dwell in contemplation of the body.

And further, whilst going, standing, sitting, or lying down, the disciple understands the expressions: "I go"; "I stand"; "I sit"; "I lie down"; he understands any position of the body. [The disciple understands that it is not a being, a real Ego, that goes, stands, etc., but that it is by a mere figure of speech that one says: "I go," "I stand," and so forth.]

And further, the disciple is clearly conscious in his going and coming; clearly conscious in looking forward and backward; clearly conscious in bending and stretching; clearly conscious in eating, drinking, chewing, and tasting; clearly conscious in discharging excrement and urine; clearly conscious in walking, standing, sitting, falling asleep and awakening; clearly conscious in speaking and in keeping silent. "In all the disciple is doing, he is clearly conscious: of his intention, of his advantage, of his duty, of the reality."

And further, the disciple contemplates this body from the sole of the foot upward, and from the top of the hair downward, with a skin stretched over it, and filled with manifold impurities: "This body consists of hairs, nails, teeth, skin, flesh, sinews, bones, marrow, kidneys, heart, liver, diaphragm, spleen, lungs, intestines, bowels, stomach, and excrement; of bile, phlegm, pus, blood, sweat, lymph, tears, semen, spittle, nasal mucus, oil of the joints, and urine." Just as if there were a sack, with openings at both ends, filled with all kinds of grain—with paddy, beans, sesamum and husked rice—and a man not blind opened it and examined its contents, thus: "That is paddy, these are beans, this is sesamum, this is husked rice": just so does the disciple investigate this body.

And further, the disciple contemplates this body with regard to the elements: "This body consists of the solid element, the liquid element, the heating element and the vibrating element." Just as a skilled butcher or butcher's apprentice, who has slaughtered a cow and divided it into separate portions, should sit down at the junction of four highroads: just so does the disciple contemplate this body with regard to the elements.

And further, just as if the disciple should see a corpse thrown into the burial-ground, one, two, or three days dead, swollen-up, blue-black in color, full of corruption he draws the conclusion as to his own body: "This my body also has this nature, has this destiny, and cannot escape it." And further, just as if the disciple should see a corpse thrown into the burial-ground, eaten by crows, hawks or vultures, by dogs or jackals, or gnawed by all kinds of worms—he draws the conclusion as to his own body: "This my body also has this nature, has this destiny, and cannot escape it."

And further, just as if the disciple should see a corpse thrown into the burial-ground, a framework of bones, flesh hanging from it, bespattered with blood, held together by the sinews; a framework of bones, stripped of flesh, bespattered with blood, held together by the sinews; a framework of bones, without flesh and blood, but still held together by the sinews; bones, disconnected and scattered in all directions, here a bone of the hand, there a bone of the foot, there a shin bone, there a thigh bone, there the pelvis, there the spine, there the skull—he draws the conclusion as to his own body: "This my body also has this nature, has this destiny, and cannot escape it."

And further, just as if the disciple should see bones lying in the burial ground, bleached and resembling shells; bones heaped together, after the lapse of years; bones weathered and crumbled to dust;—he draws the conclusion as to his own body: "This my body also has this nature, has this destiny, and cannot escape it "Thus he dwells in contemplation of the body, either with regard to his own person, or to other persons, or to both. He beholds how the body arises; beholds how it passes away; beholds the arising and passing of the body. "A body is there" this clear consciousness is present in him, because of his knowledge and mindfulness; and he lives independent, unattached to anything in the world. Thus does the disciple dwell in contemplation of the body....

Nirvana through Watching over Breathing

"Watching over In- and Outbreathing" practiced and developed, brings the four Fundamentals of Attentiveness to perfection; the four fundamentals of attentiveness, practiced and developed bring the seven Elements of Enlightenment to perfection; the seven elements of enlightenment, practiced and developed, bring Wisdom and Deliverance to perfection.

But how does Watching over In- and Outbreathing, practiced and developed, bring the four Fundamentals of Attentiveness to perfection?

I. Whenever the disciple is conscious in making a long inhalation or exhalation, or in making a short inhalation or exhalation, or is training himself to inhale or exhale whilst feeling the whole [breath]-body, or whilst calming down this bodily function—at such a time the disciple is dwelling in "contemplation of the body," of energy, clearly conscious, attentive, after subduing worldly greed and grief. For, inhalation and exhalation I call one amongst the corporeal phenomena.

II. Whenever the disciple is training himself to inhale or exhale whilst feeling rapture, or joy, or the mental functions, or whilst calming down the mental functions—at such a time he is dwelling in "contemplation of the feelings," full of energy, clearly conscious, attentive, after subduing worldly greed and grief. For, the full awareness of In- and Outbreathing I call one amongst the feelings.

III. Whenever the disciple is training himself to inhale or exhale whilst feeling the mind, or whilst gladdening the mind or whilst concentrating the mind, or whilst setting the mind free—at such a time he is dwelling in "contemplation of the mind," full of energy, clearly conscious, attentive, after subduing worldly greed and grief. For, without attentiveness and clear consciousness, I say, there is no Watching over In- and Outbreathing.

IV. Whenever the disciple is training himself to inhale or exhale whilst contemplating impermanence, or the fading away of passion, or extinction, or detachment at such a time he is dwelling in "contemplation of the phenomena," full of energy, clearly conscious, attentive, after subduing worldly greed and grief. Watching over In- and Outbreathing, thus practiced and developed, brings the four Fundamentals of Attentiveness to perfection.

But how do the four Fundamentals of Attentiveness, practiced and developed, bring the seven Elements of Enlightenment to full perfection? Whenever the disciple is dwelling in contemplation of body, feeling, mind and phenomena, strenuous, clearly conscious, attentive, after subduing worldly greed and grief—at such a time his attentiveness is undisturbed; and whenever his attentiveness is present and undisturbed, at such a time he has gained and is developing the Element of Enlightenment "Attentiveness"; and thus this element of enlightenment reaches fullest perfection.

And whenever, whilst dwelling with attentive mind, he wisely investigates, examines and thinks over the Law—at such a time he has gained and is developing the Element of Enlightenment "Investigation of the Law"; and thus this element of enlightenment reaches fullest perfection. And whenever, whilst wisely investigating, examining and thinking over the law, his energy is firm and unshaken—at such a time he has gained and is developing the Element of Enlightenment "Energy"; and thus this element of enlightenment reaches fullest perfection.

And whenever in him, whilst firm in energy, arises supersensuous rapture—at such a time he has gained and is developing the Element of Enlightenment "Rapture"; and thus this element of enlightenment reaches fullest perfection.

And whenever, whilst enraptured in mind, his spiritual frame and his mind become tranquil—at such a time he has gained and is developing the Element of Enlightenment "Tranquility"; and thus this element of enlightenment reaches fullest perfection.

And whenever, whilst being tranquilized in his spiritual frame and happy, his mind becomes concentrated—at such a time he has gained and is developing the Element of Enlightenment "Concentration"; and thus this element of enlightenment reaches fullest perfection.

And whenever he thoroughly looks with indifference on his mind thus concentrated—at such a time he has gained and is developing the Element of Enlightenment "Equanimity."

The four fundamentals of attentiveness, thus practiced and developed, bring the seven elements of enlightenment to full perfection. But how do the seven elements of enlightenment, practiced and developed, bring Wisdom and Deliverance to full perfection? There, the disciple is developing the elements of enlightenment: Attentiveness, Investigation of the Law, Energy, Rapture, Tranquility, Concentration and Equanimity, bent on detachment, on absence of desire, on extinction and renunciation. Thus practiced and developed, do the seven elements of enlightenment bring wisdom and deliverance to full perfection.

Just as the elephant hunter drives a huge stake into the ground and chains the wild elephant to it by the neck, in order to drive out of him his wonted forest ways and wishes, his forest unruliness, obstinacy and violence, and to accustom him to the environment of the village, and to teach him such good behavior as is required amongst men: in like manner also has the noble disciple to fix his mind firmly to these four fundamentals of attentiveness, so that he may drive out of himself his wonted worldly ways and wishes, his wonted worldly unruliness, obstinacy and violence, and win to the True, and realize Nirvana.

Eighth Step: Right Concentration

WHAT, now, is Right Concentration? Fixing the mind to a single object ("One-pointedness of mind"): this is concentration. The four Fundamentals of Attentiveness (seventh step): these are the objects of concentration. The four Great Efforts (sixth step): these are the requisites for concentration. The practicing, developing and cultivating of these things: this is the "Development" of concentration.

[Right Concentration has two degrees of development: 1. "Neighborhood-Concentration," which approaches the first trance, without however attaining it; 2. "Attainment Concentration," which is the concentration present in the four trances. The attainment of the trances, however, is not a requisite for the realization of the Four Ultramundane Paths of Holiness; and neither Neighborhood-Concentration nor Attainment-Concentration, as such, in any way possesses the power of conferring entry into the Four Ultramundane Paths; hence, in them is really no power to free oneself permanently from evil things. The realization of the Four Ultramundane Paths is possible only at the moment of insight into the impermanency, miserable nature, and impersonality of phenomenal process of existence. This insight is attainable only during Neighborhood-Concentration, not during Attainment-Concentration. He who has realized one or other of the Four Ultramundane Paths without ever having attained the Trances, is called a "Dry-visioned One," or one whose passions are "dried up by Insight." He, however, who after cultivating the Trances has reached one of the Ultramundane Paths, is called "one who has taken tranquility as his vehicle."]

The Four Trances

Detached from sensual objects, detached from unwholesome things, the disciple enters into the first trance, which is accompanied by "Verbal Though," and "Rumination," is born of "Detachment," and filled with "Rapture," and "Happiness." This first trance is free from five things, and five things are present. When the disciple enters the first trance, there have vanished [the 5 Hindrances]: Lust, Ill-will, Torpor and Dullness, Restlessness and Mental Worry, Doubts; and there are present: Verbal Thought, Rumination, Rapture, Happiness, and Concentration.

And further: after the subsiding of verbal thought and rumination, and by the gaining of inward tranquility and oneness of mind, he enters into a state free from verbal thought and rumination, the second trance, which is born of Concentration, and filled with Rapture and Happiness.

And further: after the fading away of rapture, he dwells in equanimity, attentive, clearly conscious; and he experiences in his person that feeling, of which the Noble Ones say: "Happy lives the man of equanimity and attentive mind"—thus he enters the third trance.

And further: after the giving up of pleasure and pain, and through the disappearance of previous joy and grief, he enters into a state beyond pleasure and pain, into the fourth trance, which is purified by equanimity and attentiveness.

[The four Trances may be obtained by means of Watching over In- and Outbreathing, as well as through the fourth sublime meditation, the "Meditation of Equanimity," and others. The three other Sublime Meditations of "Loving Kindness," "Compassion," and "Sympathetic Joy" may lead to the attainment of the first three Trances. The "Cemetery Meditations," as well as the meditation "On Loathsomeness," will produce only the First Trance. The "Analysis of the Body," and the Contemplation on the Buddha, the Law, the Holy Brotherhood, Morality, etc., will only produce Neighborhood-Concentration.]

Develop your concentration: for he who has concentration understands things according to their reality. And what are these things? The arising and passing away of corporeality, of feeling, perception, mental formations and consciousness. Thus, these five Groups of Existence must be wisely penetrated; Delusion and Craving must be wisely abandoned; Tranquility and Insight must be wisely developed. This is the Middle Path which the Perfect One has discovered, which makes one both to see and to know, and which leads to peace, to discernment, to enlightenment, to Nirvana. And following upon this path, you will put an end to suffering.

Rock and Pillar Edicts of Asoka

257–240 BCE

Document Text

Fourteen Rock Edicts

1

Beloved-of-the-Gods, King Piyadasi, has caused this Dhamma edict to be written. Here (in my domain) no living beings are to be slaughtered or offered in sacrifice. Nor should festivals be held, for Beloved-of-the-Gods, King Piyadasi, sees much to object to in such festivals, although there are some festivals that Beloved-of-the-Gods, King Piyadasi, does approve of.

Formerly, in the kitchen of Beloved-of-the-Gods, King Piyadasi, hundreds of thousands of animals were killed every day to make curry. But now with the writing of this Dhamma edict only three creatures, two peacocks and a deer are killed, and the deer not always. And in time, not even these three creatures will be killed.

2

Everywhere within Beloved-of-the-Gods, King Piyadasi's domain, and among the people beyond the borders, the Cholas, the Pandyas, the Satiyaputras, the Keralaputras, as far as Tamraparni and where the Greek king Antiochos rules, and among the kings who are neighbors of Antiochos, everywhere has Beloved-of-the-Gods, King Piyadasi, made provision for two types of medical treatment: medical treatment for humans and medical treatment for animals. Wherever medical herbs suitable for humans or animals are not available, I have had them imported and grown. Wherever medical roots or fruits are not available, I have had them imported and grown. Along roads I have had wells dug and trees planted for the benefit of humans and animals.

3

Beloved-of-the-Gods, King Piyadasi, speaks thus: Twelve years after my coronation this has been ordered.—Everywhere in my domain the Yuktas, the Rajjukas and the Pradesikas shall go on inspection tours every five years for the purpose of Dhamma instruction and also to conduct other business. Respect for mother and father is good, generosity to friends, acquaintances, relatives, Brahmans and ascetics is good, not killing living beings is good, moderation in spending and moderation in saving is good.

The Council shall notify the Yuktas about the observance of these instructions in these very words.

4

In the past, for many hundreds of years, killing or harming living beings and improper behavior towards relatives, and improper behavior towards Brahmans and ascetics has increased. But now due to Beloved-of-the-Gods, King Piyadasi's Dhamma practice, the sound of the drum has been replaced by the sound of the Dhamma. The sighting of heavenly cars, auspicious elephants, bodies of fire and other divine sightings has not happened for many hundreds of years. But now because Beloved-of-the-Gods, King Piyadasi promotes restraint in the killing and harming of living beings, proper behavior towards relatives, Brahmans and ascetics, and respect for mother, father and elders, such sightings have increased.

These and many other kinds of Dhamma practice have been encouraged by Beloved-of-the-Gods, King Piyadasi, and he will continue to promote Dhamma practice. And the sons, grandsons and great-grandsons of Beloved-of-the-Gods, King Piyadasi, too will continue to promote Dhamma practice until the end of time; living by Dhamma and virtue, they will instruct in Dhamma. Truly, this is the highest work, to instruct in Dhamma. But practicing the Dhamma cannot be done by one who is devoid of virtue and therefore its promotion and growth is commendable.

This edict has been written so that it may please my successors to devote themselves to promoting these things and not allow them to decline. Beloved-of-the-Gods, King Piyadasi, has had this written twelve years after his coronation.

5

Beloved-of-the-Gods, King Piyadasi, speaks thus: To do good is difficult. One who does good first does something hard to do. I have done many good deeds, and, if my sons, grandsons and their descendants up to the end of the world act in like manner, they too will do much good. But whoever amongst them neglects this, they will do evil. Truly, it is easy to do evil.

In the past there were no Dhamma Mahamatras but such officers were appointed by me thirteen years after my coronation. Now they work among all religions for the establishment of Dhamma, for the promotion of Dhamma, and for the welfare and happiness of all who are devoted to Dhamma. They work among the Greeks, the Kambojas, the Gandharas, the Rastrikas, the Pitinikas and other peoples on the western borders. They work among soldiers, chiefs, Brahmans, householders, the poor, the aged and those devoted to Dhamma—for their welfare and happiness—so that they may be free from harassment. They (Dhamma Mahamatras) work for the proper treatment of prisoners, towards their unfettering, and if the Mahamatras think, "This one has a family to support," "That one has been bewitched," "This one is old," then they work for the release of such prisoners. They work here, in outlying towns, in the women's quarters belonging to my brothers and sisters, and among my other relatives. They are occupied everywhere. These Dhamma Mahamatras are occupied in my domain among people devoted to Dhamma to determine who is devoted to Dhamma, who is established in Dhamma, and who is generous.

This Dhamma edict has been written on stone so that it might endure long and that my descendants might act in conformity with it.

6

Beloved-of-the-Gods, King Piyadasi, speaks thus: In the past, state business was not transacted nor were reports delivered to the king at all hours. But now I have given this order, that at any time, whether I am eating, in the women's quarters, the bed chamber, the chariot, the palanquin, in the park or wherever, reporters are to be posted with instructions to report to me the affairs of the people so that I might attend to these affairs wherever I am. And whatever I orally order in connection with donations or proclamations, or when urgent business presses itself on the Mahamatras, if disagreement or debate arises in the Council, then it must be reported to me immediately. This is what I have ordered. I am never content with exerting myself or with despatching business. Truly, I consider the welfare of all to be my duty, and the root of this is exertion and the prompt despatch of business. There is no better work than promoting the welfare of all the people and whatever efforts I am making is to repay the debt I owe to all beings to assure their happiness in this life, and attain heaven in the next.

Therefore this Dhamma edict has been written to last long and that my sons, grandsons and great-grandsons might act in conformity with it for the welfare of the world. However, this is difficult to do without great exertion.

7

Beloved-of-the-Gods, King Piyadasi, desires that all religions should reside everywhere, for all of them desire self-control and purity of heart. But people have various desires and various passions, and they may practice all of what they should or only a part of it. But one who receives great gifts yet is lacking in self-control, purity of heart, gratitude and firm devotion, such a person is mean.

8

In the past kings used to go out on pleasure tours during which there was hunting and other entertainment. But ten years after Beloved-of-the-Gods had been coronated, he went on a tour to Sambodhi and thus instituted Dhamma tours. During these tours, the following things took place: visits and gifts to Brahmans and ascetics, visits and gifts of gold to the aged, visits to people in the countryside, instructing them in Dhamma, and discussing Dhamma with them as is suitable. It is this that delights Beloved-of-the-Gods, King Piyadasi, and is, as it were, another type of revenue.

9

Beloved-of-the-Gods, King Piyadasi, speaks thus: In times of sickness, for the marriage of sons and daughters, at the birth of children, before embarking on a journey, on these and other occasions, people perform various ceremonies. Women in particular perform many vulgar and worthless ceremonies. These types of ceremonies can be performed by all means, but they bear little fruit. What does bear great fruit, however, is the ceremony of the Dhamma. This involves proper behavior towards servants and employees, respect for teachers, restraint towards living beings, and generosity towards ascetics and Brahmans. These and other things constitute the ceremony of the Dhamma. Therefore a father, a son, a brother, a master, a friend, a companion, and even a neighbor should say: "This is good, this is the ceremony that should be performed until its purpose is fulfilled, this I shall do." Other ceremonies are of doubtful fruit, for they may achieve their purpose, or they may not, and even if they do, it is only in this world. But the ceremony of the Dhamma is timeless. Even if it does not achieve its purpose in this world, it produces great merit in the next, whereas if it does achieve its purpose in this world, one gets great merit both here and there through the ceremony of the Dhamma.

10

Beloved-of-the-Gods, King Piyadasi, does not consider glory and fame to be of great account unless they are achieved through having my subjects respect Dhamma and practice Dhamma, both now and in the future. For this alone does Beloved-of-the-Gods, King Piyadasi, desire glory and fame. And whatever efforts Beloved-of-the-Gods, King Piyadasi, is making, all of that is only for the welfare of the people in the next world, and that they will have little evil. And being without merit is evil. This is difficult for either a humble person or a great person to do except with great effort, and by giving up other interests. In fact, it may be even more difficult for a great person to do.

11

Beloved-of-the-Gods, King Piyadasi, speaks thus: There is no gift like the gift of the Dhamma, (no acquaintance like) acquaintance with Dhamma, (no distribution like) distribution of Dhamma, and (no kinship like) kinship through Dhamma. And it consists of this: proper behavior towards servants and employees, respect for mother and father, generosity to friends, companions, relations, Brahmans and ascetics, and not killing living beings. Therefore a father, a son, a brother, a master, a friend, a companion or a neighbor should say: "This is good, this should be done." One benefits in this world and gains great merit in the next by giving the gift of the Dhamma.

12

Beloved-of-the-Gods, King Piyadasi, honors both ascetics and the householders of all religions, and he honors them with gifts and honors of various kinds. But Beloved-of-the-Gods, King Piyadasi, does not value gifts and honors as much as he values this—that there should be growth in the essentials of all religions. Growth in essentials can be done in different ways, but all of them have as their root restraint in speech, that is, not praising one's own religion, or condemning the religion of others without good cause. And if there is cause for criticism, it should be done in a mild way. But it is better to honor other religions for this reason. By so doing, one's own religion benefits, and so do other religions, while doing otherwise harms one's own religion and the religions of others. Whoever praises his own religion, due to excessive devotion, and condemns others with the thought "Let me glorify my own religion," only harms his own religion. Therefore contact (between religions) is good. One should listen to and respect the doctrines professed by others. Beloved-of-the-Gods, King Piyadasi, desires that all should be well-learned in the good doctrines of other religions.

Those who are content with their own religion should be told this: Beloved-of-the-Gods, King Piyadasi, does not value gifts and honors as much as he values that there should be growth in the essentials of all religions. And to this end many are working—Dhamma Mahamatras, Mahamatras in charge of the women's quarters, officers in charge of outlying areas, and other such officers. And the fruit of this is that one's own religion grows and the Dhamma is illuminated also.

13

Beloved-of-the-Gods, King Piyadasi, conquered the Kalingas eight years after his coronation. One hundred and fifty thousand were deported, 100,000 were killed and many more died (from other causes). After the Kalingas had been conquered, Beloved-of-the-Gods came to feel a strong inclination towards the Dhamma, a love for the Dhamma and for instruction in Dhamma. Now Beloved-of-the-Gods feels deep remorse for having conquered the Kalingas.

Indeed, Beloved-of-the-Gods is deeply pained by the killing, dying and deportation that take place when an unconquered country is conquered. But Beloved-of-the-Gods is pained even more by this—that Brahmans, ascetics, and householders of different religions who live in those countries, and who are respectful to superiors, to mother and father, to elders, and who behave properly and have strong loyalty towards friends, acquaintances, companions, relatives, servants and employees—that they are injured, killed or separated from their loved ones. Even those who are not affected (by all this) suffer when they see friends, acquaintances, companions and relatives affected. These misfortunes befall all (as a result of war), and this pains Beloved-of-the-Gods.

There is no country, except among the Greeks, where these two groups, Brahmans and ascetics, are not found, and there is no country where people are not devoted to one or another religion. Therefore the killing, death or deportation of a hundredth, or even a thousandth part of those who died during the conquest of Kalinga now pains Beloved-of-the-Gods. Now Beloved-of-the-Gods thinks that even those who do wrong should be forgiven where forgiveness is possible.

Even the forest people, who live in Beloved-of-the-Gods' domain, are entreated and reasoned with to act properly. They are told that despite his remorse Beloved-of-the-Gods has the power to punish them if necessary, so that they should be ashamed of their wrong and not be killed. Truly, Beloved-of-the-Gods desires non-injury, restraint and impartiality to all beings, even where wrong has been done.

Now it is conquest by Dhamma that Beloved-of-the-Gods considers to be the best conquest. And it (conquest by Dhamma) has been won here, on the borders, even six hundred yojanas away, where the Greek king Antiochos rules, beyond there where the four kings named Ptolemy, Antigonos, Magas and Alexander rule, likewise in the south among the Cholas, the Pandyas, and as far as Tamraparni. Here in the king's domain among the Greeks, the Kambojas, the Nabhakas, the Nabhapamkits, the Bhojas, the Pitinikas, the Andhras and the Palidas, everywhere people are following Beloved-of-the-Gods' instructions in Dhamma. Even where Beloved-of-the-Gods' envoys have not been, these people too, having heard of the practice of Dhamma and the ordinances and instructions in Dhamma given by Beloved-of-the-Gods, are following it and will continue to do so. This conquest has been won everywhere, and it gives great joy—the joy which only conquest by Dhamma can give. But even this joy is of little consequence. Beloved-of-the-Gods considers the great fruit to be experienced in the next world to be more important.

I have had this Dhamma edict written so that my sons and great-grandsons may not consider making new conquests, or that if military conquests are made, that they be done with forbearance and light punishment, or better still, that they consider making conquest by Dhamma only, for that bears fruit in this world and the next. May all their intense devotion be given to this which has a result in this world and the next.

14

Beloved-of-the-Gods, King Piyadasi, has had these Dhamma edicts written in brief, in medium length, and in extended form. Not all of them occur everywhere, for my domain is vast, but much has been written, and I will have still more written. And also there are some subjects here that have been spoken of again and again because of their sweetness, and so that the people may act in accordance with them. If some things written are incomplete, this is because of the locality, or in consideration of the object, or due to the fault of the scribe.

Kalinga Rock Edicts

I

Beloved-of-the-Gods says that the Mahamatras of Tosali who are judicial officers in the city are to be told this: I wish to see that everything I consider to be proper is carried out in the right way. And I consider instructing you to be the best way of accomplishing this. I have placed you over many thousands of people that you may win the people's affection.

All men are my children. What I desire for my own children, and I desire their welfare and happiness both in this world and the next, that I desire for all men. You do not understand to what extent I desire this, and if some of you do understand, you do not understand the full extent of my desire.

You must attend to this matter. While being completely law-abiding, some people are imprisoned, treated harshly and even killed without cause so that many people suffer. Therefore your aim should be to act with impartiality. It is because of these things—envy, anger, cruelty, hate, indifference, laziness or tiredness—that such a thing does not happen. Therefore your aim should be: "May these things not be in me." And the root of this is non-anger and patience. Those who are bored with the administration of justice will not be promoted; (those who are not) will move upwards and be promoted. Whoever among you understands this should say to his colleagues: "See that you do your duty properly. Such and such are Beloved-of-the-Gods' instructions." Great fruit will result from doing your duty, while failing in it will result in gaining neither heaven nor the king's pleasure. Failure in duty on your part will not please me. But done properly, it will win you heaven and you will be discharging your debts to me.

This edict is to be listened to on Tisa day, between Tisa days, and on other suitable occasions, it should be listened to even by a single person. Acting thus, you will be doing your duty.

This edict has been written for the following purpose: that the judicial officers of the city may strive to do their duty and that the people under them might not suffer unjust imprisonment or harsh treatment. To achieve this, I will send out Mahamatras every five years who are not harsh or cruel, but who are merciful and who can ascertain if the judicial officers have understood my purpose and are acting according to my instructions. Similarly, from Ujjayini, the prince will send similar persons with the same purpose without allowing three years to elapse. Likewise from Takhasila also. When these Mahamatras go on tours of inspection each year, then without neglecting their normal duties, they will ascertain if judicial officers are acting according to the king's instructions.

2

Beloved-of-the-Gods speaks thus: This royal order is to be addressed to the Mahamatras at Samapa. I wish to see that everything I consider to be proper is carried out in the right way. And I consider instructing you to be the best way of accomplishing this. All men are my children. What I desire for my own children, and I desire their welfare and happiness both in this world and the next, that I desire for all men.

The people of the unconquered territories beyond the borders might think: "What is the king's intentions towards us?" My only intention is that they live without fear of me, that they may trust me and that I may give them happiness, not sorrow. Furthermore, they should understand that the king will forgive those who can be forgiven, and that he wishes to encourage them to practice Dhamma so that they may attain happiness in this world and the next. I am telling you this so that I may discharge the debts I owe, and that in instructing you, that you may know that my vow and my promise will not be broken. Therefore acting in this way, you should perform your duties and assure them (the people beyond the borders) that: "The king is like a father. He feels towards us as he feels towards himself. We are to him like his own children."

By instructing you and informing you of my vow and my promise I shall be applying myself in complete fullness to achieving this object. You are able indeed to inspire them with confidence and to secure their welfare and happiness in this world and the next, and by acting thus, you will attain heaven as well as discharge the debts you owe to me. And so that the Mahamatras can devote themselves at all times to inspiring the border areas with confidence and encouraging them to practice Dhamma, this edict has been written here.

This edict is to be listened to every four months on Tisa day, between Tisa days, and on other suitable occasions, it should be listened to even by a single person. Acting thus, you will be doing your duty.

Minor Rock Edicts

1

Beloved-of-the-Gods speaks thus: It is now more than two and a half years since I became a lay-disciple, but until now I have not been very zealous. But now that I have visited the Sangha for more than a year, I have become very zealous. Now the people in India who have not associated with the gods do so. This is the result of zeal and it is not just the great who can do this. Even the humble, if they are zealous, can attain heaven. And this proclamation has been made with this aim. Let both humble and great be zealous, let even those on the borders know and let zeal last long. Then this zeal will increase, it will greatly increase, it will increase up to one-and-a-half times. This message has been proclaimed two hundred and fifty-six times by the king while on tour.

2

Beloved-of-the-Gods speaks thus: Father and mother should be respected and so should elders, kindness to living beings should be made strong and the truth should be spoken. In these ways, the Dhamma should be promoted. Likewise, a teacher should be honored by his pupil and proper manners should be shown towards relations. This is an ancient rule that conduces to long life. Thus should one act. Written by the scribe Chapala.

3

Piyadasi, King of Magadha, saluting the Sangha and wishing them good health and happiness, speaks thus: You know, reverend sirs, how great my faith in the Buddha, the Dhamma and Sangha is. Whatever, reverend sirs, has been spoken by Lord Buddha, all that is well-spoken. I consider it proper, reverend sirs, to advise on how the good Dhamma should last long.

These Dhamma texts—Extracts from the Discipline, the Noble Way of Life, the Fears to Come, the Poem on the Silent Sage, the Discourse on the Pure Life, Upatisa's Questions, and the Advice to Rahula which was spoken by the Buddha concerning false speech—these Dhamma texts, reverend sirs, I desire that all the monks and nuns may constantly listen to and remember. Likewise the laymen and laywomen. I have had this written that you may know my intentions.

The Seven Pillar Edicts

1

Beloved-of-the-Gods speaks thus: This Dhamma edict was written twenty-six years after my coronation. Happiness in this world and the next is difficult to obtain without much love for the Dhamma, much self-examination, much respect, much fear (of evil), and much enthusiasm. But through my instruction this regard for Dhamma and love of Dhamma has grown day by day, and will continue to grow. And my officers of high, low and middle rank are practicing and conforming to Dhamma, and are capable of inspiring others to do the same. Mahamatras in border areas are doing the same.

And these are my instructions: to protect with Dhamma, to make happiness through Dhamma and to guard with Dhamma.

2

Beloved-of-the-Gods, King Piyadasi, speaks thus: Dhamma is good, but what constitutes Dhamma? (It includes) little evil, much good, kindness, generosity, truthfulness and purity. I have given the gift of sight in various ways. To two-footed and four-footed beings, to birds and aquatic animals, I have given various things including the gift of life. And many other good deeds have been done by me.

This Dhamma edict has been written that people might follow it and it might endure for a long time. And the one who follows it properly will do something good.

3

Beloved-of-the-Gods, King Piyadasi, speaks thus: People see only their good deeds saying, "I have done this good deed." But they do not see their evil deeds saying, "I have done this evil deed" or "This is called evil." But this (tendency) is difficult to see. One should think like this: "It is these things that lead to evil, to violence, to cruelty, anger, pride and jealousy. Let me not ruin myself with these things." And further, one should think: "This leads to happiness in this world and the next."

4

Beloved-of-the-Gods speaks thus: This Dhamma edict was written twenty-six years after my coronation. My Rajjukas are working among the people, among many hundreds of thousands of people. The hearing of petitions and the administration of justice has been left to them so that they can do their duties confidently and fearlessly and so that they can work for the welfare, happiness and benefit of the people in the country. But they should remember what causes happiness and sorrow, and being themselves devoted to Dhamma, they should encourage the people in the country (to do the same), that they may attain happiness in this world and the next. These Rajjukas are eager to serve me. They also obey other officers who know my desires, who instruct the Rajjukas so that they can please me. Just as a person feels confident having entrusted his child to an expert nurse thinking: "The nurse will keep my child well," even so, the Rajjukas have been appointed by me for the welfare and happiness of the people in the country. The hearing of petitions and the administration of justice have been left to the Rajjukas so that they can do their duties unperturbed, fearlessly and confidently. It is my desire that there should be uniformity in law and uniformity in sentencing. I even go this far, to grant a three-day stay for those in prison who have been tried and sentenced to death. During this time their relatives can make appeals to have the prisoners' lives spared. If there is none to appeal on their behalf, the prisoners can give gifts in order to make merit for the next world, or observe fasts. Indeed, it is my wish that in this way, even if a prisoner's time is limited, he can prepare for the next world, and that people's Dhamma practice, self-control and generosity may grow.

5

Beloved-of-the-Gods, King Piyadasi, speaks thus: Twenty-six years after my coronation various animals were declared to be protected—parrots, mainas, aruna, ruddy geese, wild ducks, nandimukhas, gelatas, bats, queen ants, terrapins, boneless fish, vedareyaka, gangapuputaka, sankiya fish, tortoises, porcupines, squirrels, deer, bulls, okapinda, wild asses, wild pigeons, domestic pigeons and all four-footed creatures that are neither useful nor edible. Those nanny goats, ewes and sows which are with young or giving milk to their young are protected, and so are young ones less than six months old. Cocks are not to be caponized, husks hiding living beings are not to be burnt and forests are not to be burnt either without reason or to kill creatures. One animal is not to be fed to another. On the three Caturmasis, the three days of Tisa and during the fourteenth and fifteenth of the Uposatha, fish are protected and not to be sold. During these days animals are not to be killed in the elephant reserves or the fish reserves either. On the eighth of every fortnight, on the fourteenth and fifteenth, on Tisa, Punarvasu, the three Caturmasis and other auspicious days, bulls are not to be castrated, billy goats, rams, boars and other animals that are usually castrated are not to be. On Tisa, Punarvasu, Caturmasis and the fortnight of Caturmasis, horses and bullocks are not to be branded.

In the twenty-six years since my coronation prisoners have been given amnesty on twenty-five occasions.

6

Beloved-of-the-Gods speaks thus: Twelve years after my coronation I started to have Dhamma edicts written for the welfare and happiness of the people, and so that not transgressing them they might grow in the Dhamma. Thinking: "How can the welfare and happiness of the people be secured?" I give attention to my relatives, to those dwelling near and those dwelling far, so I can lead them to happiness and then I act accordingly. I do the same for all groups. I have honored all religions with various honors. But I consider it best to meet with people personally.

This Dhamma edict was written twenty-six years after my coronation.

7

Beloved-of-the-Gods speaks thus: In the past kings desired that the people might grow through the promotion of the Dhamma. But despite this, people did not grow through the promotion of the Dhamma. Beloved-of-the-Gods, King Piyadasi, said concerning this: "It occurs to me that in the past kings desired that the people might grow through the promotion of the Dhamma. But despite this, people did not grow through the promotion of the Dhamma. Now how can the people be encouraged to follow it? How can the people be encouraged to grow through the promotion of the Dhamma? How can I elevate them by promoting the Dhamma?" Beloved-of-the-Gods, King Piyadasi, further said concerning this: "It occurs to me that I shall have proclamations on Dhamma announced and instruction on Dhamma given. When people hear these, they will follow them, elevate themselves and grow considerably through the promotion of the Dhamma." It is for this purpose that proclamations on Dhamma have been announced and various instructions on Dhamma have been given and that officers who work among many promote and explain them in detail. The Rajjukas who work among hundreds of thousands of people have likewise been ordered: "In this way and that encourage those who are devoted to Dhamma." Beloved-of-the-Gods speaks thus: "Having this object in view, I have set up Dhamma pillars, appointed Dhamma Mahamatras, and announced Dhamma proclamations."

Beloved-of-the-Gods, King Piyadasi, says: Along roads I have had banyan trees planted so that they can give shade to animals and men, and I have had mango groves planted. At intervals of eight krosas, I have had wells dug, rest-houses built, and in various places, I have had watering-places made for the use of animals and men. But these are but minor achievements. Such things to make the people happy have been done by former kings. I have done these things for this purpose, that the people might practice the Dhamma. Beloved-of-the-Gods, King Piyadasi, speaks thus: My Dhamma Mahamatras too are occupied with various good works among the ascetics and householders of all religions. I have ordered that they should be occupied with the affairs of the Sangha. I have also ordered that they should be occupied with the affairs of the Brahmans and the Ajivikas. I have ordered that they be occupied with the Niganthas. In fact, I have ordered that different Mahamatras be occupied with the particular affairs of all different religions. And my Dhamma Mahamatras likewise are occupied with these and other religions.

Beloved-of-the-Gods, King Piyadasi, speaks thus: These and other principal officers are occupied with the distribution of gifts, mine as well as those of the queens. In my women's quarters, they organize various charitable activities here and in the provinces. I have also ordered my sons and the sons of other queens to distribute gifts so that noble deeds of Dhamma and the practice of Dhamma may be promoted. And noble deeds of Dhamma and the practice of Dhamma consist of having kindness, generosity, truthfulness, purity, gentleness and goodness increase among the people.

Beloved-of-the-Gods, King Piyadasi, speaks thus: Whatever good deeds have been done by me, those the people accept and those they follow. Therefore they have progressed and will continue to progress by being respectful to mother and father, respectful to elders, by courtesy to the aged and proper behavior towards Brahmans and ascetics, towards the poor and distressed, and even towards servants and employees.

Beloved-of-the-Gods, King Piyadasi, speaks thus: This progress among the people through Dhamma has been done by two means, by Dhamma regulations and by persuasion. Of these, Dhamma regulation is of little effect, while persuasion has much more effect. The Dhamma regulations I have given are that various animals must be protected. And I have given many other Dhamma regulations also. But it is by persuasion that progress among the people through Dhamma has had a greater effect in respect of harmlessness to living beings and non-killing of living beings.

Concerning this, Beloved-of-the-Gods says: Wherever there are stone pillars or stone slabs, there this Dhamma edict is to be engraved so that it may long endure. It has been engraved so that it may endure as long as my sons and great-grandsons live and as long as the sun and the moon shine, and so that people may practice it as instructed. For by practicing it happiness will be attained in this world and the next.

This Dhamma edict has been written by me twenty-seven years after my coronation.

Minor Pillar Edicts

1

Twenty years after his coronation, Beloved-of-the-Gods, King Piyadasi, visited this place and worshipped because here the Buddha, the sage of the Sakyans, was born. He had a stone figure and a pillar set up and because the Lord was born here, the village of Lumbini was exempted from tax and required to pay only one eighth of the produce.

2

Beloved-of-the-Gods commands: The Mahamatras at Kosambi (are to be told: Whoever splits the Sangha) which is now united, is not to be admitted into the Sangha. Whoever, whether monk or nun, splits the Sangha is to be made to wear white clothes and to reside somewhere other than in a monastery.

Analects of Confucius

ca. 479–249 BCE

Document Text

Book 1

The Master said, "Is it not pleasant to learn with a constant perseverance and application?

"Is it not delightful to have friends coming from distant quarters?

"Is he not a man of complete virtue, who feels no discomposure though men may take no note of him?"

The philosopher Yu said, "They are few who, being filial and fraternal, are fond of offending against their superiors. There have been none, who, not liking to offend against their superiors, have been fond of stirring up confusion.

"The superior man bends his attention to what is radical. That being established, all practical courses naturally grow up. Filial piety and fraternal submission—are they not the root of all benevolent actions?"

The Master said, "Fine words and an insinuating appearance are seldom associated with true virtue."

The philosopher Tsang said, "I daily examine myself on three points: whether, in transacting business for others, I may have been not faithful; whether, in intercourse with friends, I may have been not sincere; whether I may have not mastered and practiced the instructions of my teacher."

The Master said, "To rule a country of a thousand chariots, there must be reverent attention to business, and sincerity; economy in expenditure, and love for men; and the employment of the people at the proper seasons."

The Master said, "A youth, when at home, should be filial, and, abroad, respectful to his elders. He should be earnest and truthful. He should overflow in love to all, and cultivate the friendship of the good. When he has time and opportunity, after the performance of these things, he should employ them in polite studies."

Tsze-hsia said, "If a man withdraws his mind from the love of beauty, and applies it as sincerely to the love of the virtuous; if, in serving his parents, he can exert his utmost strength; if, in serving his prince, he can devote his life; if, in his intercourse with his friends, his words are sincere: although men say that he has not learned, I will certainly say that he has.

The Master said, "If the scholar be not grave, he will not call forth any veneration, and his learning will not be solid.

"Hold faithfulness and sincerity as first principles.

"Have no friends not equal to yourself.

"When you have faults, do not fear to abandon them."

The philosopher Tsang said, "Let there be a careful attention to perform the funeral rites to parents, and let them be followed when long gone with the ceremonies of sacrifice; then the virtue of the people will resume its proper excellence."

Tsze-ch'in asked Tsze-kung saying, "When our master comes to any country, he does not fail to learn all about its government. Does he ask his information? or is it given to him?"

Tsze-kung said, "Our master is benign, upright, courteous, temperate, and complaisant and thus he gets his information. The master's mode of asking information, is it not different from that of other men?"

The Master said, "While a man's father is alive, look at the bent of his will; when his father is dead, look at his conduct. If for three years he does not alter from the way of his father, he may be called filial."

The philosopher Yu said, "In practicing the rules of propriety, a natural ease is to be prized. In the ways prescribed by the ancient kings, this is the excellent quality, and in things small and great we follow them.

"Yet it is not to be observed in all cases. If one, knowing how such ease should be prized, manifests it, without regulating it by the rules of propriety, this likewise is not to be done."

The philosopher Yu said, "When agreements are made according to what is right, what is spoken can be made good. When respect is shown according to what is proper, one keeps far from shame and disgrace. When the parties upon whom a man leans are proper persons to be intimate with, he can make them his guides and masters."

The Master said, "He who aims to be a man of complete virtue in his food does not seek to gratify his appetite, nor in his dwelling place does he seek the appliances of ease; he is earnest in what he is doing, and careful in his speech; he frequents the company of men of principle that he may be rectified: such a person may be said indeed to love to learn."

Tsze-kung said, "What do you pronounce concerning the poor man who yet does not flatter, and the rich man who is not proud?" The Master replied, "They will do; but they are not equal to him, who, though poor, is yet cheerful, and to him, who, though rich, loves the rules of propriety."

Tsze-kung replied, "It is said in the Book of Poetry, 'As you cut and then file, as you carve and then polish.' The meaning is the same, I apprehend, as that which you have just expressed."

The Master said, "With one like Ts'ze, I can begin to talk about the odes. I told him one point, and he knew its proper sequence."

The Master said, "I will not be afflicted at men's not knowing me; I will be afflicted that I do not know men."

Book 2

The Master said, "He who exercises government by means of his virtue may be compared to the north polar star, which keeps its place and all the stars turn towards it."

The Master said, "In the Book of Poetry are three hundred pieces, but the design of them all may be embraced in one sentence 'Having no depraved thoughts.'"

The Master said, "If the people be led by laws, and uniformity sought to be given them by punishments, they will try to avoid the punishment, but have no sense of shame.

"If they be led by virtue, and uniformity sought to be given them by the rules of propriety, they will have the sense of shame, and moreover will become good."

The Master said, "At fifteen, I had my mind bent on learning.

"At thirty, I stood firm.

"At forty, I had no doubts.

"At fifty, I knew the decrees of Heaven.

"At sixty, my ear was an obedient organ for the reception of truth.

"At seventy, I could follow what my heart desired, without transgressing what was right."

Mang I asked what filial piety was. The Master said, "It is not being disobedient."

Soon after, as Fan Ch'ih was driving him, the Master told him, saying, "Mang-sun asked me what filial piety was, and I answered him, 'not being disobedient.'"

Fan Ch'ih said, "What did you mean?" The Master replied, "That parents, when alive, be served according to propriety; that, when dead, they should be buried according to propriety; and that they should be sacrificed to according to propriety."

Mang Wu asked what filial piety was. The Master said, "Parents are anxious lest their children should be sick."

Tsze-yu asked what filial piety was. The Master said, "The filial piety nowadays means the support of one's parents. But dogs and horses likewise are able to do something in the way of support; without reverence, what is there to distinguish the one support given from the other?"

Tsze-hsia asked what filial piety was. The Master said, "The difficulty is with the countenance. If, when their elders have any troublesome affairs, the young take the toil of them, and if, when the young have wine and food, they set them before their elders, is THIS to be considered filial piety?"

The Master said, "I have talked with Hui for a whole day, and he has not made any objection to anything I said, as if he were stupid. He has retired, and I have examined his conduct when away from me, and found him able to illustrate my teachings. Hui!-He is not stupid."

The Master said, "See what a man does.

"Mark his motives.

"Examine in what things he rests.

"How can a man conceal his character? How can a man conceal his character?"

The Master said, "If a man keeps cherishing his old knowledge, so as continually to be acquiring new, he may be a teacher of others."

The Master said, "The accomplished scholar is not a utensil."

Tsze-kung asked what constituted the superior man. The Master said, "He acts before he speaks, and afterwards speaks according to his actions."

The Master said, "The superior man is catholic and not partisan. The mean man is partisan and not catholic."

The Master said, "Learning without thought is labor lost; thought without learning is perilous."

The Master said, "The study of strange doctrines is injurious indeed!"

The Master said, "Yu, shall I teach you what knowledge is? When you know a thing, to hold that you know it; and when you do not know a thing, to allow that you do not know it; this is knowledge."

Tsze-chang was learning with a view to official emolument.

The Master said, "Hear much and put aside the points of which you stand in doubt, while you speak cautiously at the same time of the others: then you will afford few occasions for blame. See much and put aside the things which seem perilous, while you are cautious at the same time in carrying the others into practice: then you will have few occasions for repentance. When one gives few occasions for blame in his words, and few occasions for repentance in his conduct, he is in the way to get emolument."

The Duke Ai asked, saying, "What should be done in order to secure the submission of the people?" Confucius replied, "Advance the upright and set aside the crooked, then the people will submit. Advance the crooked and set aside the upright, then the people will not submit."

Chi K'ang asked how to cause the people to reverence their ruler, to be faithful to him, and to go on to nerve themselves to virtue. The Master said, "Let him preside over them with gravity; then they will reverence him. Let him be filial and kind to all; then they will be faithful to him. Let him advance the good and teach the incompetent; then they will eagerly seek to be virtuous."

Some one addressed Confucius, saying, "Sir, why are you not engaged in the government?"

The Master said, "What does the Shu-ching say of filial piety? 'You are filial, you discharge your brotherly duties. These qualities are displayed in government.' This then also constitutes the exercise of government. Why must there be THAT—making one be in the government?"

The Master said, "I do not know how a man without truthfulness is to get on. How can a large carriage be made to go without the crossbar for yoking the oxen to, or a small carriage without the arrangement for yoking the horses?"

Tsze-chang asked whether the affairs of ten ages after could be known.

Confucius said, "The Yin dynasty followed the regulations of the Hsia: wherein it took from or added to them may be known. The Chau dynasty has followed the regulations of Yin: wherein it took from or added to them may be known. Some other may follow the Chau, but though it should be at the distance of a hundred ages, its affairs may be known."

The Master said, "For a man to sacrifice to a spirit which does not belong to him is flattery.

"To see what is right and not to do it is want of courage."

Book 3

Confucius said of the head of the Chi family, who had eight rows of pantomimes in his area, "If he can bear to do this, what may he not bear to do?"

The three families used the Yungode, while the vessels were being removed, at the conclusion of the sacrifice. The Master said, "'Assisting are the princes; the son of heaven looks profound and grave'; what application can these words have in the hall of the three families?"

The Master said, "If a man be without the virtues proper to humanity, what has he to do with the rites of propriety? If a man be without the virtues proper to humanity, what has he to do with music?"

Lin Fang asked what was the first thing to be attended to in ceremonies.

The Master said, "A great question indeed!

"In festive ceremonies, it is better to be sparing than extravagant. In the ceremonies of mourning, it is better that there be deep sorrow than in minute attention to observances."

The Master said, "The rude tribes of the east and north have their princes, and are not like the States of our great land which are without them."

The chief of the Chi family was about to sacrifice to the T'ai mountain. The Master said to Zan Yu, "Can you not save him from this?" He answered, "I cannot." Confucius said, "Alas! will you say that the T'ai mountain is not so discerning as Lin Fang?"

The Master said, "The student of virtue has no contentions. If it be said he cannot avoid them, shall this be in archery? But he bows complaisantly to his competitors; thus he ascends the hall, descends, and exacts the forfeit of drinking. In his contention, he is still the Chun-tsze."

Tsze-hsia asked, saying, "What is the meaning of the passage—'The pretty dimples of her artful smile! The well-defined black and white of her eye! The plain ground for the colors?'"

The Master said, "The business of laying on the colors follows the preparation of the plain ground."

"Ceremonies then are a subsequent thing?" The Master said, "It is Shang who can bring out my meaning. Now I can begin to talk about the odes with him."

The Master said, "I could describe the ceremonies of the Hsia dynasty, but Chi cannot sufficiently attest my words. I could describe the ceremonies of the Yin dynasty, but Sung cannot sufficiently attest my words. They cannot do so because of the insufficiency of their records and wise men. If those were sufficient, I could adduce them in support of my words."

The Master said, "At the great sacrifice, after the pouring out of the libation, I have no wish to look on."

Some one asked the meaning of the great sacrifice. The Master said, "I do not know. He who knew its meaning would find it as easy to govern the kingdom as to look on this"—pointing to his palm.

He sacrificed to the dead, as if they were present. He sacrificed to the spirits, as if the spirits were present.

The Master said, "I consider my not being present at the sacrifice, as if I did not sacrifice."

Wang-sun Chia asked, saying, "What is the meaning of the saying, 'It is better to pay court to the furnace then to the southwest corner?'"

The Master said, "Not so. He who offends against Heaven has none to whom he can pray."

The Master said, "Chau had the advantage of viewing the two past dynasties. How complete and elegant are its regulations! I follow Chau."

The Master, when he entered the grand temple, asked about everything. Some one said, "Who say that the son of the man of Tsau knows the rules of propriety! He has entered the grand temple and asks about everything." The Master heard the remark, and said, "This is a rule of propriety."

The Master said, "In archery it is not going through the leather which is the principal thing, because people's strength is not equal. This was the old way."

Tsze-kung wished to do away with the offering of a sheep connected with the inauguration of the first day of each month.

The Master said, "Ts'ze, you love the sheep; I love the ceremony."

The Master said, "The full observance of the rules of propriety in serving one's prince is accounted by people to be flattery."

The Duke Ting asked how a prince should employ his ministers, and how ministers should serve their prince. Confucius replied, "A prince should employ his minister according to according to the rules of propriety; ministers should serve their prince with faithfulness."

The Master said, "The Kwan Tsu is expressive of enjoyment without being licentious, and of grief without being hurtfully excessive."

The Duke Ai asked Tsai Wo about the altars of the spirits of the land. Tsai Wo replied, "The Hsia sovereign planted the pine tree about them; the men of the Yin planted the cypress; and the men of the Chau planted the chestnut tree, meaning thereby to cause the people to be in awe."

When the Master heard it, he said, "Things that are done, it is needless to speak about;

things that have had their course, it is needless to remonstrate about; things that are past, it is needless to blame."

The Master said, "Small indeed was the capacity of Kwan Chung!"

Some one said, "Was Kwan Chung parsimonious?" "Kwan," was the reply, "had the San Kwei, and his officers performed no double duties; how can he be considered parsimonious?"

"Then, did Kwan Chung know the rules of propriety?" The Master said, "The princes of States have a screen intercepting the view at their gates. Kwan had likewise a screen at his gate. The princes of States on any friendly meeting between two of them, had a stand on which to place their inverted cups. Kwan had also such a stand. If Kwan knew the rules of propriety, who does not know them?"

The Master instructing the grand music master of Lu said, "How to play music may be known. At the commencement of the piece, all the parts should sound together. As it proceeds, they should be in harmony while severally distinct and flowing without break, and thus on to the conclusion."

The border warden at Yi requested to be introduced to the Master, saying, "When men of superior virtue have come to this, I have never been denied the privilege of seeing them." The followers of the sage introduced him, and when he came out from the interview, he said, "My friends, why are you distressed by your master's loss of office? The kingdom has long been without the principles of truth and right; Heaven is going to use your master as a bell with its wooden tongue."

The Master said of the Shao that it was perfectly beautiful and also perfectly good. He said of the Wu that it was perfectly beautiful but not perfectly good.

The Master said, "High station filled without indulgent generosity; ceremonies performed without reverence; mourning conducted without sorrow; wherewith should I contemplate such ways?"

Book 4

The Master said, "It is virtuous manners which constitute the excellence of a neighborhood. If a man in selecting a residence do not fix on one where such prevail, how can he be wise?"

The Master said, "Those who are without virtue cannot abide long either in a condition of poverty and hardship, or in a condition of enjoyment.

The virtuous rest in virtue; the wise desire virtue."

The Master said, "It is only the truly virtuous man, who can love, or who can hate, others."

The Master said, "If the will be set on virtue, there will be no practice of wickedness."

The Master said, "Riches and honors are what men desire. If they cannot be obtained in the proper way, they should not be held. Poverty and meanness are what men dislike. If they cannot be avoided in the proper way, they should not be avoided.

"If a superior man abandon virtue, how can he fulfill the requirements of that name?

"The superior man does not, even for the space of a single meal, act contrary to virtue. In moments of haste, he cleaves to it. In seasons of danger, he cleaves to it."

The Master said, "I have not seen a person who loved virtue, or one who hated what was not virtuous. He who loved virtue, would esteem nothing above it. He who hated what is not virtuous, would practice virtue in such a way that he would not allow anything that is not virtuous to approach his person.

"Is any one able for one day to apply his strength to virtue? I have not seen the case in which his strength would be insufficient.

"Should there possibly be any such case, I have not seen it."

The Master said, "The faults of men are characteristic of the class to which they belong. By observing a man's faults, it may be known that he is virtuous."

The Master said, "If a man in the morning hear the right way, he may die in the evening hear regret."

The Master said, "A scholar, whose mind is set on truth, and who is ashamed of bad clothes and bad food, is not fit to be discoursed with."

The Master said, "The superior man, in the world, does not set his mind either for anything, or against anything; what is right he will follow."

The Master said, "The superior man thinks of virtue; the small man thinks of comfort. The superior man thinks of the sanctions of law; the small man thinks of favors which he may receive."

The Master said: "He who acts with a constant view to his own advantage will be much murmured against."

The Master said, "If a prince is able to govern his kingdom with the complaisance proper to the rules of propriety, what difficulty will he have?

If he cannot govern it with that complaisance, what has he to do with the rules of propriety?"

The Master said, "A man should say, I am not concerned that I have no place, I am concerned how I may fit myself for one. I am not concerned that I am not known, I seek to be worthy to be known."

The Master said, "Shan, my doctrine is that of an all-pervading unity." The disciple Tsang replied, "Yes."

The Master went out, and the other disciples asked, saying, "What do his words mean?" Tsang said, "The doctrine of our master is to be true to the principles of our nature and the benevolent exercise of them to others—this and nothing more."

The Master said, "The mind of the superior man is conversant with righteousness; the mind of the mean man is conversant with gain."

The Master said, "When we see men of worth, we should think of equaling them; when we see men of a contrary character, we should turn inwards and examine ourselves."

The Master said, "In serving his parents, a son may remonstrate with them, but gently; when he sees that they do not incline to follow his advice, he shows an increased degree of reverence, but does not abandon his purpose; and should they punish him, he does not allow himself to murmur."

The Master said, "While his parents are alive, the son may not go abroad to a distance. If he does go abroad, he must have a fixed place to which he goes."

The Master said, "If the son for three years does not alter from the way of his father, he may be called filial."

The Master said, "The years of parents may by no means not be kept in the memory, as an occasion at once for joy and for fear."

The Master said, "The reason why the ancients did not readily give utterance to their words, was that they feared lest their actions should not come up to them."

The Master said, "The cautious seldom err."

The Master said, "The superior man wishes to be slow in his speech and earnest in his conduct."

The Master said, "Virtue is not left to stand alone. He who practices it will have neighbors."

Tsze-yu said, "In serving a prince, frequent remonstrances lead to disgrace. Between friends, frequent reproofs make the friendship distant."

Book 5

The Master said of Kung-ye Ch'ang that he might be wived; although he was put in bonds, he had not been guilty of any crime. Accordingly, he gave him his own daughter to wife.

Of Nan Yung he said that if the country were well governed he would not be out of office, and if it were in governed, he would escape punishment and disgrace. He gave him the daughter of his own elder brother to wife.

The Master said of Tsze-chien, "Of superior virtue indeed is such a man! If there were not virtuous men in Lu, how could this man have acquired this character?"

Tsze-kung asked, "What do you say of me, Ts'ze!" The Master said, "You are a utensil." "What utensil?" "A gemmed sacrificial utensil."

Some one said, "Yung is truly virtuous, but he is not ready with his tongue."

The Master said, "What is the good of being ready with the tongue? They who encounter men with smartness of speech for the most part procure themselves hatred. I know not whether he be truly virtuous, but why should he show readiness of the tongue?"

The Master was wishing Ch'i-tiao K'ai to enter an official employment. He replied, "I am not yet able to rest in the assurance of this." The Master was pleased.

The Master said, "My doctrines make no way. I will get upon a raft, and float about on the sea. He that will accompany me will be Yu, I dare say." Tsze-lu hearing this was glad, upon which the Master said, "Yu is fonder of daring than I am. He does not exercise his judgment upon matters."

Mang Wu asked about Tsze-lu, whether he was perfectly virtuous. The Master said, "I do not know."

He asked again, when the Master replied, "In a kingdom of a thousand chariots, Yu might be employed to manage the military levies, but I do not know whether he be perfectly virtuous."

"And what do you say of Ch'iu?" The Master replied, "In a city of a thousand families, or a clan of a hundred chariots, Ch'iu might be employed as governor, but I do not know whether he is perfectly virtuous."

"What do you say of Ch'ih?" The Master replied, "With his sash girt and standing in a court, Ch'ih might be employed to converse with the visitors and guests, but I do not know whether he is perfectly virtuous."

The Master said to Tsze-kung, "Which do you consider superior, yourself or Hui?"

Tsze-kung replied, "How dare I compare myself with Hui? Hui hears one point and knows all about a subject; I hear one point, and know a second."

The Master said, "You are not equal to him. I grant you, you are not equal to him."

Tsai Yu being asleep during the daytime, the Master said, "Rotten wood cannot be carved; a wall of dirty earth will not receive the trowel.

This Yu—what is the use of my reproving him?"

The Master said, "At first, my way with men was to hear their words, and give them credit for their conduct. Now my way is to hear their words, and look at their conduct. It is from Yu that I have learned to make this change."

The Master said, "I have not seen a firm and unbending man." Some one replied, "There is Shan Ch'ang." "Ch'ang," said the Master, "is under the influence of his passions; how can he be pronounced firm and unbending?"

Tsze-kung said, "What I do not wish men to do to me, I also wish not to do to men." The Master said, "Ts'ze, you have not attained to that."

Tsze-kung said, "The Master's personal displays of his principles and ordinary descriptions of them may be heard. His discourses about man's nature, and the way of Heaven, cannot be heard."

When Tsze-lu heard anything, if he had not yet succeeded in carrying it into practice, he was only afraid lest he should hear something else.

Tsze-kung asked, saying, "On what ground did Kung-wan get that title of Wan?"

The Master said, "He was of an active nature and yet fond of learning, and he was not ashamed to ask and learn of his inferiors! On these grounds he has been styled Wan."

The Master said of Tsze-ch'an that he had four of the characteristics of a superior man—in his conduct of himself, he was humble; in serving his superior, he was respectful; in nourishing the people, he was kind; in ordering the people, he was just."

The Master said, "Yen P'ing knew well how to maintain friendly intercourse. The acquaintance might be long, but he showed the same respect as at first."

The Master said, "Tsang Wan kept a large tortoise in a house, on the capitals of the pillars of which he had hills made, and with representations of duckweed on the small pillars above the beams supporting the rafters. Of what sort was his wisdom?"

Tsze-chang asked, saying, "The minister Tsze-wan thrice took office, and manifested no joy in his countenance. Thrice he retired from office, and manifested no displeasure. He made it a point to inform the new minister of the way in which he had conducted the government; what do you say of him?" The Master replied. "He was loyal." "Was he perfectly virtuous?" "I do not know. How can he be pronounced perfectly virtuous?"

Tsze-chang proceeded, "When the officer Ch'ui killed the prince of Ch'i, Ch'an Wan, though he was the owner of forty horses, abandoned them and left the country. Coming to another state, he said, 'They are here like our great officer, Ch'ui,' and left it. He came to a second state, and with the same observation left it also; what do you say of him?" The Master replied, "He was pure." "Was he perfectly virtuous?" "I do not know. How can he be pronounced perfectly virtuous?"

Chi Wan thought thrice, and then acted. When the Master was informed of it, he said, "Twice may do."

The Master said, "When good order prevailed in his country, Ning Wu acted the part of a wise man. When his country was in disorder, he acted the part of a stupid man. Others may equal his wisdom, but they cannot equal his stupidity."

When the Master was in Ch'an, he said, "Let me return! Let me return! The little children of my school are ambitious and too hasty. They are accomplished and complete so far, but they do not know how to restrict and shape themselves."

The Master said, "Po-i and Shu-ch'i did not keep the former wickednesses of men in mind, and hence the resentments directed towards them were few."

The Master said, "Who says of Weishang Kao that he is upright? One begged some vinegar of him, and he begged it of a neighbor and gave it to the man."

The Master said, "Fine words, an insinuating appearance, and excessive respect—Tso Ch'iu-ming was ashamed of them. I also am ashamed of them. To conceal resentment against a person, and appear friendly with him—Tso Ch'iu-ming was ashamed of such conduct. I also am ashamed of it."

Yen Yuan and Chi Lu being by his side, the Master said to them, "Come, let each of you tell his wishes."

Tsze-lu said, "I should like, having chariots and horses, and light fur clothes, to share them with my friends, and though they should spoil them, I would not be displeased."

Yen Yuan said, "I should like not to boast of my excellence, nor to make a display of my meritorious deeds."

Tsze-lu then said, "I should like, sir, to hear your wishes." The Master said, "They are, in regard to the aged, to give them rest; in regard to friends, to show them sincerity; in regard to the young, to treat them tenderly."

The Master said, "It is all over. I have not yet seen one who could perceive his faults, and inwardly accuse himself."

The Master said, "In a hamlet of ten families, there may be found one honorable and sincere as I am, but not so fond of learning."

Book 6

The Master said, "There is Yung! He might occupy the place of a prince."

Chung-kung asked about Tsze-sang Po-tsze. The Master said, "He may pass. He does not mind small matters."

Chung-kung said, "If a man cherish in himself a reverential feeling of the necessity of attention to business, though he may be easy in small matters in his government of the people, that may be allowed. But if he cherish in himself that easy feeling, and also carry it out in his practice, is not such an easy mode of procedure excessive?"

The Master said, "Yung's words are right."

The Duke Ai asked which of the disciples loved to learn.

Confucius replied to him, "There was Yen Hui; he loved to learn. He did not transfer his anger; he did not repeat a fault. Unfortunately, his appointed time was short and he died; and now there is not such another. I have not yet heard of any one who loves to learn as he did."

Tsze-hwa being employed on a mission to Ch'i, the disciple Zan requested grain for his mother. The Master said, "Give her a fu." Yen requested more. "Give her a yi," said the Master. Yen gave her five ping.

The Master said, "When Ch'ih was proceeding to Ch'i, he had fat horses to his carriage, and wore light furs. I have heard that a superior man helps the distressed, but does not add to the wealth of the rich."

Yuan Sze being made governor of his town by the Master, he gave him nine hundred measures of grain, but Sze declined them.

The Master said, "Do not decline them. May you not give them away in the neighborhoods, hamlets, towns, and villages?"

The Master, speaking of Chung-kung, said, "If the calf of a brindled cow be red and horned, although men may not wish to use it, would the spirits of the mountains and rivers put it aside?"

The Master said, "Such was Hui that for three months there would be nothing in his mind contrary to perfect virtue. The others may attain to this on some days or in some months, but nothing more."

Chi K'ang asked about Chung-yu, whether he was fit to be employed as an officer of government. The Master said, "Yu is a man of decision; what difficulty would he find in being an officer of government?" K'ang asked, "Is Ts'ze fit to be employed as an officer of government?" and was answered, "Ts'ze is a man of intelligence; what difficulty would he find in being an officer of government?" And to the same question about Ch'iu the Master gave the same reply, saying, "Ch'iu is a man of various ability."

The chief of the Chi family sent to ask Min Tsze-ch'ien to be governor of Pi. Min Tszech'ien said, "Decline the offer for me politely. If any one come again to me with a second invitation, I shall be obliged to go and live on the banks of the Wan."

Po-niu being ill, the Master went to ask for him. He took hold of his hand through the window, and said, "It is killing him. It is the appointment of Heaven, alas! That such a man should have such a sickness! That such a man should have such a sickness!"

The Master said, "Admirable indeed was the virtue of Hui! With a single bamboo dish of rice, a single gourd dish of drink, and living in his mean narrow lane, while others could not have endured the distress, he did not allow his joy to be affected by it. Admirable indeed was the virtue of Hui!"

Yen Ch'iu said, "It is not that I do not delight in your doctrines, but my strength is insufficient." The Master said, "Those whose strength is insufficient give over in the middle of the way but now you limit yourself."

The Master said to Tsze-hsia, "Do you be a scholar after the style of the superior man, and not after that of the mean man."

Tsze-yu being governor of Wu-ch'ang, the Master said to him, "Have you got good men there?" He answered, "There is Tan-t'ai Miehming, who never in walking takes a short cut, and never comes to my office, excepting on public business."

The Master said, "Mang Chih-fan does not boast of his merit. Being in the rear on an occasion of flight, when they were about to enter the gate, he whipped up his horse, saying, "It is not that I dare to be last. My horse would not advance."

The Master said, "Without the specious speech of the litanist T'o and the beauty of the prince Chao of Sung, it is difficult to escape in the present age."

The Master said, "Who can go out but by the door? How is it that men will not walk according to these ways?"

The Master said, "Where the solid qualities are in excess of accomplishments, we have rusticity; where the accomplishments are in excess of the solid qualities, we have the manners of a clerk. When the accomplishments and solid qualities are equally blended, we then have the man of virtue."

The Master said, "Man is born for uprightness. If a man lose his uprightness, and yet live, his escape from death is the effect of mere good fortune."

The Master said, "They who know the truth are not equal to those who love it, and they who love it are not equal to those who delight in it."

The Master said, "To those whose talents are above mediocrity, the highest subjects may be announced. To those who are below mediocrity, the highest subjects may not be announced."

Fan Ch'ih asked what constituted wisdom. The Master said, "To give one's self earnestly to the duties due to men, and, while respecting spiritual beings, to keep aloof from them, may be called wisdom." He asked about perfect virtue. The Master said, "The man of virtue makes the difficulty to be overcome his first business, and success only a subsequent consideration; this may be called perfect virtue."

The Master said, "The wise find pleasure in water; the virtuous find pleasure in hills. The wise are active; the virtuous are tranquil. The wise are joyful; the virtuous are long-lived."

The Master said, "Ch'i, by one change, would come to the State of Lu. Lu, by one change, would come to a State where true principles predominated."

The Master said, "A cornered vessel without corners—a strange cornered vessel! A strange cornered vessel!"

Tsai Wo asked, saying, "A benevolent man, though it be told him, 'There is a man in the well' will go in after him, I suppose." Confucius said,

"Why should he do so?" A superior man may be made to go to the well, but he cannot be made to go down into it. He may be imposed upon, but he cannot be fooled."

The Master said, "The superior man, extensively studying all learning, and keeping himself under the restraint of the rules of propriety, may thus likewise not overstep what is right."

The Master having visited Nan-tsze, Tsze-lu was displeased, on which the Master swore, saying, "Wherein I have done improperly, may Heaven reject me, may Heaven reject me!"

The Master said, "Perfect is the virtue which is according to the Constant Mean! Rare for a long time has been its practice among the people."

Tsze-kung said, "Suppose the case of a man extensively conferring benefits on the people, and able to assist all, what would you say of him?

Might he be called perfectly virtuous?" The Master said, "Why speak only of virtue in connection with him? Must he not have the qualities of a sage? Even Yao and Shun were still solicitous about this.

"Now the man of perfect virtue, wishing to be established himself, seeks also to establish others; wishing to be enlarged himself, he seeks also to enlarge others.

"To be able to judge of others by what is nigh in ourselves—this may be called the art of virtue."

Book 7

The Master said, "A transmitter and not a maker, believing in and loving the ancients, I venture to compare myself with our old P'ang."

The Master said, "The silent treasuring up of knowledge; learning without satiety; and instructing others without being wearied: which one of these things belongs to me?"

The Master said, "The leaving virtue without proper cultivation; the not thoroughly discussing what is learned; not being able to move towards righteousness of which a knowledge is gained; and not being able to change what is not good—these are the things which occasion me solicitude."

When the Master was unoccupied with business, his manner was easy, and he looked pleased.

The Master said, "Extreme is my decay. For a long time, I have not dreamed, as I was wont to do, that I saw the duke of Chau."

The Master said, "Let the will be set on the path of duty.

"Let every attainment in what is good be firmly grasped.

"Let perfect virtue be accorded with.

"Let relaxation and enjoyment be found in the polite arts."

The Master said, "From the man bringing his bundle of dried flesh for my teaching upwards, I have never refused instruction to any one."

The Master said, "I do not open up the truth to one who is not eager to get knowledge, nor help out any one who is not anxious to explain himself. When I have presented one corner of a subject to any one, and he cannot from it learn the other three, I do not repeat my lesson."

When the Master was eating by the side of a mourner, he never ate to the full.

He did not sing on the same day in which he had been weeping.

The Master said to Yen Yuan, "When called to office, to undertake its duties; when not so called, to he retired; it is only I and you who have attained to this."

Tsze-lu said, "If you had the conduct of the armies of a great state, whom would you have to act with you?"

The Master said, "I would not have him to act with me, who will unarmed attack a tiger, or cross a river without a boat, dying without any regret. My associate must be the man who proceeds to action full of solicitude, who is fond of adjusting his plans, and then carries them into execution."

The Master said, "If the search for riches is sure to be successful, though I should become a groom with whip in hand to get them, I will do so. As the search may not be successful, I will follow after that which I love."

The things in reference to which the Master exercised the greatest caution were fasting, war, and sickness.

When the Master was in Ch'i, he heard the Shao, and for three months did not know the taste of flesh. "I did not think'" he said, "that music could have been made so excellent as this."

Yen Yu said, "Is our Master for the ruler of Wei?" Tsze-kung said, "Oh! I will ask him."

He went in accordingly, and said, "What sort of men were Po-i and Shu-ch'i?" "They were ancient worthies," said the Master. "Did they have any repinings because of their course?" The Master again replied, "They sought to act virtuously, and they did so; what was there for them to repine about?" On this, Tsze-kung went out and said, "Our Master is not for him."

The Master said, "With coarse rice to eat, with water to drink, and my bended arm for a pillow—I have still joy in the midst of these things. Riches and honors acquired by unrighteousness, are to me as a floating cloud."

The Master said, "If some years were added to my life, I would give fifty to the study of the Yi, and then I might come to be without great faults."

The Master's frequent themes of discourse were the Odes, the History, and the maintenance of the Rules of Propriety. On all these he frequently discoursed.

The Duke of Sheh asked Tsze-lu about Confucius, and Tsze-lu did not answer him.

The Master said, "Why did you not say to him, He is simply a man, who in his eager pursuit of knowledge forgets his food, who in the joy of its attainment forgets his sorrows, and who does not perceive that old age is coming on?"

The Master said, "I am not one who was born in the possession of knowledge; I am one who is fond of antiquity, and earnest in seeking it there."

The subjects on which the Master did not talk, were extraordinary things, feats of strength, disorder, and spiritual beings.

The Master said, "When I walk along with two others, they may serve me as my teachers. I will select their good qualities and follow them, their bad qualities and avoid them."

The Master said, "Heaven produced the virtue that is in me. Hwan T'ui—what can he do to me?"

The Master said, "Do you think, my disciples, that I have any concealments? I conceal nothing from you. There is nothing which I do that is not shown to you, my disciples; that is my way."

There were four things which the Master taught—letters, ethics, devotion of soul, and truthfulness.

The Master said, "A sage it is not mine to see; could I see a man of real talent and virtue, that would satisfy me."

The Master said, "A good man it is not mine to see; could I see a man possessed of constancy, that would satisfy me.

"Having not and yet affecting to have, empty and yet affecting to be full, straitened and yet affecting to be at ease—it is difficult with such characteristics to have constancy."

The Master angled, but did not use a net. He shot, but not at birds perching.

The Master said, "There may be those who act without knowing why. I do not do so. Hearing much and selecting what is good and following it; seeing much and keeping it in memory: this is the second style of knowledge."

It was difficult to talk profitably and reputably with the people of Hu-hsiang, and a lad of that place having had an interview with the Master, the disciples doubted.

The Master said, "I admit people's approach to me without committing myself as to what they may do when they have retired. Why must one be so severe? If a man purify himself to wait upon me, I receive him so purified, without guaranteeing his past conduct."

The Master said, "Is virtue a thing remote? I wish to be virtuous, and lo! virtue is at hand."

The minister of crime of Ch'an asked whether the duke Chao knew propriety, and Confucius said, "He knew propriety."

Confucius having retired, the minister bowed to Wu-ma Ch'i to come forward, and said, "I have heard that the superior man is not a partisan. May the superior man be a partisan also? The prince married a daughter of the house of WU, of the same surname with himself, and called her 'The elder Tsze of Wu.' If the prince knew propriety, who does not know it?"

Wu-ma Ch'i reported these remarks, and the Master said, "I am fortunate! If I have any errors, people are sure to know them."

When the Master was in company with a person who was singing, if he sang well, he would make him repeat the song, while he accompanied it with his own voice.

The Master said, "In letters I am perhaps equal to other men, but the character of the superior man, carrying out in his conduct what he professes, is what I have not yet attained to."

The Master said, "The sage and the man of perfect virtue—how dare I rank myself with them? It may simply be said of me, that I strive to become such without satiety, and teach others without weariness." Kung-hsi Hwa said, "This is just what we, the disciples, cannot imitate you in."

The Master being very sick, Tsze-lu asked leave to pray for him. He said, "May such a thing be done?" Tsze-lu replied, "It may. In the Eulogies it is said, 'Prayer has been made for thee to the spirits of the upper and lower worlds.'" The Master said, "My praying has been for a long time."

The Master said, "Extravagance leads to insubordination, and parsimony to meanness. It is better to be mean than to be insubordinate."

The Master said, "The superior man is satisfied and composed; the mean man is always full of distress."

The Master was mild, and yet dignified; majestic, and yet not fierce; respectful, and yet easy.

Book 8

The Master said, "T'ai-po may be said to have reached the highest point of virtuous action. Thrice he declined the kingdom, and the people in ignorance of his motives could not express their approbation of his conduct."

The Master said, "Respectfulness, without the rules of propriety, becomes laborious bustle; carefulness, without the rules of propriety, becomes timidity; boldness, without the rules of propriety, becomes insubordination; straightforwardness, without the rules of propriety, becomes rudeness.

"When those who are in high stations perform well all their duties to their relations, the people are aroused to virtue. When old friends are not neglected by them, the people are preserved from meanness."

The philosopher Tsang being ill, he cared to him the disciples of his school, and said, "Uncover my feet, uncover my hands. It is said in the Book of Poetry, 'We should be apprehensive and cautious, as if on the brink of a deep gulf, as if treading on thin ice, I and so have I been.

Now and hereafter, I know my escape from all injury to my person. O ye, my little children."

The philosopher Tsang being ill, Meng Chang went to ask how he was.

Tsang said to him, "When a bird is about to die, its notes are mournful; when a man is about to die, his words are good.

"There are three principles of conduct which the man of high rank should consider specially important—that in his deportment and manner he keep from violence and heedlessness; that in regulating his countenance he keep near to sincerity; and that in his words and tones he keep far from lowness and impropriety. As to such matters as attending to the sacrificial vessels, there are the proper officers for them."

The philosopher Tsang said, "Gifted with ability, and yet putting questions to those who were not so; possessed of much, and yet putting questions to those possessed of little; having, as though he had not; full, and yet counting himself as empty; offended against, and yet entering into no altercation; formerly I had a friend who pursued this style of conduct."

The philosopher Tsang said, "Suppose that there is an individual who can be entrusted with the charge of a young orphan prince, and can be commissioned with authority over a state of a hundred li, and whom no emergency however great can drive from his principles: is such a man a superior man? He is a superior man indeed."

The philosopher Tsang said, "The officer may not be without breadth of mind and vigorous endurance. His burden is heavy and his course is long.

"Perfect virtue is the burden which he considers it is his to sustain; is it not heavy? Only with death does his course stop; is it not long?

The Master said, "It is by the Odes that the mind is aroused.

"It is by the Rules of Propriety that the character is established.

"It is from Music that the finish is received."

The Master said, "The people may be made to follow a path of action, but they may not be made to understand it."

The Master said, "The man who is fond of daring and is dissatisfied with poverty, will proceed to insubordination. So will the man who is not virtuous, when you carry your dislike of him to an extreme."

The Master said, "Though a man have abilities as admirable as those of the Duke of Chau, yet if he be proud and niggardly, those other things are really not worth being looked at."

The Master said, "It is not easy to find a man who has learned for three years without coming to be good."

The Master said, "With sincere faith he unites the love of learning; holding firm to death, he is perfecting the excellence of his course.

"Such an one will not enter a tottering state, nor dwell in a disorganized one. When right principles of government prevail in the kingdom, he will show himself; when they are prostrated, he will keep concealed.

"When a country is well governed, poverty and a mean condition are things to be ashamed of. When a country is ill governed, riches and honor are things to be ashamed of."

The Master said, "He who is not in any particular office has nothing to do with plans for the administration of its duties."

The Master said, "When the music master Chih first entered on his office, the finish of the Kwan Tsu was magnificent; how it filled the ears!"

The Master said, "Ardent and yet not upright, stupid and yet not attentive; simple and yet not sincere—such persons I do not understand."

The Master said, "Learn as if you could not reach your object, and were always fearing also lest you should lose it."

The Master said, "How majestic was the manner in which Shun and Yu held possession of the empire, as if it were nothing to them!

The Master said, "Great indeed was Yao as a sovereign! How majestic was he! It is only Heaven that is grand, and only Yao corresponded to it. How vast was his virtue! The people could find no name for it.

"How majestic was he in the works which he accomplished! How glorious in the elegant regulations which he instituted!"

Shun had five ministers, and the empire was well governed.

King Wu said, "I have ten able ministers."

Confucius said, "Is not the saying that talents are difficult to find, true? Only when the dynasties of T'ang and Yu met, were they more abundant than in this of Chau, yet there was a woman among them. The able ministers were no more than nine men.

"King Wan possessed two of the three parts of the empire, and with those he served the dynasty of Yin. The virtue of the house of Chau may be said to have reached the highest point indeed."

The Master said, "I can find no flaw in the character of Yu. He used himself coarse food and drink, but displayed the utmost filial piety towards the spirits. His ordinary garments were poor, but he displayed the utmost elegance in his sacrificial cap and apron. He lived in a low, mean house, but expended all his strength on the ditches and water channels. I can find nothing like a flaw in Yu."

Book 9

The subjects of which the Master seldom spoke were profitableness, and also the appointments of Heaven, and perfect virtue.

A man of the village of Ta-hsiang said, "Great indeed is the philosopher K'ung! His learning is extensive, and yet he does not render his name famous by any particular thing."

The Master heard the observation, and said to his disciples, "What shall I practice? Shall I practice charioteering, or shall I practice archery? I will practice charioteering."

The Master said, "The linen cap is that prescribed by the rules of ceremony, but now a silk one is worn. It is economical, and I follow the common practice.

"The rules of ceremony prescribe the bowing below the hall, but now the practice is to bow only after ascending it. That is arrogant. I continue to bow below the hall, though I oppose the common practice."

There were four things from which the Master was entirely free. He had no foregone conclusions, no arbitrary predeterminations, no obstinacy, and no egoism.

The Master was put in fear in K'wang.

He said, "After the death of King Wan, was not the cause of truth lodged here in me?

"If Heaven had wished to let this cause of truth perish, then I, a future mortal! should not have got such a relation to that cause. While Heaven does not let the cause of truth perish, what can the people of K'wang do to me?"

A high officer asked Tsze-kung, saying, "May we not say that your Master is a sage? How various is his ability!"

Tsze-kung said, "Certainly Heaven has endowed him unlimitedly. He is about a sage. And, moreover, his ability is various."

The Master heard of the conversation and said, "Does the high officer know me? When I was young, my condition was low, and I acquired my ability in many things, but they were mean matters. Must the superior man have such variety of ability? He does not need variety of ability.

Lao said, "The Master said, 'Having no official employment, I acquired many arts.'"

The Master said, "Am I indeed possessed of knowledge? I am not knowing. But if a mean person, who appears quite empty-like, ask anything of me, I set it forth from one end to the other, and exhaust it."

The Master said, "The Fang bird does not come; the river sends forth no map—it is all over with me!"

When the Master saw a person in a mourning dress, or any one with the cap and upper and lower garments of full dress, or a blind person, on observing them approaching, though they were younger than himself, he would rise up, and if he had to pass by them, he would do so hastily.

Yen Yuan, in admiration of the Master's doctrines, sighed and said, "I looked up to them, and they seemed to become more high; I tried to penetrate them, and they seemed to become more firm; I looked at them before me, and suddenly they seemed to be behind.

"The Master, by orderly method, skillfully leads men on. He enlarged my mind with learning, and taught me the restraints of propriety.

"When I wish to give over the study of his doctrines, I cannot do so, and having exerted all my ability, there seems something to stand right up before me; but though I wish to follow and lay hold of it, I really find no way to do so."

The Master being very ill, Tsze-lu wished the disciples to act as ministers to him.

During a remission of his illness, he said, "Long has the conduct of Yu been deceitful! By pretending to have ministers when I have them not, whom should I impose upon? Should I impose upon Heaven?

"Moreover, than that I should die in the hands of ministers, is it not better that I should die in the hands of you, my disciples? And though I may not get a great burial, shall I die upon the road?"

Tsze-kung said, "There is a beautiful gem here. Should I lay it up in a case and keep it? or should I seek for a good price and sell it?" The Master said, "Sell it! Sell it! But I would wait for one to offer the price."

The Master was wishing to go and live among the nine wild tribes of the east.

Some one said, "They are rude. How can you do such a thing?" The Master said, "If a superior man dwelt among them, what rudeness would there be?"

The Master said, "I returned from Wei to Lu, and then the music was reformed, and the pieces in the Royal songs and Praise songs all found their proper places."

The Master said, "Abroad, to serve the high ministers and nobles; at home, to serve one's father and elder brothers; in all duties to the dead, not to dare not to exert one's self; and not to be overcome of wine: which one of these things do I attain to?"

The Master standing by a stream, said, "It passes on just like this, not ceasing day or night!"

The Master said, "I have not seen one who loves virtue as he loves beauty."

The Master said, "The prosecution of learning may be compared to what may happen in raising a mound. If there want but one basket of earth to complete the work, and I stop, the stopping is my own work. It may be compared to throwing down the earth on the level ground.

Though but one basketful is thrown at a time, the advancing with it my own going forward."

The Master said, "Never flagging when I set forth anything to him; ah! that is Hui." The Master said of Yen Yuan, "Alas! I saw his constant advance. I never saw him stop in his progress."

The Master said, "There are cases in which the blade springs, but the plant does not go on to flower! There are cases where it flowers but fruit is not subsequently produced!"

The Master said, "A youth is to be regarded with respect. How do we know that his future will not be equal to our present? If he reach the age of forty or fifty, and has not made himself heard of, then indeed he will not be worth being regarded with respect."

The Master said, "Can men refuse to assent to the words of strict admonition? But it is reforming the conduct because of them which is valuable. Can men refuse to be pleased with words of gentle advice? But it is unfolding their aim which is valuable.

If a man be pleased with these words, but does not unfold their aim, and assents to those, but does not reform his conduct, I can really do nothing with him."

The Master said, "Hold faithfulness and sincerity as first principles. Have no friends not equal to yourself. When you have faults, do not fear to abandon them."

The Master said, "The commander of the forces of a large state may be carried off, but the will of even a common man cannot be taken from him."

The Master said, "Dressed himself in a tattered robe quilted with hemp, yet standing by the side of men dressed in furs, and not ashamed; ah! it is Yu who is equal to this!

"He dislikes none, he covets nothing—what can he do but what is good!"

Tsze-lu kept continually repeating these words of the ode, when the Master said, "Those things are by no means sufficient to constitute perfect excellence."

The Master said, "When the year becomes cold, then we know how the pine and the cypress are the last to lose their leaves."

The Master said, "The wise are free from perplexities; the virtuous from anxiety; and the bold from fear."

The Master said, "There are some with whom we may study in common, but we shall find them unable to go along with us to principles.

Perhaps we may go on with them to principles, but we shall find them unable to get established in those along with us. Or if we may get so established along with them, we shall find them unable to weigh occurring events along with us."

"How the flowers of the aspen-plum flutter and turn! Do I not think of you? But your house is distant."

The Master said, "It is the want of thought about it. How is it distant?"

. . .

Book 12

. . .

Chung-kung asked about perfect virtue. The Master said, "It is, when you go abroad, to behave to every one as if you were receiving a great guest; to employ the people as if you were assisting at a great sacrifice; not to do to others as you would not wish done to yourself; to have no murmuring against you in the country, and none in the family." Chung-kung said, "Though I am deficient in intelligence and vigor, I will make it my business to practice this lesson...."

The Duke Ching, of Ch'i, asked Confucius about government.

Confucius replied, "There is government, when the prince is prince, and the minister is minister; when the father is father, and the son is son."

"Good!" said the duke; "if, indeed, the prince be not prince, the minister not minister, the father not father, and the son not son, although I have my revenue, can I enjoy it?..."

Chi K'ang asked Confucius about government, saying, "What do you say to killing the unprincipled for the good of the principled?" Confucius replied, "Sir, in carrying on your government, why should you use killing at all? Let your evinced desires be for what is good, and the people will be good. The relation between superiors and inferiors is like that between the wind and the grass. The grass must bend, when the wind blows across it."

Mandate of Heaven

ca. 475–221 BCE

Document Text

I. In the third month, at the commencement of *the government of* the duke of Chow in the new city of Luo, he announced *the royal will* to the officers of the Shang dynasty, *saying*, "The king speaks to this effect:—'Ye numerous officers who remain from the dynasty of Yin, great ruin came down on Yin from the want of pity in compassionate Heaven, and we, the princes of Chow, received its favouring decree. We accordingly felt charged with its bright terrors; carried out the punishments which kings inflict; rightly disposed of the appointment of Yin; and finished *the work* of God. Now, ye numerous officers, it was not that our small country dared to aim at the appointment of Yin. But Heaven was not with *Yin*, for indeed it would not strengthen its misrule. It *therefore* helped us;—did we dare to seek the throne of ourselves? God was not for *Yin*, as appeared from the conduct of our inferior people, in which there is the brilliant dreadfulness of Heaven.

II. 'I have heard the saying—God leads men to tranquil security; but the sovereign of Hea would not move to such security, whereupon God sent down *corrections*, indicating His mind to him. *Këe*, however, would not be warned by God, but proceeded to greater dissoluteness and sloth and excuses for himself. Then Heaven no longer regarded nor heard him, but disallowed his great appointment, and inflicted extreme punishment. Hereupon it charged your founder, T'ang [Tang] the Successful, to set Hea [Xia] aside, and by means of able men to rule the empire. From T'ang the Successful down to the emperor Yih, every sovereign sought to make his virtue illustrious, and duly attended to the sacrifices. And thus it was that while Heaven exerted a great establishing influence, preserving and regulating the house of Yin, its sovereigns on their part were humbly careful not to lose the favour of God, and strove to manifest a good doing corresponding to that of Heaven. But in these times, their successor showed himself greatly ignorant of *the ways of* Heaven, and much less could it be expected of him that he would be regardful of the earnest labours of his fathers for the country. Greatly abandoned to dissolute idleness, he paid no regard to the bright principles of Heaven, nor the awfulness of the people. On this account God no longer protected him, but sent down the great ruin which we have witnessed. Heaven was not with him because he did not seek to illustrate his virtue. *Indeed*, with regard to the overthrow of all States, great and small, throughout the four quarters of the empire, in every case there are reasons to be alleged for their punishment.'"

"The king speaks to this effect:—'Ye numerous officers of Yin, the case now is this, that the sovereigns of our Chow, from their great goodness were charged with the work of God. There was the charge to them, Cut off Yin. *They proceeded to perform it,* and announced the correcting work to God. In our affairs we have followed no double aims:—ye of the royal house *of Yin* must follow us.

III. 'May I not say that you were very lawless? I did not *want to* remove you. The thing came from your own city. When I consider also how Heaven has drawn near to Yin with *so* great tribulations, it must be that there was *there* what was not right.'"

"The king says, 'Ho! I declare to you, ye numerous officers, it is simply on account of these things that I have removed and settled you in the west;—it was not that I, the one man, considered it a part of my virtue to make you untranquil. The thing was from the decree of Heaven; do not resist me; I dare not have any further *change for you*. Do not murmur against me. Ye know that your fathers of the Yin dynasty had their archives and narratives *showing* how Yin superseded the appointment of Hea. Ye now indeed say further, "*The officers of* Hea were chosen and promoted to the imperial court, or had their places among the mass of officers." I, the one man, listen only to the virtuous and employ them; and it was with this view that I presumed to seek you out in *your* heavenly city of Shang. I thereby follow the ancient *example*, and have pity on you. *Your present non-employment* is no fault of mine; it is by the decree of Heaven.'"

"The king says, 'Ye numerous officers, formerly, when I came from Yen, I greatly mitigated the penalty in favour of the lives of the people of your four countries. At the same time I made evident the punishment appointed by Heaven, and removed you to this distant abode, that you might be near the ministers who had served in our honoured *capital*, and *learn* their much obedience.'"

"The king says, 'I declare to you, ye numerous officers of Yin,—now I have not put you to death, and therefore I repeat to you my charge again. I have built this great city here in Luo, considering that there was no other place in which to receive my guests from the four quarters, and also that you, ye numerous officers, might here with zealous activity, perform the part of ministers to us with much obedience. You have still here I may say your grounds, and here you may still rest in your duties and dwellings.

If you can reverently obey, Heaven will favour and compassionate you. If you cannot reverently obey, you will not only not have your lands, but I will also carry to the utmost Heaven's inflictions on your persona. Now you may here dwell in your villages, and perpetuate your families; you may pursue your occupations and enjoy your years in this Luo; your children also will prosper:—*all* from your being removed here.'"

"The king says,—; and again he says, 'Whatsoever I have spoken, is all on account of *my anxiety about* your residence *here*.'"

Canon of Filial Piety

ca. 300–239 BCE

Document Text

The Scope and Meaning of the Treatise

Once, when Zhong Ni was unoccupied, and his disciple Zeng was sitting by in attendance on him, the Master said, "The ancient kings had a perfect virtue and all-embracing rule of conduct, through which they were in accord with all under Heaven. By the practice of it the people were brought to live in peace and harmony, and there was no ill-will between superiors and inferiors. Do you know what it was?"

Zeng rose from his mat and said, "How should I, Shen, who am so devoid of intelligence, be able to know this?"

The Master said, "It was filial piety. Now filial piety is the root of all virtue, and the stem out of which grows all moral teaching. Sit down again, and I will explain the subject to you. Our bodies—to every hair and bit of skin—are received by us from our parents, and we must not presume to injure or wound them. This is the beginning of filial piety. When we have established our character by the practice of the filial course, so as to make our name famous in future ages and thereby glorify our parents, this is the end of filial piety. It commences with the service of parents; it proceeds to the service of the ruler; it is completed by the establishment of character.

It is said in the Major Odes of the Kingdom: Ever think of your ancestor, cultivating your virtue."

Filial Piety in the Son of Heaven

The Master said, "He who loves his parents will not dare to incur the risk of being hated by any man, and he who reveres his parents will not dare to incur the risk of being condemned by any man. When the love and reverence of the Son of Heaven are thus carried to the utmost in the service of his parents, the lessons of his virtue affect all the people, and he becomes a pattern to all within the four seas. This is the filial piety of the Son of Heaven.

It is said in the Marquis of Fu on Punishments: The one man will have felicity, and the millions of the people will depend on what ensures his happiness."

Filial Piety in High Ministers and Great Officers

"They do not presume to wear robes other than those appointed by the laws of the ancient kings, nor to speak words other than those sanctioned by their speech, nor to exhibit conduct other than that exemplified by their virtuous ways. Thus none of their words being contrary to those sanctions, and none of their actions contrary to the right way, from their mouths there comes no exceptionable speech, and in their conduct there are found no exceptionable actions. Their words may fill all under Heaven, and no error of speech will be found in them. Their actions may fill all under Heaven, and no dissatisfaction or dislike will be awakened by them. When these three things—their robes, their words, and their conduct—are all complete as they should be, they can then preserve their ancestral temples. This is the filial piety of high ministers and great officers.

It is said in the Book of Poetry: He is never idle, day or night, in the service of the one man."

Filial Piety in Inferior Officers

"As they serve their fathers, so they serve their mothers, and they love them equally. As they serve their fathers, so they serve their rulers, and they reverence them equally. Hence love is what is chiefly rendered to the mother, and reverence is what is chiefly rendered to the ruler, while both of these things are given to the father. Therefore when they serve their ruler with filial piety, they are loyal; when they serve their superiors with reverence, they are obedient. Not failing in this loyalty and obedience in serving those above them, they are then able to preserve their emoluments and positions, and to maintain their sacrifices. This is the filial piety of inferior officers.

It is said in the Book of Poetry: Rising early and going to sleep late, Do not disgrace those who gave you birth."

Filial Piety in the Common People

"They follow the course of Heaven in the revolving seasons; they distinguish the advantages afforded by different soils; they are careful of their conduct and economical in their expenditure—in order to nourish their parents. This is the filial piety of the common people. Therefore from the Son of Heaven down to the common people, there never has been one whose filial piety was without its beginning and end on whom calamity did not come."

Filial Piety in Relation to the Three Powers

The disciple Zeng said, "Immense indeed is the greatness of filial piety!"

The Master replied, "Yes, filial piety is the constant method of Heaven, the righteousness of Earth, and the practical duty of Man. Heaven and Earth invariably pursue the course that may be thus described, and the people take it as their pattern. The ancient kings imitated the brilliant luminaries of Heaven and acted in accordance with the varying advantages afforded by Earth, so that they were in accord with all under Heaven, and in consequence their teachings, without being severe, were successful, and their government, without being rigorous, secured perfect order.

The ancient kings, seeing how their teachings could transform the people, set before them therefore an example of the most extended love, and none of the people neglected their parents. They set forth to them the nature of virtue and righteousness, and the people roused themselves to the practice of them. They went before them with reverence and yielding courtesy, and the people had no contentions. They led them on by the rules of propriety and by music, and the people were harmonious and benignant. They showed them what they loved and what they disliked, and the people understood their prohibitions.

It is said in the Book of Poetry: Awe-inspiring are you, O Grand-Master Yin, and the people all look up to you."

Filial Piety in Government

The Master said, "Anciently, when the intelligent kings by means of filial piety ruled all under Heaven, they did not dare to receive with disrespect the ministers of small states. How much less would they do so to the dukes, marquises, counts, and barons! Thus it was that they got the princes of the myriad states with joyful hearts to assist them in the sacrificial services to their royal predecessors.

The rulers of states did not dare to slight wifeless men and widows. How much less would they slight their officers and the people! Thus it was that they got all their people with joyful hearts to assist them in serving the rulers, their predecessors.

The heads of clans did not dare to slight their servants and concubines. How much less would they slight their wives and sons! Thus it was that they got their men with joyful hearts to assist them in the service of their parents.

In such a state of things, while alive, parents reposed in the glory of their sons, and, when sacrificed to, their disembodied spirits enjoyed their offerings. Therefore for all under Heaven peace and harmony prevailed; disasters and calamities did not occur; misfortunes and rebellions did not arise.

It is said in the Book of Poetry: To an upright, virtuous conduct all in the four quarters of the state render obedient homage."

The Government of the Sages

The disciple Zeng said, "I venture to ask whether in the virtue of the sages there was not something greater than filial piety."

The Master replied, "Of all creatures with their different natures produced by Heaven and Earth, man is the noblest. Of all the actions of man there is none greater than filial piety. In filial piety there is nothing greater than the reverential awe of one's father. In the reverential awe shown to one's father there is nothing greater than the making him the correlate of Heaven. The duke of Zhou was the man who first did this.

Formerly the duke of Zhou at the border altar sacrificed to Hou Ji as the correlate of Heaven, and in the Brilliant Hall he honored king Wen and sacrificed to him as the correlate of God. The consequence was that from all the states within the four seas, every prince came in the discharge of his duty to assist in those sacrifices. In the virtue of the sages what besides was there greater than filial piety?

Now the feeling of affection grows up at the parents' knees, and as the duty of nourishing those parents is exercised, the affection daily merges in awe. The sages proceeded from the feeling of awe to teach the duties of reverence, and from that of affection to teach those of love. The teachings of the sages, without being severe, were successful, and their government, without being rigorous, was effective. What they proceeded from was the root of filial piety implanted by Heaven.

The relation and duties between father and son, thus belonging to the Heaven-conferred nature, contain in them the principle of righteousness between ruler and subject. The son derives his life from his parents, and no greater gift could possibly be transmitted. His ruler and parent in one, his father deals with him accordingly, and no generosity could be greater than this. Hence, he who does not love his parents, but loves other men, is called a rebel against virtue, and he who does not revere his parents, but reveres other men, is called a rebel against propriety. When the ruler himself thus acts contrary to the principles which should place him in accord with all men, he presents nothing for the people to imitate. He has nothing to do with what is good, but entirely and only with what is injurious to virtue. Though he may get his will, and be above others, the superior man does not give him his approval.

It is not so with the superior man. He speaks, having thought whether the words should be spoken; he acts, having thought whether his actions are sure to give pleasure. His virtue and righteousness are such as will be honored; what he initiates and does is fit to be imitated; his deportment is worthy of contemplation; his movements in advancing or retiring are all according to the proper rule. In this way does he present himself to the people, who both revere and love him, imitate and become like him. Thus he is able to make his teaching of virtue successful, and his government and orders to be carried into effect.

It is said in the Book of Poetry: The virtuous man, the princely one, Has nothing wrong in his deportment."

An Orderly Description of the Acts of Filial Piety

The Master said, "The service which a filial son does to his parents is as follows: In his general conduct to them, he manifests the utmost reverence. In his nourishing of them, his endeavor is to give them the utmost pleasure. When they are ill, he feels the greatest anxiety. In mourning for them dead, he exhibits every demonstration of grief. In sacrificing to them, he displays the utmost solemnity. When a son is complete in these five things, he may be pronounced able to serve his parents.

He who thus serves his parents, in a high situation will be free from pride, in a low situation will be free from insubordination, and among his equals will not be quarrelsome. In a high situation pride leads to ruin; in a low situation insubordination leads to punishment; among equals quarrelsomeness leads to the wielding of weapons. If those three things be not put away, though a son every day contribute beef, mutton, and pork to nourish his parents, he is not filial."

Filial Piety in Relation to the Five Punishments

The Master said, "There are three thousand offenses against which the five punishments are directed, and there is not one of them greater than being unfilial.

When constraint is put upon a ruler, that is the disowning of his superiority. When the authority of the sages is disallowed, that is the disowning of all law. When filial piety is put aside, that is the disowning of the principle of affection. These three things pave the way to anarchy."

Amplification of "the All-embracing Rule of Conduct" in Chapter I

The Master said, "For teaching the people to be affectionate and loving, there is nothing better than filial piety. For teaching them the observance of propriety and submissiveness, there is nothing better than fraternal duty. For changing their manners and altering their customs, there is nothing better than music. For securing the repose of superiors and the good order of the people, there is nothing better than the rules of propriety.

The rules of propriety are simply the development of the principle of reverence. Therefore the reverence paid to a father makes all sons pleased. The reverence paid to an elder brother makes all younger brothers pleased. The reverence paid to a ruler makes all subjects pleased. The reverence paid to the one man makes thousands and myriads of men pleased. The reverence is paid to a few, and the pleasure extends to many. This is what is meant by an "All-embracing Rule of Conduct."'

Amplification of "the Perfect Virtue" in Chapter I

The Master said, "The teaching of filial piety by the superior man does not require that he should go to family after family and daily see the members of each. His teaching of filial piety is a tribute of reverence to all the fathers under Heaven. His teaching of fraternal submission is a tribute of reverence to all the elder brothers under Heaven. His teaching of the duty of a subject is a tribute of reverence to all the rulers under Heaven.

It is said in the Book of Poetry: The happy and courteous sovereign is the parent of the people. If it were not a perfect virtue, how could it be recognized as in accordance with their nature by the people so extensively as this?"

Amplification of "Making Our Name Famous" in Chapter I

The Master said, "The filial piety with which the superior man serves his parents may be transferred as loyalty to the ruler. The fraternal duty with which he serves his elder brother may be transferred as submissive deference to elders. His regulation of his family may be transferred as good government in any official position. Therefore, when his conduct is thus successful in his inner private circle, his name will be established and transmitted to future generations."

Filial Piety in Relation to Reproof and Remonstrance

The disciple Zeng said, "I have heard your instructions on the affection of love, on respect and reverence, on giving repose to the minds of our parents, and on making our names famous. I would venture to ask if simple obedience to the orders of one's father can be pronounced filial piety."

The Master replied, "What words are these! What words are these! Anciently, if the Son of Heaven had seven ministers who would remonstrate with him, although he had not right methods of government, he would not lose his possession of the kingdom. If the prince of a state had five such ministers, though his measures might be equally wrong, he would not lose his state. If a great officer had three, he would not, in a similar case, lose the headship of his clan. If an inferior officer had a friend who would remonstrate with him, a good name would not cease to be connected with his character. And the father who had a son that would remonstrate with him would not sink into the gulf of unrighteous deeds. Therefore when a case of unrighteous conduct is concerned, a son must by no means keep from remonstrating with his father, nor a minister from remonstrating with his ruler. Hence, since remonstrance is required in the case of unrighteous conduct, how can simple obedience to the orders of a father be accounted filial piety?"

The Influence of Filial Piety and the Response to It

The Master said, "Anciently, the intelligent kings served their fathers with filial piety, and therefore they served Heaven with intelligence. They served their mothers with filial piety, and therefore they served Earth with discrimination. They pursued the right course with reference to their own seniors and juniors, and therefore they secured the regulation of the relations between superiors and inferiors throughout the kingdom. When Heaven and Earth were served with intelligence and discrimination, the spiritual intelligences displayed their retributive power. Therefore even the Son of Heaven must have some whom he honors; that is, he has his uncles of his surname. He must have some to whom he concedes the precedence; that is, he has his cousins, who bear the same surname and are older than himself. In the ancestral temple he manifests the utmost reverence, showing that he does not forget his parents. He cultivates his person and is careful of his conduct, fearing lest he should disgrace his predecessors. When in the ancestral temple he exhibits the utmost reverence, the spirits of the departed manifest themselves. Perfect filial piety and fraternal duty reach to and move the spiritual intelligences and diffuse their light on all within the four seas. They penetrate everywhere.

It is said in the Book of Poetry: From the west to the east, from the south to the north, there was not a thought but did him homage."

The Service of the Ruler

The Master said, "The superior man serves his ruler in such a way that, when at court in his presence, his thought is how to discharge his loyal duty to the utmost, and when he retires from it, his thought is how to amend his errors. He carries out with deference the measures springing from his excellent qualities and rectifies him only to save him from what are evil. Hence, as the superior and inferior, they are able to have an affection for each other.

It is said in the Book of Poetry: In my heart I love him, and why should I not say so? In the core of my heart I keep him, and never will forget him."

Filial Piety in Mourning for Parents

The Master said, "When a filial son is mourning for a parent, he wails, but not with a prolonged sobbing. In the movements of ceremony he pays no attention to his appearance. His words are without elegance of phrase. He cannot bear to wear fine clothes. When he hears music, he feels no delight. When he eats a delicacy, he is not conscious of its flavor. Such is the nature of grief and sorrow.

After three days he may partake of food, for thus the people are taught that the living should not be injured on account of the dead, and that emaciation must not be carried to the extinction of life. Such is the rule of the sages. The period of mourning does not go beyond three years, to show the people that it must have an end.

An inner and outer coffin are made; the grave-clothes also are put on, and the shroud; and the body is lifted into the coffin. The sacrificial vessels, round and square, are regularly set forth, and the sight of them fills the mourners with fresh distress. The women beat their breasts, and the men stamp with their feet, wailing and weeping, while they sorrowfully escort the coffin to the grave. They consult the tortoise-shell to determine the grave and the ground about it, and there they lay the body in peace. They prepare the ancestral temple to receive the tablet of the departed, and there they present offerings to the disembodied spirit. In spring and autumn they offer sacrifices, thinking of the deceased as the seasons come round.

The services of love and reverence to parents when alive, and those of grief and sorrow to them when dead: these completely discharge the fundamental duty of living men. The righteous claims of life and death are all satisfied, and the filial son's service of his parents is completed."

Han Feizi

ca. 230 BCE

Document Text

"The Five Vermin"

There was a farmer of Song who tilled the land, and in his field was a stump. One day a rabbit, racing across the field, bumped into the stump, broke its neck, and died. Thereupon the farmer laid aside his plow and took up watch beside the stump, hoping that he would get another rabbit in the same way. But he got no more rabbits, and instead became the laughingstock of Song. Those who think they can take the ways of the ancient kings and use them to govern the people of today all belong in the category of stump-watchers! . . .

When Yao ruled the world, he left the thatch of his roof untrimmed, and the raw timber of his beams was left unplaned. He ate coarse millet and a soup of greens, wore deerskin in the winter days and rough fiber robes in summer. Even a lowly gatekeeper was no worse clothed and provided for than he. When Yu ruled the world, he took plow and spade in hand to lead his people, working until there was no more down on his thighs or hair on his shins. Even the toil of a slave taken prisoner in the wars was no bitterer than his. Therefore those men in ancient times who abdicated and relinquished the rule of the world were, in a manner of speaking, merely forsaking the life of a gatekeeper and escaping from the toil of a slave. Therefore they thought little of handing over the rule of the world to someone else. Nowadays, however, the magistrate of a district dies and his sons and grandsons are able to go riding about in carriages for generations after. Therefore people prize such offices. In the matter of relinquishing things, people thought nothing of stepping down from the position of Son of Heaven in ancient times, yet they are very reluctant to give up the post of district magistrate today; this is because of the difference in the actual benefits received. . . .

When men lightly relinquish the position of Son of Heaven, it is not because they are high-minded but because the advantages of the post are slight; when men strive for sinecures in the government, it is not because they are base but because the power they will acquire is great.

When the sage rules, he takes into consideration the quantity of things and deliberates on scarcity and plenty. Though his punishments may be light, this is not due to his compassion; though his penalties may be severe, this is not because he is cruel; he simply follows the custom appropriate to the time. Circumstances change according to the age, and ways of dealing with them change with the circumstances. . . .

Past and present have different customs; new and old adopt different measures. To try to use the ways of a generous and lenient government to rule the people of a critical age is like trying to drive a runaway horse without using reins or whip. This is the misfortune that ignorance invites.

Now the Confucians and the Mohists all praise the ancient kings for their universal love of the world, saying that they looked after the people as parents look after a beloved child. And how do they prove this contention? They say, "Whenever the minister of justice administered some punishment, the ruler would purposely cancel all musical performances; and whenever the ruler learned that the death sentence had been passed on someone, he would shed tears." For this reason they praise the ancient kings.

Now if ruler and subject must become like father and son before there can be order, then we must suppose that there is no such thing as an unruly father or son. Among human affections none takes priority over the love of parents for their children. But though all parents may show love for their children, the children are not always well behaved.... And if such love cannot prevent children from becoming unruly, then how can it bring the people to order?...

Humaneness may make one shed tears and be reluctant to apply penalties, but law makes it clear that such penalties must be applied. The ancient kings allowed law to be supreme and did not give in to their tearful longings. Hence it is obvious that humaneness cannot be used to achieve order in the state....

Now here is a young man of bad character. His parents rail at him, but he does not reform; the neighbors scold, but he is unmoved; his teachers instruct him, but he refuses to change his ways. Thus, although three fine influences are brought to bear on him—the love of his parents, the efforts of the neighbors, the wisdom of his teachers—yet he remains unmoved and refuses to change so much as a hair on his shin. But let the district magistrate send out the government soldiers to enforce the law and search for evildoers, and then he is filled with terror, reforms his conduct, and changes his ways. Thus the love of parents is not enough to make children learn what is right, but must be backed up by the strict penalties of the local officials; for people by nature grow proud on love, but they listen to authority....

The best rewards are those that are generous and predictable, so that the people may profit by them. The best penalties are those that are severe and inescapable, so that the people will fear them. The best laws are those that are uniform and inflexible, so that the people can understand them....

Those who practice humaneness and rightness should not be praised, for to praise them is to cast aspersion on military achievements; men of literary accomplishment should not be employed in the government, for to employ them is to bring confusion to the law. In the state of Chu there was a man named Honest Gong. When his father stole a sheep, he reported the theft to the authorities. But the local magistrate, considering that the man was honest in the service of his sovereign but a villain to his own father, replied, "Put him to death!" and the man was accordingly sentenced and executed. Thus we see that a man who is an honest subject of his sovereign may be an infamous son to his father.

There was a man of Lu who accompanied his sovereign to war. Three times he went into battle, and three times he ran away. When Confucius asked him the reason, he replied, "I have an aged father, and if I should die, there would be no one to take care of him." Confucius, considering the man filial, recommended him and had him promoted to a post in the government. Thus we see that a man who is a filial son to his father may be a traitorous subject to his lord.

The magistrate of Chu executed a man, and as a result the felonies of the state were never reported to the authorities; Confucius rewarded a man, and as a result the people of Lu thought nothing of surrendering or running away in battle. Since the interests of superior and inferior are as disparate as all this, it is hopeless for the ruler to praise the actions of the private individual and at the same time try to ensure blessing to the state's altars of the soil and grain.

In ancient times when Cang Jie created the system of writing, he used the character for "private" to express the idea of self-centeredness, and combined the elements for "private" and "opposed to" to form the character for "public." The fact that public and private are mutually opposed was already well understood at the time of Cang Jie. To regard the two as being identical in interest is a disaster that comes from lack of consideration. . . .

The world calls worthy those whose conduct is marked by integrity and good faith, and wise those whose words are subtle and mysterious. But even the wisest man has difficulty understanding words that are subtle and mysterious. Now if you want to set up laws for the masses and you try to base them on doctrines that even the wisest men have difficulty in understanding, how can the common people comprehend them? . . . Now in administering your rule and dealing with the people, if you do not speak in terms that any man or woman can plainly understand, but long to apply the doctrines of the wise men, then you will defeat your own efforts at rule. Subtle and mysterious words are no business of the people.

If people regard those who act with integrity and good faith as worthy, it must be because they value men who have no deceit, and they value men of no deceit because they themselves have no means to protect themselves from deceit. The common people in selecting their friends, for example, have no wealth by which to win others over, and no authority by which to intimidate others. For that reason they seek for men who are without deceit to be their friends. But the ruler occupies a position whereby he may impose his will upon others, and he has the whole wealth of the nation at his disposal; he may dispense lavish rewards and severe penalties and, by wielding these two handles, may illuminate all things through his wise policies. In that case, even traitorous ministers like Tian Chang and Zihan would not dare to deceive him. Why should he have to wait for men who are by nature not deceitful?

Hardly ten men of true integrity and good faith can be found today, and yet the offices of the state number in the hundreds. If they must be filled by men of integrity and good faith, then there will never be enough men to go around; and if the offices are left unfilled, then those whose business it is to govern will dwindle in numbers while disorderly men increase. Therefore the way of the enlightened ruler is to unify the laws instead of seeking for wise men, to lay down firm policies instead of longing for men of good faith. Hence his laws never fail him, and there is no felony or deceit among his officials....

Now the people of the state all discuss good government, and everyone has a copy of the works on law by Shang Yang and Guan Zhong in his house, and yet the state gets poorer and poorer, for though many people talk about farming, very few put their hands to a plow. The people of the state all discuss military affairs, and everyone has a copy of the works of Sun Wu and Wu Qi in his house, and yet the armies grow weaker and weaker, for though many people talk about war, few buckle on armor. Therefore an enlightened ruler will make use of men's strength but will not heed their words, will reward their accomplishments but will prohibit useless activities. Then the people will be willing to exert themselves to the point of death in the service of their sovereign.

Farming requires a lot of hard work, but people will do it because they say, "This way we can get rich." War is a dangerous undertaking, but people will take part in it because they say, "This way we can become eminent." Now if men who devote themselves to literature or study the art of persuasive speaking are able to get the fruits of wealth without the hard work of the farmer and can gain the advantages of eminence without the danger of battle, then who will not take up such pursuits? So for every man who works with his hands there will be a hundred devoting themselves to the pursuit of wisdom. If those who pursue wisdom are numerous, the laws will be defeated, and if those who labor with their hands are few, the state will grow poor. Hence the age will become disordered.

Therefore, in the state of an enlightened ruler there are no books written on bamboo slips; law supplies the only instruction. There are no sermons on the former kings; the officials serve as the only teachers. There are no fierce feuds of private swordsmen; cutting off the heads of the enemy is the only deed of valor. Hence, when the people of such a state make a speech, they say nothing that is in contradiction to the law; when they act, it is in some way that will bring useful results; and when they do brave deeds, they do them in the army. Therefore, in times of peace the state is rich, and in times of trouble its armies are strong. . . .

These are the customs of a disordered state: Its scholars praise the ways of the former kings and imitate their humaneness and rightness, put on a fair appearance and speak in elegant phrases, thus casting doubt upon the laws of the time and causing the ruler to be of two minds. Its speechmakers propound false schemes and borrow influence from abroad, furthering their private interests and forgetting the welfare of the state's altars of the soil and grain. Its swordsmen gather bands of followers about them and perform deeds of honor, making a fine name for themselves and violating the prohibitions of the five government bureaus. Those of its people who are worried about military service flock to the gates of private individuals and pour out their wealth in bribes to influential men who will plead for them, in this way escaping the hardship of battle. Its merchants and artisans spend their time making articles of no practical use and gathering stores of luxury goods, accumulating riches, waiting for the best time to sell, and exploiting the farmers.

These five groups are the vermin of the state. If the rulers do not wipe out such vermin, and in their place encourage men of integrity and public spirit, then they should not be surprised, when they look about the area within the four seas, to see states perish and ruling houses wane and die.

Huan Kuan: Discourses on Salt and Iron

74–49 BCE

Document Text

Chapter I. The Basic Argument

a. It so happened that in the sixth year of the *shih-yüan* era an Imperial edict directed the Chancellor and the Imperial secretaries to confer with the recommended Worthies and Literati, and to enquire of them as to the rankling grievances among the people.

b. The Literati responded as follows: It is our humble opinion that the principle of ruling men lies in nipping in the bud wantonness and frivolity, in extending wide the elementals of virtue, in discouraging mercantile pursuits, and in displaying benevolence and righteousness. Let lucre never be paraded before the eyes of the people; only then will enlightenment flourish and folkways improve.

c. But now, with the system of the salt and iron monopolies, the liquor excise, and equable marketing, established in the provinces and the demesnes, the Government has entered into financial competition with the people, dissipating primordial candor and simplicity and sanctioning propensities to selfishness and greed. As a result few among our people take up the fundamental pursuits of life, while many flock to the non-essential. Now sturdy natural qualities decay as artificiality thrives, and rural values decline when industrialism flourishes. When industrialism is cultivated, the people become frivolous; when the values of rural life are developed, the people are simple and unsophisticated. The people being unsophisticated, wealth will abound; when the people are extravagant, cold and hunger will follow. We pray that the salt, iron and liquor monopolies and the system of equable marketing be abolished so that the rural pursuits may be encouraged, people be deterred from entering the secondary occupations, and national agriculture be materially and financially benefited.

d. The Lord Grand Secretary said: When the Hsiung Nu rebelled against our authority and frequently raided and devastated the frontier settlements, to be constantly on the watch for them was a great strain upon the soldiery of the Middle Kingdom; but without measures of precaution being taken, these forays and depredations would never cease. The late Emperor, grieving at the long suffering of the denizens of the marches who live in fear of capture by the barbarians, caused consequently forts and seried signal stations to be built, where garrisons were held ready against the nomads. When the revenue for the defence of the frontier fell short, the salt and iron monopoly was established, the liquor excise and the system of equable marketing introduced; goods were multiplied and wealth increased so as to furnish the frontier expenses.

e. Now our critics here, who demand that these measures be abolished, at home would have the hoard of the treasury entirely depleted, and abroad would deprive the border of provision for its defence; they would expose our soldiers who defend the barriers and mount the walls to all the hunger and cold of the borderland. How else do they expect to provide for them? It is not expedient to abolish these measures!

f. The Literati: Confucius observed that the ruler of a kingdom or the chief of a house is not concerned about his people being few, but about lack of equitable treatment; nor is he concerned about poverty, but over the presence of discontentment. Thus the Son of Heaven should not speak about much and little, the feudal lords should not talk about advantage and detriment, ministers about gain and loss, but they should cultivate benevolence and righteousness, to set an example to the people, and extend wide their virtuous conduct to gain the people's confidence. Then will nearby folk lovingly flock to them and distant peoples joyfully submit to their authority. Therefore the master conqueror does not fight; the expert warrior needs no soldiers; the truly great commander requires not to set his troops in battle array. Cultivate virtue in the temple and the hall; then you need only to show a bold front to the enemy and your troops will return home in victory. The Prince who practices benevolent administration should be matchless in the world; for him, what use is expenditure?

g. The Lord Grand Secretary: The Hsiung Nu, savage and wily, boldly push through the barriers and harass the Middle Kingdom, massacring the provincial population and killing the keepers of the Northern Marches. They long deserve punishment for their unruliness and lawlessness. But Your Majesty graciously took pity on the insufficiency of the multitude and did not suffer his lords and knights to be exposed in the desert plains, yet unflinchingly You cherish the purpose of raising strong armies and driving the Hsiung Nu before You to their original haunts in the north. I again assert that the proposal to do away with the salt and iron monopoly and equable marketing would grievously diminish our frontier supplies and impair our military plans. I can not consider favorably a proposal so heartlessly dismissing the frontier question.

h. The Literati: The ancients held in honor virtuous methods and discredited resort to arms. Thus Confucius said: If remoter people are not submissive, all the influences of civil culture and virtue are to be cultivated to attract them to be so; and when they have been so attracted, they must be made contented and tranquil? Now these virtuous principles are discarded and reliance put on military force; troops are raised to attack the enemy and garrisons are stationed to make ready for him. It is the long drawn-out service of our troops in the field and the ceaseless transportation for the needs of the commissariat that cause our soldiers on the marches to suffer from hunger and cold abroad, while the common people are burdened with labor at home. The establishment of the salt and iron monopoly and the institution of finance officials to supply the army needs were not permanent schemes; it is therefore desirable that they now be abolished.

i. The Lord Grand Secretary: The ancient founders of the Commonwealth made open the ways for both fundamental and branch industries and facilitated equitable distribution of goods. Markets and courts were provided to harmonize various demands; there people of all classes gathered together and all goods collected, so that farmer, merchant, and worker could each obtain what he desired; the exchange completed, everyone went back to his occupation. Facilitate exchange so that the people will be unflagging in industry says the Book of Changes. Thus without artisans, the farmers will be deprived of the use of implements; without merchants, all prized commodities will be cut off. The former would lead to stoppage of grain production, the latter to exhaustion of wealth. It is clear that the salt and iron monopoly and equable marketing are really intended for the circulation of amassed wealth and the regulation of the consumption according to the urgency of the need. It is inexpedient to abolish them.

j. The Literati: Lead the people with virtue and the people will return to honest simplicity; entice the people with gain, and they will become vicious. Vicious habits would lead them away from righteousness to follow after gain, with the result that people will swarm on the road and throng at the markets. A poor country may appear plentiful, not because it possesses abundant wealth, but because wants multiply and people become reckless, said Lao-tzŭ. Hence the true King promotes rural pursuits and discourages branch industries; he checks the people's desires through the principles of propriety and righteousness and provides a market for grain in exchange for other commodities, where there is no place for merchants to circulate useless goods, and for artisans to make useless implements. Thus merchants are for the purpose of draining stagnation and the artisans for providing tools; they should not become the principal concern of the government.

k. The Lord Grand Secretary: Kuan-tzŭ is reported to have said: A country may possess a wealth of fertile land and yet its people may be underfed—the reason lying in lack of an adequate supply of agricultural implements. It may possess rich natural resources in its mountains and seas and yet the people may be deficient in wealth—the reason being in the insufficient number of artisans and merchants. The scarlet lacquer and pennant feathers of Lung and Shu, the leather goods, bone and ivory of Ching and Yang, the cedars, lindera, and bamboo rods of Chiang-nan, the fish, salt, rugs, and furs of Yen and Ch'i, the lustrine yarn, linen, and hemp-cloth of Yen and Yü, are all necessary commodities to maintain our lives and provide for our death. But we depend upon the merchants for their distribution and on the artisans for giving them their finished forms. This is why the Sages availed them of boats and bridges to negotiate rivers and gulleys, and domesticated cattle and horses for travel over mountains and plateaux. Thus by penetrating to distant lands and exploring remote places, they were able to exchange all goods to the benefit of the people. Hence His late Majesty established officers in control of iron to meet the farmer's needs and provided equable marketing to make sufficient the people's wealth. Thus, the salt and iron monopoly and the equable marketing supported by the myriad people and looked to as the source of supply, cannot conveniently be abolished.

l. The Literati: That a country possesses a wealth of fertile land and yet its people are underfed is due to the fact that merchants and workers have prospered unduly while the fundamental occupations have been neglected. That a country possesses rich natural resources in its mountains and seas and yet its people lack capital is because the people's necessities have not been attended to, while luxuries and fancy articles have multiplied. The fountain-head of a river cannot fill a leaking cup; mountains and seas cannot overwhelm streams and valleys. This is why P'an Kêng practised communal living, Shun hid away gold, and Kao Tsu forbade merchants and shopkeepers to be officials. Their purpose was to discourage habits of greed and fortify the spirit of extreme earnestness. Now with all the discriminations against the market people, and stoppage of the sources of profit, people still do evil. What if the ruling classes should pursue profit themselves? The Chuan says, When the princes take delight in profit, the ministers become mean; when the ministers become mean, the minor officers become greedy; when the minor officers become greedy, the people become thieves. Thus to open the way for profit is to provide a ladder to popular misdemeanor.

m. The Lord Grand Secretary: Formerly the Princes in the provinces and the demesnes sent in their respective products as tribute. The transportation was vexacious and disorganized; the goods were usually of distressingly bad quality, often failing to repay their transport costs. Therefore Transportation Officers have been provided in every province to assist in the delivery and transportation and for the speeding of the tribute from distant parts. So the system came to be known as equable marketing. A Receiving Bureau has been established at the capital to monopolize all the commodities, buying when prices are low, and selling when prices are high, with the result that the Government suffers no loss and the merchants cannot speculate for profit. This is therefore known as the balancing standard. With the balancing standard people are safeguarded from unemployment; with the equable marketing people have evenly distributed labor. Both of these measures are intended to equilibrate all goods and convenience the people, and not to open the way to profit and provide a ladder to popular misdemeanor.

n. The Literati: The Ancients in levying upon and taxing the people would look for what the latter were skilled in, and not seek for those things in which they were not adept. Thus the farmers contributed the fruits of their labor, the weaving women, their products. Now the Government leaves alone what the people have and exacts what they have not, with the result that the people sell their products at a cheap price to satisfy demands from above. Recently in some of the provinces and demesnes they ordered the people to make woven goods. The officers then caused the producers various embarassments and bargained with them. What was collected by the officers was not only the silk from Ch'i and T'ao, or cloth from Shu and Han, but also other goods manufactured by the people which were mischievously sold at a standard price. Thus the farmers suffer twice over while the weaving women are doubly taxed. We have not yet seen that your marketing is "equable". As to the second measure under discussion, the government officers swarm out to close the door, gain control of the market and corner all commodities. With commodities cornered, prices soar; with prices rising, the merchants make private deals by way of speculation. Thus the officers are lenient to the cunning capitalists, and the merchants store up goods and accumulate commodities waiting for a time of need. Nimble traders and unscrupulous officials buy in cheap to get high returns. We have not yet seen that your standard is "balanced". For it seems that in ancient times equable marketing was to bring about equitable division of labor and facilitate transportation of tribute; it was surely not for profit or to make trade in commodities.

Han Yu: "Memorial on the Buddha's Bones"

819

Document Text

Your servant says:

He humbly believes that Buddhism is a religion of the barbarians, which spread to the Middle Kingdom in Later Han [25—220 ce] times. It did not exist in antiquity. In the ancient past, the Yellow Emperor [Huang Di] reigned for 100 years, and lived 110 years; Shaohao reigned for 80 years, and lived 100 years; Zhuanxu reigned for 79 years, and lived 98 years; Di Ku reigned for 70 years, and lived 105 years; Di Yao reigned for 98 years, and lived 118 years; both Di Shun and Yu lived 100 years. This was a time of great tranquility under heaven. The people enjoyed peace, happiness, and longevity while there was no Buddha in the Middle Kingdom.

Thereafter King Tang of Yin too lived 100 years. Tang's grandson Taiwu reigned for 75 years while Wuding reigned for 59 years. History does not record their ages, which, judging by their reign periods, should not be shorter than 100 years. King Wen of Zhou lived 97 years, and King Wu 93 years, while King Mu reigned for 100 years. During this period the law of the Buddha did not enter the Middle Kingdom, nor did Buddha worship bring about all this.

During the reign of Emperor Ming of Han [r. 57—75 ce] the law of the Buddha began to make its appearance. Emperor Ming reigned for only 18 years. Thereafter chaos and destruction continued, and reign periods were short-lived. During and after the period of the Song [420—479], Qi [479—502], Liang [502—557], Chen [557—589], and the Yuan Wei [Northern Wei, 386—534] dynasties, as people became more devoted to Buddha worship, reign periods became particularly short. Only Wudi of Liang [r. 502—549] reigned for 48 years. During his reign on three occasions he gave up his own body for the Buddha. At the Ancestral Temple sacrifices, he stopped making animal offerings, and limited himself to one meal of vegetables and fruits every day. With Hou Jing [502—552] closing in on him, Wudi ended up dying of starvation at Taicheng. His country too was destroyed soon after. Buddha worship is for the purpose of bringing good fortune, but it only results in more misfortune. In view of this, it is evident that the Buddha is not worth worshiping.

Upon taking over the imperial mantle from the Sui, [Tang] Gaozu [Li Yuan, r. 618—626] discussed the elimination [of Buddhism]. At that time, the ministers and courtiers were not farsighted enough to comprehend the profundity of the Way of the ancient sages and the exigencies of the past and present so as to elucidate the sagely wisdom and correct that abuse. So the effort did not go any further, to your servant's constant regret.

I humble myself in front of the divine, holy, brilliant, and martial presence of Your Imperial Majesty, who is wise and sagely, and excels in literary accomplishment and the art of war. In the past thousands of years, no one can compare with [Your Majesty]. Not long after you ascended the throne you began to disallow ordinations of people as Buddhist monks and nuns or Daoist adepts. Nor did you permit the creation of Buddhist monasteries and Daoist abbeys. Once your servant believed that the wish of Gaozu would certainly be realized under Your Majesty's hand. Nowadays, even though that has not come to pass, there is no reason to encourage it [Buddhism] to flourish again.

Now I have heard that Your Majesty instructed various monks to greet the Buddhist relic at Fengxiang, mounted a loft-building to view it, and took it in both hands into the Great Within. In addition, [Your Majesty] ordered various monasteries to take turns to receive and worship the relic.

Although your servant is extremely foolish, he still knows that Your Majesty will not be deluded by the Buddha into worshiping [the relic] like this in the hope of achieving happiness and auspiciousness. This is simply a frivolous gimmick and a deceitful and exotic spectacle set up for the officials and commoners of the capital in an attempt to humor some people at a time when the harvest is good and people are happy. It cannot be true that [Your Majesty], so sagely and brilliant, believes in this sort of thing.

However, the people are inherently ignorant, susceptible to delusion, and difficult to reason with. If they should behold Your Majesty like this, they would talk about devotedly worshiping the Buddha. Everyone would say, "Even the great sage Son of Heaven is devout in his faith; who are we the ordinary people to grudge our own bodies and lives?" They would sear the tops of their heads and burn their fingers, gathering in crowds of tens or hundreds. They would doff their clothes to scatter their money, from morning till night. They would emulate one another for fear of being left behind. Old and young would all run about [doing this], abandoning their proper occupations.

If this is not henceforth banned, it [the relic] will go the rounds among various monasteries. By then, there will be people who sever their arms and cut out their flesh to make offerings [to the relic]. Corrupting our accepted mores and customs and making ourselves a laughingstock everywhere—this is no small matter.

The Buddha was originally a man of the barbarians who did not speak the language of the Middle Kingdom and was dressed in clothes of a different cut from ours. Neither did he cite the edifying discourses of the ancient sovereigns, nor did he don their proper attire. He was ignorant of the sense of duty between sovereign and subject, and the affections between father and son. If he were alive today, and were on a state mission to visit the court in the capital, and if Your Majesty would generously receive him, [Your Majesty] would merely grant him one audience in the Hall of Manifest Government [Xuanzheng dian]. After one banquet was held at the Office of Foreign Relations, and one set of attire was conferred on him, [Your Majesty] would have guards escort him out of the country so that he would not be able to delude the masses.

All the more, now that he has been dead for long, how can his withered and decayed bones and baleful and filthy remains be allowed into the forbidden palace? Confucius said, "Revere ghosts and spirits but keep them at a distance." In antiquity, when the various princes were about to hold mourning ceremonies in their states, even they would request shamans to use peach-wood charms and magic brooms to eradicate the ill-omened before they proceeded. Today for no good reason the decayed and filthy object was brought to light for Your Majesty's viewing. It was neither proceeded by shamans nor exorcised by peach-wood charms and magic brooms. No ministers have ever talked about its wrongs, and no censors have ever cited its faults. Your servant is truly mortified by this.

I pray that [Your Majesty] will have the relic delivered to the government agency concerned, which will depose of it in water or fire so as to permanently destroy its roots. If [Your Majesty] puts to rest doubts under Heaven and stops once and for all [Buddhism] from deluding posterity, all under Heaven will be aware of the achievement by you the great sage, which is hundreds of millions of times greater than that of ordinary people. Isn't that wonderful? Isn't that cause for joy?

If the Buddha should possess soul and the power to cause misfortunes, let all such calamities be visited upon your servant. Let Heaven be the witness: your servant shall never regret it.

With great gratitude and extreme sincerity, I present this memorial for Your Majesty's consideration.

Your servant in genuine fear and trepidation.

Twelve Tables of Roman Law

451 BCE

Document Text

Table I.

Concerning the summons to court.

Law I.

When anyone summons another before the tribunal of a judge, the latter must, without hesitation, immediately appear.

Law II.

If, after having been summoned, he does not appear, or refuses to come before the tribunal of the judge, let the party who summoned him call upon any citizens who are present to bear witness. Then let him seize his reluctant adversary; so that he may be brought into court, as a captive, by apparent force.

Law III.

When anyone who has been summoned to court is guilty of evasion, or attempts to flee, let him be arrested by the plaintiff.

Law IV.

If bodily infirmity or advanced age should prevent the party summoned to court from appearing, let him who summoned him furnish him with an animal, as a means of transport. If he is unwilling to accept it, the plaintiff cannot legally be compelled to provide the defendant with a vehicle constructed of boards, or a covered litter.

Law V.

If he who is summoned has either a sponsor or a defender, let him be dismissed, and his representative can take his place in court.

Law VI.

The defender, or the surety of a wealthy man, must himself be rich; but anyone who desires to do so can come to the assistance of a person who is poor, and occupy his place.

Law VII.

When litigants wish to settle their dispute among themselves, even while they are on their way to appear before the Praetor, they shall have the right to make peace; and whatever agreement they enter into, it shall be considered just, and shall be confirmed.

Law VIII.

If the plaintiff and defendant do not settle their dispute, as above mentioned, let them state their cases either in the *Comitium* or the Forum, by making a brief statement in the presence of the judge, between the rising of the sun and noon; and, both of them being present, let them speak so that each party may hear.

Law IX.

In the afternoon, let the judge grant the right to bring the action, and render his decision in the presence of the plaintiff and the defendant.

Law X.

The setting of the sun shall be the extreme limit of time within which a judge must render his decision.

Table II.

Concerning judgments and thefts.

Law I.

When issue has been joined in the presence of the judge, sureties and their substitutes for appearance at the trial must be furnished on both sides. The parties shall appear in person, unless prevented by disease of a serious character; or where vows which they have taken must be discharged to the Gods; or where the proceedings are interrupted through their absence on business for the State; or where a day has been appointed by them to meet an alien.

Law II.

If any of the above mentioned occurrences takes place, that is, if one of the parties is seriously ill, or a vow has to be performed, or one of them is absent on business for the State, or a day has been appointed for an interview with an alien, so that the judge, the arbiter, or the defendant is prevented from being present, and the furnishing of security is postponed on this account, the hearing of the case shall be deferred.

Law III.

Where anyone is deprived of the evidence of a witness let him call him with a loud voice in front of his house, on three market-days.

Law IV.

Where anyone commits a theft by night, and having been caught in the act is killed, he is legally killed.

Law V.

If anyone commits a theft during the day, and is caught in the act, he shall be scourged, and given up as a slave to the person against whom the theft was committed. If he who perpetrated the theft is a slave, he shall be beaten with rods and hurled from the Tarpeian Rock. If he is under the age of puberty, the Praetor shall decide whether he shall be scourged, and surrendered by way of reparation for the injury.

Law VI.

When any persons commit a theft during the day and in the light, whether they be freemen or slaves, of full age or minors, and attempt to defend themselves with weapons, or with any kind of implements; and the party against whom the violence is committed raises the cry of thief, and calls upon other persons, if any are present, to come to his assistance; and this is done, and the thieves are killed by him in the defence of his person and property, it is legal, and no liability attaches to the homicide.

Law VII.

If a theft be detected by means of a dish and a girdle, it is the same as manifest theft, and shall be punished as such.

Law VII.

When anyone accuses and convicts another of theft which is not manifest, and no stolen property is found, judgment shall be rendered to compel the thief to pay double the value of what was stolen.

Law IX.

Where anyone secretly cuts down trees belonging to another, he shall pay twenty-five *asses* for each tree cut down.

Law X.

Where anyone, in order to favor a thief, makes a compromise for the loss sustained, he cannot afterwards prosecute him for theft.

Law XI.

Stolen property shall always be his to whom it formerly belonged; nor can the lawful owner ever be deprived of it by long possession, without regard to its duration; nor can it ever be acquired by another, no matter in what way this may take place.

Table III.

Concerning property which is lent.

Law I.

When anyone, with fraudulent intent, appropriates property deposited with him for safe keeping, he shall be condemned to pay double its value.

Law II.

When anyone collects interest on money loaned at a higher rate per annum than that of the *unciae*, he shall pay quadruple the amount by way of penalty.

Law III.

An alien cannot acquire the property of another by usucaption; but a Roman citizen, who is the lawful owner of the property, shall always have the right to demand it from him.

Law IV.

Where anyone, having acknowledged a debt, has a judgment rendered against him requiring payment, thirty days shall be given to him in which to pay the money and satisfy the judgment.

Law V.

After the term of thirty days granted by the law to debtors who have had judgment rendered against them has expired, and in the meantime, they have not satisfied the judgment, their creditors shall be permitted to forcibly seize them and bring them again into court.

Law VI.

When a defendant, after thirty days have elapsed, is brought into court a second time by the plaintiff, and does not satisfy the judgment; or, in the meantime, another party, or his surety does not pay it out of his own money, the creditor, or the plaintiff, after the debtor has been delivered up to him, can take the latter with him and bind him or place him in fetters; provided his chains are not of more than fifteen pounds weight; he can, however, place him in others which are lighter, if he desires to do so.

Law VII.

If, after a debtor has been delivered up to his creditor, or has been placed in chains, he desires to obtain food and has the means, he shall be permitted to support himself out of his own property. But if he has nothing on which to live, his creditor, who holds him in chains, shall give him a pound of grain every day, or he can give him more than a pound, if he wishes to do so.

Law VIII.

In the meantime, the party who has been delivered up to his creditor can make terms with him. If he does not, he shall be kept in chains for sixty days; and for three consecutive market-days he shall be brought before the Praetor in the place of assembly in the Forum, and the amount of the judgment against him shall be publicly proclaimed.

Law IX.

After he has been kept in chains for sixty days, and the sum for which he is liable has been three times publicly proclaimed in the Forum, he shall be condemned to be reduced to slavery by him to whom he was delivered up; or, if the latter prefers, he can be sold beyond the Tiber.

Law X.

Where a party is delivered up to several persons, on account of a debt, after he has been exposed in the Forum on three market days, they shall be permitted to divide their debtor into different parts, if they desire to do so; and if anyone of them should, by the division, obtain more or less than he is entitled to, he shall not be responsible.

Table IV.

Concerning the rights of a father, and of marriage.

Law I.

A father shall have the right of life and death over his son born in lawful marriage, and shall also have the power to render him independent, after he has been sold three times.

Law II.

If a father sells his son three times, the latter shall be free from paternal authority.

Law III.

A father shall immediately put to death a son recently born, who is a monster, or has a form different from that of members of the human race.

Law IV.

When a woman brings forth a son within the next ten months after the death of her husband, he shall be born in lawful marriage, and shall be the legal heir of his estate.

Table V.

Concerning estates and guardianships.

Law I.

No matter in what way the head of a household may dispose of his estate, and appoint heirs to the same, or guardians; it shall have the force and effect of law.

Law II.

Where a father dies intestate, without leaving any proper heir, his nearest agnate, or, if there is none, the next of kin among his family, shall be his heir. /

Law III.

When a freedman dies intestate, and does not leave any proper heir, but his patron, or the children of the latter survive him; the inheritance of the estate of the freedman shall be adjudged to the next of kin of the patron.

Law IV.

When a creditor or a debtor dies, his heirs can only sue, or be sued, in proportion to their shares in the estate; and any claims, or remaining property, shall be divided among them in the same proportion.

Law V.

Where co-heirs desire to obtain their shares of the property of an estate, which has not yet been divided, it shall be divided. In order that this may be properly done and no loss be sustained by the litigants, the Praetor shall appoint three arbiters, who can give to each one that to which he is entitled in accordance with law and equity.

Law VI.

When the head of a family dies intestate, and leaves a proper heir who has not reached the age of puberty, his nearest agnate shall obtain the guardianship.

Law VII.

When no guardian has been appointed for an insane person, or a spendthrift, his nearest agnates, or if there are none, his other relatives, must take charge of his property.

Table VI.

Concerning ownership and possession.

Law I.

When anyone contracts a legal obligation with reference to his property, or sells it, by making a verbal statement or agreement concerning the same, this shall have the force and effect of law. If the party should afterwards deny his statements, and legal proceedings are instituted, he shall, by way of penalty, pay double the value of the property in question.

Law II.

Where a slave is ordered to be free by a will, upon his compliance with a certain condition, and he complies with the condition; or if, after having paid his price to the purchaser, he claims his liberty, he shall be free.

Law III.

Where property has been sold, even though it may have been delivered, it shall by no means be acquired by the purchaser until the price has been paid, or a surety or a pledge has been given, and the vendor satisfied in this manner.

Law IV.

Immovable property shall be acquired by usucaption after the lapse of two years; other property after the lapse of one year.

Law V.

Where a woman, who has not been united to a man in marriage, lives with him for an entire year without the usucaption of her being interrupted for three nights, she shall pass into his power as his legal wife.

Law VI.

Where parties have a dispute with reference to property before the tribunal of the Praetor, both of them shall be permitted to state their claims in the presence of witnesses.

Law VII.

Where anyone demands freedom for another against the claim of servitude, the Praetor shall render judgment in favor of liberty.

Law VIII.

No material forming part of either a building or a vineyard shall be removed therefrom. Any one who, without the knowledge or consent of the owner, attaches a beam or anything else to his house or vineyard, shall be condemned to pay double its value.

Law IX.

Timbers which have been dressed and prepared for building purposes, but which have not yet been attached to a building or a vineyard can legally be recovered by the owner, if they are stolen from him.

Law X.

If a husband desires to divorce his wife, and dissolve his marriage, he must give a reason for doing so.

Table VII.

Concerning crimes.

Law I.

If a quadruped causes injury to anyone, let the owner tender him the estimated amount of the damage; and if he is unwilling to accept it, the owner shall, by way of reparation, surrender the animal that caused the injury.

Law II.

If you cause any unlawful damage . . . accidentally and unintentionally, you must make good the loss, either by tendering what has caused it, or by payment.

Law III.

Anyone who, by means of incantations and magic arts, prevents grain or crops of any kind belonging to another from growing, shall be sacrificed to Ceres.

Law IV.

If anyone who has arrived at puberty, secretly, and by night, destroys or cuts and appropriates to his own use, the crop of another, which the owner of the land has laboriously obtained by plowing and the cultivation of the soil, he shall be sacrificed to Ceres, and hung.

If he is under the age of puberty, and not yet old enough to be accountable, he shall be scourged, in the discretion of the Praetor, and shall make good the loss by paying double its amount.

Law V.

Anyone who turns cattle on the land of another, for the purpose of pasture, shall surrender the cattle, by way of reparation.

Law VI.

Anyone who, knowingly and maliciously, burns a building, or a heap of grain left near a building, after having been placed in chains and scourged, shall be put to death by fire. If, however, he caused the damage by accident, and without malice, he shall make it good; or, if he has not the means to do so, he shall receive a lighter punishment.

Law VII.

When a person, in any way, causes an injury to another which is not serious, he shall be punished with a fine of twenty *asses*.

Law VIII.

When anyone publicly abuses another in a loud voice, or writes a poem for the purpose of insulting him, or rendering him infamous, he shall be beaten with a rod until he dies.

Law IX.

When anyone breaks a member of another, and is unwilling to come to make a settlement with him, he shall be punished by the law of retaliation.

Law X.

When anyone knocks a tooth out of the gum of a freeman, he shall be fined three hundred *asses*; if he knocks one out of the gum of a slave, he shall be fined a hundred and fifty *asses*.

Law XI.

If anyone, after having been asked, appears either as a witness or a balance-holder, at a sale, or the execution of a will, and refuses to testify when this is required to prove the genuineness of the transaction, he shall become infamous, and cannot afterwards give evidence.

Law XII.

Anyone who gives false testimony shall be hurled from the Tarpeian Rock.

Law XIII.

If anyone knowingly and maliciously kills a freeman, he shall be guilty of a capital crime. If he kills him by accident, without malice and unintentionally, let him substitute a ram to be sacrificed publicly by way of expiation for the homicide of the deceased, and for the purpose of appeasing the children of the latter.

Law XIV.

Anyone who annoys another by means of magic incantations or diabolical arts, and renders him inactive, or ill; or who prepares or administers poison to him, is guilty of a capital crime, and shall be punished with death.

Law XV.

Anyone who kills an ascendant, shall have his head wrapped in a cloth, and after having been sewed up in a sack, shall be thrown into the water.

Law XVI.

Where anyone is guilty of fraud in the administration of a guardianship, he shall be considered infamous; and, even after the guardianship has been terminated, if any theft is proved to have been committed, he shall, by the payment of double damages, be compelled to make good the loss which he caused.

Law XVII.

When a patron defrauds his client, he shall be dedicated to the infernal gods.

Table VIII.

Concerning the laws of real property.

Law I.

A space of two feet and a half must be left between neighboring buildings.

Law II.

Societies and associations which have the right to assemble, can make, promulgate, and confirm for themselves such contracts and rules as they may desire; provided nothing is done by them contrary to public enactments, or which does not violate the common law.

Law III.

The space of five feet shall be left between adjoining fields, by means of which the owners can visit their property, or drive and plow around it. No one shall ever have the right to acquire this space by usucaption.

Law IV.

If any persons are in possession of adjoining fields, and a dispute arises with reference to the boundaries of the same, the Praetor shall appoint three arbiters, who shall take cognizance of the case, and, after the boundaries have been established, he shall assign to each party that to which he is entitled.

Law V.

When a tree overhangs the land of a neighbor, so as to cause injury by its branches and its shade, it shall be cut off fifteen feet from the ground.

Law VI.

When the fruit of a tree falls upon the premises of a neighbor, the owner of the tree shall have a right to gather and remove it.

Law VII.

When rain falls upon the land of one person in such a quantity as to cause water to rise and injure the property of another, the Praetor shall appoint three arbiters for the purpose of confining the water, and providing against damage to the other party.

Law VIII.

Where a road runs in a straight line, it shall be eight feet, and where it curves, it shall be sixteen feet in width.

Law IX.

When a man's land lies adjacent to the highway, he can enclose it in any way that he chooses; but if he neglects to do so, any other person can drive an animal over the land wherever he pleases.

Table IX.

Concerning public law.

Law I.

No privileges, or statutes, shall be enacted in favor of private persons, to the injury of others contrary to the law common to all citizens, and which individuals, no matter of what rank, have a right to make use of.

Law II.

The same rights shall be conferred upon, and the same laws shall be considered to have been enacted for all the people residing in and beyond Latium, that have been enacted for good and steadfast Roman citizens.

Law III.

When a judge, or an arbiter appointed to hear a case, accepts money, or other gifts, for the purpose of influencing his decision, he shall suffer the penalty of death.

Law IV.

No decision with reference to the life or liberty of a Roman citizen shall be rendered except by the vote of the Greater *Comitia*.

Law V.

Public accusers in capital cases shall be appointed by the people.

Law VI.

If anyone should cause nocturnal assemblies in the City, he shall be put to death.

Law VII.

If anyone should stir up war against his country, or delivers a Roman citizen into the hands of the enemy, he shall be punished with death.

Table X.

Concerning religious law.

Law I.

An oath shall have the greatest force and effect, for the purpose of compelling good faith.

Law II.

Where a family adopts private religious rites every member of it can, afterwards, always make use of them.

Law III.

No burial or cremation of a corpse shall take place in a city.

Law IV.

No greater expenses or mourning than is proper shall be permitted in funeral ceremonies.

Law V.

No one shall, hereafter, exceed the limit established by these laws for the celebration of funeral rites.

Law VI.

Wood employed for the purpose of constructing a funeral pyre shall not be hewn, but shall be rough and unpolished.

Law VII.

When a corpse is prepared for burial at home, not more than three women with their heads covered with mourning veils shall be permitted to perform this service. The body may be enveloped in purple robes, and when borne outside, ten flute players, at the most, shall accompany the funeral procession.

Law VIII.

Women shall not during a funeral lacerate their faces, or tear their cheeks with their nails; nor shall they utter loud cries bewailing the dead.

Law IX.

No bones shall be taken from the body of a person who is dead, or from his ashes after cremation, in order that funeral ceremonies may again be held elsewhere. When, however, anyone dies in a foreign country, or is killed in war, a part of his remains may be transferred to the burial place of his ancestors.

Law X.

The body of no dead slave shall be anointed; nor shall any drinking take place at his funeral, nor a banquet of any kind be instituted in his honor.

Law XI.

No wine flavored with myrrh, or any other precious beverage, shall be poured upon a corpse while it is burning; nor shall the funeral pile be sprinkled with wine.

Law XII.

Large wreaths shall not be borne at a funeral; nor shall perfumes be burned on the altars.

Law XIII.

Anyone who has rendered himself deserving of a wreath, as the reward of bravery in war, or through his having been the victor in public contests or games, whether he has obtained it through his own exertions or by means of others in his own name, and by his own money, through his horses, or his slaves, shall have a right to have the said wreath placed upon his dead body, or upon that of any of his ascendants, as long as the corpse is at his home, as well as when it is borne away; so that, during his obsequies, he may enjoy the honor which in his lifetime he acquired by his bravery or his good fortune.

Law XIV.

Only one funeral of an individual can take place; and it shall not be permitted to prepare several biers.

Law XV.

Gold, no matter in what form it may be present, shall, by all means, be removed from the corpse at the time of the funeral; but if anyone's teeth should be fastened with gold, it shall be lawful either to burn, or to bury it with the body.

Law XVI.

No one, without the knowledge or consent of the owner, shall erect a funeral pyre, or a tomb, nearer than sixty feet to the building of another.

Law XVII.

No one can acquire by usucaption either the vestibule or approach to a tomb, or the tomb itself.

Law XVIII.

No assembly of the people shall take place during the obsequies of any man distinguished in the State.

Table XI.

Supplement to the five preceding ones.

Law I.

Affairs of great importance shall not be transacted without the vote of the people, with whom rests the power to appoint magistrates, to condemn citizens, and to enact laws. Laws subsequently passed always take preference over former ones.

Law II.

Those who belong to the Senatorial Order and are styled Fathers, shall not contract marriage with plebeians.

Table XII.

Supplement to the five preceding ones.

Law I.

No one shall render sacred any property with reference to which there is a controversy in court, where issue has already been joined; and if anyone does render such property sacred, he shall pay double its value as a penalty.

Law II.

If the claim of anyone in whose favor judgment was rendered after the property had been illegally seized, or after possession of the same had been delivered, is found to be false, the Praetor shall appoint three arbiters, by whose award double the amount of the profits shall be restored by him in whose favor the judgment was rendered.

Law III.

If a slave, with the knowledge of his master, should commit a theft, or cause damage to anyone, his master shall be given up to the other party by way of reparation for the theft, injury, or damage committed by the slave.

Marcus Cato (the Elder): On Agriculture

ca. 160 BCE

Document Text

It is true that to obtain money by trade is sometimes more profitable, were it not so hazardous; and likewise money-lending, if it were as honourable. Our ancestors held this view and embodied it in their laws, which required that the thief be mulcted double and the usurer fourfold; how much less desirable a citizen they considered the usurer than the thief, one may judge from this. And when they would praise a worthy man their praise took this form: "good husbandman, good farmer"; one so praised was thought to have received the greatest commendation. The trader I consider to be an energetic man, and one bent on making money; but, as I said above, it is a dangerous career and one subject to disaster. On the other hand, it is from the farming class that the bravest men and the sturdiest soldiers come, their calling is most highly respected, their livelihood is most assured and is looked on with the least hostility, and those who are engaged in that pursuit are least inclined to be disaffected. And now, to come back to my subject, the above will serve as an introduction to what I have undertaken. When you are thinking of acquiring a farm, keep in mind these points: that you be not over-eager in buying nor spare your pains in examining, and that you consider it not sufficient to go over it once. However often you go, a good piece of land will please you more at each visit. Notice how the neighbours keep up their places; if the district is good, they should be well kept. Go in and keep your eyes open, so that you may be able to find your way out. It should have a good climate, not subject to storms; the soil should be good, and naturally strong. If possible, it should lie at the foot of a mountain and face south; the situation should be healthful, there should be a good supply of labourers, it should be well watered, and near it there should be a flourishing town, or the sea, or a navigable stream, or a good and much travelled road. It should lie among those farms which do not often change owners; where those who have sold farms are sorry to have done so. It should be well furnished with buildings. Do not be hasty in despising the methods of management adopted by others. It will be better to purchase from an owner who is a good farmer and a good builder. When you reach the steading, observe whether there are numerous oil presses and wine vats; if there are not, you may infer that the amount of the yield is in proportion. The farm should be one of no great equipment, but should be well situated. See that it be equipped as economically as possible, and that the land be not extravagant. Remember that a farm is like a man—however great the income, if there is extravagance but little is left. If you ask me what is the best kind of farm, I should say: a hundred iugera of land, comprising all sorts of soils, and in a good situation; a vineyard comes first if it produces bountifully wine of a good quality; second, a watered garden; third, an osier-bed; fourth, an olive yard; fifth, a meadow; sixth, grain land; seventh, a wood lot; eighth, an arbustum; ninth, a mast grove.

When the master arrives at the farmstead, after paying his respects to the god of the household, let him go over the whole farm, if possible, on the same day; if not, at least on the next. When he has learned the condition of the farm, what work has been accomplished and what remains to be done, let him call in his overseer the next day and inquire of him what part of the work has been completed, what has been left undone; whether what has been finished was done betimes, and whether it is possible to complete the rest; and what was the yield of wine, grain, and all other products. Having gone into this, he should make a calculation of the labourers and the time consumed. If the amount of work does not seem satisfactory, the overseer claims that he has done his best, but that the slaves have not been well, the weather has been bad, slaves have run away, he has had public work to do; when he has given these and many other excuses, call the overseer back to your estimate of the work done and the hands employed. If it has been a rainy season, remind him of the work that could have been done on rainy days: scrubbing and pitching wine vats, cleaning the farmstead, shifting grain, hauling out manure, making a manure pit, cleaning seed, mending old harness and making new; and that the hands ought to have mended their smocks and hoods. Remind him, also, that on feast days old ditches might have been cleaned, road work done, brambles cut, the garden spaded, a meadow cleared, faggots bundled, thorns rooted out, spelt ground, and general cleaning done. When the slaves were sick, such large rations should not have been issued. After this has been gone into calmly, give orders for the completion of what work remains; run over the cash accounts, grain accounts, and purchases of fodder; run over the wine accounts, the oil accounts—what has been sold, what collected, balance due, and what is left that is saleable; where security for an account should be taken, let it be taken; and let the supplies on hand be checked over. Give orders that whatever may be lacking for the current year be supplied; that what is superfluous be sold; that whatever work should be let out be let. Give directions as to what work you want done on the place, and what you want let out, and leave the directions in writing. Look over the live stock and hold a sale. Sell your oil, if the price is satisfactory, and sell the surplus of your wine and grain. Sell worn-out oxen, blemished cattle, blemished sheep, wool, hides, an old wagon, old tools, an old slave, a sickly slave, and whatever else is superfluous. The master should have the selling habit, not the buying habit.

In his youth the owner should devote his attention to planting. He should think a long time about building, but planting is a thing not to be thought about but done. When you reach the age of thirty-six you should build, if you have your land planted. In building, you should see that the steading does not lag behind the farm nor the farm behind the steading. It is well for the master to have a well-built barn and storage room and plenty of vats for oil and wine, so that he may hold his products for good prices; it will redound to his wealth, his self-respect, and his reputation. He should have good presses, so that the work may be done thoroughly. Let the olives be pressed immediately, to prevent the oil from spoiling. Remember that high winds come every year and are apt to beat off the olives; if you gather them at once and the presses are ready, there will be no loss on account of the storm, and the oil will be greener and better. If the olives remain too long on the ground or the floor they will spoil, and the oil will be rancid. Any sort of olive will produce a good and greener oil if it is pressed betimes. For an oliveyard of 120 iugera there should be two pressing equipments, if the trees are vigorous, thickly planted, and well cultivated. The mills should be stout and of different sizes, so that if the stones become worn you may change. Each should have its own leather ropes, six sets of hand bars, six double sets of pins, and leather belts. Greek blocks run on double ropes of Spanish broom; you can work more rapidly with eight pulleys above, and six below; if you wish to use wheels it will work more slowly but with less effort.

...

The following is the Roman formula to be observed in thinning a grove: A pig is to be sacrificed, and the following prayer uttered: "Whether thou be god or goddess to whom this grove is dedicated, as it is thy right to receive a sacrifice of a pig for the thinning of this sacred grove, and to this intent, whether I or one at my bidding do it, may it be rightly done. To this end, in offering this pig to thee I humbly beg that thou wilt be gracious and merciful to me, to my house and household, and to my children. Wilt thou deign to receive this pig which I offer thee to this end."

If you wish to till the ground, offer a second sacrifice in the same way, with the addition of the words: "for the sake of doing this work." So long as the work continues, the ritual must be performed in some part of the land every day; and if you miss a day, or if public or domestic feast days intervene, a new offering must be made.

The following is the formula for purifying land: Bidding the suovetaurilia to be led around, use the words: "That with the good help of the gods success may crown our work, I bid thee, Manius, to take care to purify my farm, my land, my ground with this suovetaurilia, in whatever part thou thinkest best for them to be driven or carried around." Make a prayer with wine to Janus and Jupiter, and say: "Father Mars, I pray and beseech thee that thou be gracious and merciful to me, my house, and my household; to which intent I have bidden this suovetaurilia to be led around my land, my ground, my farm; that thou keep away, ward off, and remove sickness, seen and unseen, barrenness and destruction, ruin and unseasonable influence; and that thou permit my harvests, my grain, my vineyards, and my plantations to flourish and to come to good issue, preserve in health my shepherds and my flocks, and give good health and strength to me, my house, and my household. To this intent, to the intent of purifying my farm, my land, my ground, and of making an expiation, as I have said, deign to accept the offering of these suckling victims; Father Mars, to the same intent deign to accept the offering of these suckling offering." Also heap the cakes with the knife and see that the oblation cake be hard by, then present the victims. When you offer up the pig, the lamb, and the calf, use this formula: "To this intent design to accept the offering of these victims." . . . If favourable omens are not obtained in response to all, speak thus: "Father Mars, if aught hath not pleased thee in the offering of those sucklings, I make atonement with these victims." If there is doubt about one or two, use these words: "Father Mars, inasmuch as thou wast not pleased by the offering of that pig, I make atonement with this pig."

Marcus Aurelius: Meditations

170-180

Document Text

Book II

Begin the morning by saying to thyself, I shall meet with the busy-body, the ungrateful, arrogant, deceitful, envious, unsocial. All these things happen to them by reason of their ignorance of what is good and evil. But I who have seen the nature of the good that it is beautiful, and of the bad that it is ugly, and the nature of him who does wrong, that it is akin to me, not only of the same blood or seed, but that it participates in the same intelligence and the same portion of the divinity, I can neither be injured by any of them, for no one can fix on me what is ugly, nor can I be angry with my kinsman, nor hate him, For we are made for co-operation, like feet, like hands, like eyelids, like the rows of the upper and lower teeth. To act against one another then is contrary to nature; and it is acting against one another to be vexed and to turn away.

Whatever this is that I am, it is a little flesh and breath, and the ruling part. Throw away thy books; no longer distract thyself: it is not allowed; but as if thou wast now dying, despise the flesh; it is blood and bones and a network, a contexture of nerves, veins, and arteries. See the breath also, what kind of a thing it is, air, and not always the same, but every moment sent out and again sucked in. The third then is the ruling part: consider thus: Thou art an old man; no longer let this be a slave, no longer be pulled by the strings like a puppet to unsocial movements, no longer either be dissatisfied with thy present lot, or shrink from the future.

All that is from the gods is full of Providence. That which is from fortune is not separated from nature or without an interweaving and involution with the things which are ordered by Providence. From thence all things flow; and there is besides necessity, and that which is for the advantage of the whole universe, of which thou art a part. But that is good for every part of nature which the nature of the whole brings, and what serves to maintain this nature. Now the universe is preserved, as by the changes of the elements so by the changes of things compounded of the elements. Let these principles be enough for thee, let them always be fixed opinions. But cast away the thirst after books, that thou mayest not die murmuring, but cheerfully, truly, and from thy heart thankful to the gods.

Remember how long thou hast been putting off these things, and how often thou hast received an opportunity from the gods, and yet dost not use it. Thou must now at last perceive of what universe thou art a part, and of what administrator of the universe thy existence is an efflux, and that a limit of time is fixed for thee, which if thou dost not use for clearing away the clouds from thy mind, it will go and thou wilt go, and it will never return.

Every moment think steadily as a Roman and a man to do what thou hast in hand with perfect and simple dignity, and feeling of affection, and freedom, and justice; and to give thyself relief from all other thoughts. And thou wilt give thyself relief, if thou doest every act of thy life as if it were the last, laying aside all carelessness and passionate aversion from the commands of reason, and all hypocrisy, and self-love, and discontent with the portion which has been given to thee. Thou seest how few the things are, the which if a man lays hold of, he is able to live a life which flows in quiet, and is like the existence of the gods; for the gods on their part will require nothing more from him who observes these things.

Do wrong to thyself, do wrong to thyself, my soul; but thou wilt no longer have the opportunity of honouring thyself. Every man's life is sufficient. But thine is nearly finished, though thy soul reverences not itself but places thy felicity in the souls of others.

Do the things external which fall upon thee distract thee? Give thyself time to learn something new and good, and cease to be whirled around. But then thou must also avoid being carried about the other way. For those too are triflers who have wearied themselves in life by their activity, and yet have no object to which to direct every movement, and, in a word, all their thoughts.

Through not observing what is in the mind of another a man has seldom been seen to be unhappy; but those who do not observe the movements of their own minds must of necessity be unhappy.

This thou must always bear in mind, what is the nature of the whole, and what is my nature, and how this is related to that, and what kind of a part it is of what kind of a whole; and that there is no one who hinders thee from always doing and saying the things which are according to the nature of which thou art a part. . . .

Since it is possible that thou mayest depart from life this very moment, regulate every act and thought accordingly. But to go away from among men, if there are gods, is not a thing to be afraid of, for the gods will not involve thee in evil; but if indeed they do not exist, or if they have no concern about human affairs, what is it to me to live in a universe devoid of gods or devoid of Providence? But in truth they do exist, and they do care for human things, and they have put all the means in man's power to enable him not to fall into real evils. And as to the rest, if there was anything evil, they would have provided for this also, that it should be altogether in a man's power not to fall into it. Now that which does not make a man worse, how can it make a man's life worse? But neither through ignorance, nor having the knowledge, but not the power to guard against or correct these things, is it possible that the nature of the universe has overlooked them; nor is it possible that it has made so great a mistake, either through want of power or want of skill, that good and evil should happen indiscriminately to the good and the bad. But death certainly, and life, honour and dishonour, pain and pleasure, all these things equally happen to good men and bad, being things which make us neither better nor worse. Therefore they are neither good nor evil.

How quickly all things disappear, in the universe the bodies themselves, but in time the remembrance of them; what is the nature of all sensible things, and particularly those which attract with the bait of pleasure or terrify by pain, or are noised abroad by vapoury fame; how worthless, and contemptible, and sordid, and perishable, and dead they are—all this it is the part of the intellectual faculty to observe. To observe too who these are whose opinions and voices give reputation; what death is, and the fact that, if a man looks at it in itself, and by the abstractive power of reflection resolves into their parts all the things which present themselves to the imagination in it, he will then consider it to be nothing else than an operation of nature; and if any one is afraid of an operation of nature, he is a child. This, however, is not only an operation of nature, but it is also a thing which conduces to the purposes of nature. To observe too how man comes near to the deity, and by what part of him, and when this part of man is so disposed.

Nothing is more wretched than a man who traverses everything in a round, and pries into the things beneath the earth, as the poet says, and seeks by conjecture what is in the minds of his neighbours, without perceiving that it is sufficient to attend to the daemon within him, and to reverence it sincerely. And reverence of the daemon consists in keeping it pure from passion and thoughtlessness, and dissatisfaction with what comes from gods and men. For the things from the gods merit veneration for their excellence; and the things from men should be dear to us by reason of kinship; and sometimes even, in a manner, they move our pity by reason of men's ignorance of good and bad; this defect being not less than that which deprives us of the power of distinguishing things that are white and black. . . .

The soul of man does violence to itself, first of all, when it becomes an abscess and, as it were, a tumour on the universe, so far as it can. For to be vexed at anything which happens is a separation of ourselves from nature, in some part of which the natures of all other things are contained. In the next place, the soul does violence to itself when it turns away from any man, or even moves towards him with the intention of injuring, such as are the souls of those who are angry. In the third place, the soul does violence to itself when it is overpowered by pleasure or by pain. Fourthly, when it plays a part, and does or says anything insincerely and untruly. Fifthly, when it allows any act of its own and any movement to be without an aim, and does anything thoughtlessly and without considering what it is, it being right that even the smallest things be done with reference to an end; and the end of rational animals is to follow the reason and the law of the most ancient city and polity.

Of human life the time is a point, and the substance is in a flux, and the perception dull, and the composition of the whole body subject to putrefaction, and the soul a whirl, and fortune hard to divine, and fame a thing devoid of judgement. And, to say all in a word, everything which belongs to the body is a stream, and what belongs to the soul is a dream and vapour, and life is a warfare and a stranger's sojourn, and after-fame is oblivion. What then is that which is able to conduct a man? One thing and only one, philosophy. But this consists in keeping the daemon within a man free from violence and unharmed, superior to pains and pleasures, doing nothing without purpose, nor yet falsely and with hypocrisy, not feeling the need of another man's doing or not doing anything; and besides, accepting all that happens, and all that is allotted, as coming from thence, wherever it is, from whence he himself came; and, finally, waiting for death with a cheerful mind, as being nothing else than a dissolution of the elements of which every living being is compounded. But if there is no harm to the elements themselves in each continually changing into another, why should a man have any apprehension about the change and dissolution of all the elements? For it is according to nature, and nothing is evil which is according to nature. . . .

Book III

. . .

Labour not unwillingly, nor without regard to the common interest, nor without due consideration, nor with distraction; nor let studied ornament set off thy thoughts, and be not either a man of many words, or busy about too many things. And further, let the deity which is in thee be the guardian of a living being, manly and of ripe age, and engaged in matter political, and a Roman, and a ruler, who has taken his post like a man waiting for the signal which summons him from life, and ready to go, having need neither of oath nor of any man's testimony. Be cheerful also, and seek not external help nor the tranquility which others give. A man then must stand erect, not be kept erect by others.

If thou findest in human life anything better than justice, truth, temperance, fortitude, and, in a word, anything better than thy own mind's self-satisfaction in the things which it enables thee to do according to right reason, and in the condition that is assigned to thee without thy own choice; if, I say, thou seest anything better than this, turn to it with all thy soul, and enjoy that which thou hast found to be the best. But if nothing appears to be better than the deity which is planted in thee, which has subjected to itself all thy appetites, and carefully examines all the impressions, and, as Socrates said, has detached itself from the persuasions of sense, and has submitted itself to the gods, and cares for mankind; if thou findest everything else smaller and of less value than this, give place to nothing else, for if thou dost once diverge and incline to it, thou wilt no longer without distraction be able to give the preference to that good thing which is thy proper possession and thy own; for it is not right that anything of any other kind, such as praise from the many, or power, or enjoyment of pleasure, should come into competition with that which is rationally and politically or practically good. All these things, even though they may seem to adapt themselves to the better things in a small degree, obtain the superiority all at once, and carry us away. But do thou, I say, simply and freely choose the better, and hold to it.—But that which is useful is the better.—Well then, if it is useful to thee as a rational being, keep to it; but if it is only useful to thee as an animal, say so, and maintain thy judgement without arrogance: only take care that thou makest the inquiry by a sure method.

Never value anything as profitable to thyself which shall compel thee to break thy promise, to lose thy self-respect, to hate any man, to suspect, to curse, to act the hypocrite, to desire anything which needs walls and curtains: for he who has preferred to everything intelligence and daemon and the worship of its excellence, acts no tragic part, does not groan, will not need either solitude or much company; and, what is chief of all, he will live without either pursuing or flying from death; but whether for a longer or a shorter time he shall have the soul inclosed in the body, he cares not at all: for even if he must depart immediately, he will go as readily as if he were going to do anything else which can be done with decency and order; taking care of this only all through life, that his thoughts turn not away from anything which belongs to an intelligent animal and a member of a civil community....

Book IV

That which rules within, when it is according to nature, is so affected with respect to the events which happen, that it always easily adapts itself to that which is and is presented to it. For it requires no definite material, but it moves towards its purpose, under certain conditions however; and it makes a material for itself out of that which opposes it, as fire lays hold of what falls into it, by which a small light would have been extinguished: but when the fire is strong, it soon appropriates to itself the matter which is heaped on it, and consumes it, and rises higher by means of this very material.

Let no act be done without a purpose, nor otherwise than according to the perfect principles of art.

Men seek retreats for themselves, houses in the country, sea-shores, and mountains; and thou too art wont to desire such things very much. But this is altogether a mark of the most common sort of men, for it is in thy power whenever thou shalt choose to retire into thyself. For nowhere either with more quiet or more freedom from trouble does a man retire than into his own soul, particularly when he has within him such thoughts that by looking into them he is immediately in perfect tranquility; and I affirm that tranquility is nothing else than the good ordering of the mind. Constantly then give to thyself this retreat, and renew thyself; and let thy principles be brief and fundamental, which, as soon as thou shalt recur to them, will be sufficient to cleanse the soul completely, and to send thee back free from all discontent with the things to which thou returnest. For with what art thou discontented? With the badness of men? Recall to thy mind this conclusion, that rational animals exist for one another, and that to endure is a part of justice, and that men do wrong involuntarily; and consider how many already, after mutual enmity, suspicion, hatred, and fighting, have been stretched dead, reduced to ashes; and be quiet at last.—But perhaps thou art dissatisfied with that which is assigned to thee out of the universe.—Recall to thy recollection this alternative; either there is providence or atoms, fortuitous concurrence of things; or remember the arguments by which it has been proved that the world is a kind of political community, and be quiet at last.—But perhaps corporeal things will still fasten upon thee.—Consider then further that the mind mingles not with the breath, whether moving gently or violently, when it has once drawn itself apart and discovered its own power, and think also of all that thou hast heard and assented to about pain and pleasure, and be quiet at last.—But perhaps the desire of the thing called fame will torment thee.—See how soon everything is forgotten, and look at the chaos of infinite time on each side of the present, and the emptiness of applause, and the changeableness and want of judgement in those who pretend to give praise, and the narrowness of the space within which it is circumscribed, and be quiet at last. For the whole earth is a point, and how small a nook in it is this thy dwelling, and how few are there in it, and what kind of people are they who will praise thee....

Consider that everything which happens, happens justly, and if thou observest carefully, thou wilt find it to be so. I do not say only with respect to the continuity of the series of things, but with respect to what is just, and as if it were done by one who assigns to each thing its value. Observe then as thou hast begun; and whatever thou doest, do it in conjunction with this, the being good, and in the sense in which a man is properly understood to be good. Keep to this in every action.

Do not have such an opinion of things as he has who does thee wrong, or such as he wishes thee to have, but look at them as they are in truth.

A man should always have these two rules in readiness; the one, to do only whatever the reason of the ruling and legislating faculty may suggest for the use of men; the other, to change thy opinion, if there is any one at hand who sets thee right and moves thee from any opinion. But this change of opinion must proceed only from a certain persuasion, as of what is just or of common advantage, and the like, not because it appears pleasant or brings reputation....

Try how the life of the good man suits thee, the life of him who is satisfied with his portion out of the whole, and satisfied with his own just acts and benevolent disposition.

Hast thou seen those things? Look also at these. Do not disturb thyself. Make thyself all simplicity. Does any one do wrong? It is to himself that he does the wrong. Has anything happened to thee? Well; out of the universe from the beginning everything which happens has been apportioned and spun out to thee. In a word, thy life is short. Thou must turn to profit the present by the aid of reason and justice. Be sober in thy relaxation.

Either it is a well-arranged universe or a chaos huddled together, but still a universe. But can a certain order subsist in thee, and disorder in the All? And this too when all things are so separated and diffused and sympathetic.

A black character, a womanish character, a stubborn character, bestial, childish, animal, stupid, counterfeit, scurrilous, fraudulent, tyrannical.

If he is a stranger to the universe who does not know what is in it, no less is he a stranger who does not know what is going on in it. He is a runaway, who flies from social reason; he is blind, who shuts the eyes of the understanding; he is poor, who has need of another, and has not from himself all things which are useful for life. He is an abscess on the universe who withdraws and separates himself from the reason of our common nature through being displeased with the things which happen, for the same nature produces this, and has produced thee too: he is a piece rent asunder from the state, who tears his own soul from that of reasonable animals, which is one.

The one is a philosopher without a tunic, and the other without a book: here is another half naked: Bread I have not, he says, and I abide by reason.—And I do not get the means of living out of my learning, and I abide by my reason.

Book V

In the morning when thou risest unwillingly, let this thought be present—I am rising to the work of a human being. Why then am I dissatisfied if I am going to do the things for which I exist and for which I was brought into the world? Or have I been made for this, to lie in the bed-clothes and keep myself warm?—But this is more pleasant.— Dost thou exist then to take thy pleasure, and not at all for action or exertion? Dost thou not see the little plants, the little birds, the ants, the spiders, the bees working together to put in order their several parts of the universe? And art thou unwilling to do the work of a human being, and dost thou not make haste to do that which is according to thy nature?—But it is necessary to take rest also.—It is necessary: however nature has fixed bounds to this too: she has fixed bounds both to eating and drinking, and yet thou goest beyond these bounds, beyond what is sufficient; yet in thy acts it is not so, but thou stoppest short of what thou canst do. So thou lovest not thyself, for if thou didst, thou wouldst love thy nature and her will. But those who love their several arts exhaust themselves in working at them unwashed and without food; but thou valuest thy own own nature less than the turner values the turning art, or the dancer the dancing art, or the lover of money values his money, or the vainglorious man his little glory. And such men, when they have a violent affection to a thing, choose neither to eat nor to sleep rather than to perfect the things which they care for. But are the acts which concern society more vile in thy eyes and less worthy of thy labour?

Book VI

Look within. Let neither the peculiar quality of anything nor its value escape thee.

All existing things soon change, and they will either be reduced to vapour, if indeed all substance is one, or they will be dispersed.

The reason which governs knows what its own disposition is, and what it does, and on what material it works.

The best way of avenging thyself is not to become like the wrong doer.

Take pleasure in one thing and rest in it, in passing from one social act to another social act, thinking of God.

The ruling principle is that which rouses and turns itself, and while it makes itself such as it is and such as it wills to be, it also makes everything which happens appear to itself to be such as it wills.

In conformity to the nature of the universe every single thing is accomplished, for certainly it is not in conformity to any other nature that each thing is accomplished, either a nature which externally comprehends this, or a nature which is comprehended within this nature, or a nature external and independent of this.

The universe is either a confusion, and a mutual involution of things, and a dispersion; or it is unity and order and providence. If then it is the former, why do I desire to tarry in a fortuitous combination of things and such a disorder? And why do I care about anything else than how I shall at last become earth? And why am I disturbed, for the dispersion of my elements will happen whatever I do. But if the other supposition is true, I venerate, and I am firm, and I trust in him who governs.

When thou hast been compelled by circumstances to be disturbed in a manner, quickly return to thyself and do not continue out of tune longer than the compulsion lasts: for thou wilt have more mastery over the harmony by continually recurring to it....

Most of the things which the multitude admire are referred to objects of the most general kind, those which are held together by cohesion or natural organization, such as stones, wood, fig-trees, vines, olives. But those which are admired by men who are a little more reasonable are referred to the things which are held together by a living principle, as flocks, herds. Those which are admired by men who are still more instructed are the things which are held together by a rational soul, not however a universal soul, but rational so far as it is a soul skilled in some art, or expert in some other way, or simply rational so far as it possesses a number of slaves. But he who values rational soul, a soul universal and fitted for political life, regards nothing else except this; and above all things he keeps his soul in a condition and in an activity conformable to reason and social life, and he co-operates to this end with those who are of the same kind as himself....

Death is a cessation of the impressions through the senses, and of the pulling of the strings which move the appetites, and of the discursive movements of the thoughts, and of the service to the flesh.

It is a shame for the soul to be first to give way in this life, when thy body does not give way.

Take care that thou art not made into a Caesar, that thou art not dyed with this dye; for such things happen. Keep thyself then simple, good, pure, serious, free from affectation, a friend of justice, a worshipper of the gods, kind, affectionate, strenuous in all proper acts. Strive to continue to be such as philosophy wished to make thee. Reverence the gods, and help men. Short is life. There is only one fruit of this terrene life, a pious disposition and social acts. Do everything as a disciple of Antoninus. Remember his constancy in every act which was conformable to reason, and his evenness in all things, and his piety, and the serenity of his countenance, and his sweetness, and his disregard of empty fame, and his efforts to understand things; and how he would never let anything pass without having first most carefully examined it and clearly understood it; and how he bore with those who blamed him unjustly without blaming them in return; how he did nothing in a hurry; and how he listened not to calumnies, and how exact an examiner of manners and actions he was; and not given to reproach people, nor timid, nor suspicious, nor a sophist; and with how little he was satisfied, such as lodging, bed, dress, food, servants; and how laborious and patient; and how he was able on account of his sparing diet to hold out to the evening, not even requiring to relieve himself by any evacuations except at the usual hour; and his firmness and uniformity in his friendships; and how he tolerated freedom of speech in those who opposed his opinions; and the pleasure that he had when any man showed him anything better; and how religious he was without superstition. Imitate all this that thou mayest have as good a conscience, when thy last hour comes, as he had....

I consist of a little body and a soul. Now to this little body all things are indifferent, for it is not able to perceive differences. But to the understanding those things only are indifferent, which are not the works of its own activity. But whatever things are the works of its own activity, all these are in its power. And of these however only those which are done with reference to the present; for as to the future and the past activities of the mind, even these are for the present indifferent.

Neither the labour which the hand does nor that of the foot is contrary to nature, so long as the foot does the foot's work and the hand the hand's. So then neither to a man as a man is his labour contrary to nature, so long as it does the things of a man. But if the labour is not contrary to his nature, neither is it an evil to him.

How many pleasures have been enjoyed by robbers, patricides, tyrants.

Dost thou not see how the handicraftsmen accommodate themselves up to a certain point to those who are not skilled in their craft—nevertheless they cling to the reason (the principles) of their art and do not endure to depart from it? Is it not strange if the architect and the physician shall have more respect to the reason (the principles) of their own arts than man to his own reason, which is common to him and the gods?

Asia, Europe are corners of the universe: all the sea a drop in the universe; Athos a little clod of the universe: all the present time is a point in eternity. All things are little, changeable, perishable. All things come from thence, from that universal ruling power either directly proceeding or by way of sequence. And accordingly the lion's gaping jaws, and that which is poisonous, and every harmful thing, as a thorn, as mud, are after-products of the grand and beautiful. Do not then imagine that they are of another kind from that which thou dost venerate, but form a just opinion of the source of all.

He who has seen present things has seen all, both everything which has taken place from all eternity and everything which will be for time without end; for all things are of one kin and of one form.

Frequently consider the connexion of all things in the universe and their relation to one another. For in a manner all things are implicated with one another, and all in this way are friendly to one another; for one thing comes in order after another, and this is by virtue of the active movement and mutual conspiration and the unity of the substance.

Adapt thyself to the things with which thy lot has been cast: and the men among whom thou hast received thy portion, love them, but do it truly, sincerely.

Every instrument, tool, vessel, if it does that for which it has been made, is well, and yet he who made it is not there. But in the things which are held together by nature there is within and there abides in them the power which made them; wherefore the more is it fit to reverence this power, and to think, that, if thou dost live and act according to its will, everything in thee is in conformity to intelligence. And thus also in the universe the things which belong to it are in conformity to intelligence.

Whatever of the things which are not within thy power thou shalt suppose to be good for thee or evil, it must of necessity be that, if such a bad thing befall thee or the loss of such a good thing, thou wilt blame the gods, and hate men too, those who are the cause of the misfortune or the loss, or those who are suspected of being likely to be the cause; and indeed we do much injustice, because we make a difference between these things. But if we judge only those things which are in our power to be good or bad, there remains no reason either for finding fault with God or standing in a hostile attitude to man.

Pliny the Younger and Emperor Trajan: Letters on Treatment of the Christians

112

Document Text

Pliny to Emperor Trajan

It is my invariable rule, Sir, to refer to you in all matters where I feel doubtful; for who is more capable of removing my scruples, or informing my ignorance? Having never been present at any trials concerning those who profess Christianity, I am unacquainted not only with the nature of their crimes, or the measure of their punishment, but how far it is proper to enter into an examination concerning them. Whether, therefore, any difference is usually made with respect to ages, or no distinction is to be observed between the young and the adult; whether repentance entitles them to a pardon; or if a man has been once a Christian, it avails nothing to desist from his error; whether the very profession of Christianity, unattended with any criminal act, or only the crimes themselves inherent in the profession are punishable; on all these points I am in great doubt. In the meanwhile, the method I have observed towards those who have been brought before me as Christians is this: I asked them whether they were Christians; if they admitted it, I repeated the question twice, and threatened them with punishment; if they persisted, I ordered them to be at once punished: for I was persuaded, whatever the nature of their opinions might be, a contumacious and inflexible obstinacy certainly deserved correction. There were others also brought before me possessed with the same infatuation, but being Roman citizens, I directed them to be sent to Rome. But this crime spreading (as is usually the case) while it was actually under prosecution, several instances of the same nature occurred. An anonymous information was laid before me containing a charge against several persons, who upon examination denied they were Christians, or had ever been so. They repeated after me an invocation to the gods, and offered religious rites with wine and incense before your statue (which for that purpose I had ordered to be brought, together with those of the gods), and even reviled the name of Christ: whereas there is no forcing, it is said, those who are really Christians into any of these compliances: I thought it proper, therefore, to discharge them. Some among those who were accused by a witness in person at first confessed themselves Christians, but immediately after denied it; the rest owned indeed that they had been of that number formerly, but had now (some above three, others more, and a few above twenty years ago) renounced that error. They all worshipped your statue and the images of the gods, uttering imprecations at the same time against the name of Christ. They affirmed the whole of their guilt, or their error, was, that they met on a stated day before it was light, and addressed a form of prayer to Christ, as to a divinity, binding themselves by a solemn oath, not for the purposes of any wicked design, but never to commit any fraud, theft, or adultery, never to falsify their word, nor deny a trust when they should be called upon to deliver it up; after which it was their custom to separate, and then reassemble, to eat in common a harmless meal. From this custom, however, they desisted after the publication of my edict, by which, according to your commands, I forbade the meeting of any assemblies. After receiving this account, I judged it so much the more necessary to endeavor to extort the real truth, by putting two female slaves to the torture, who were said to officiate' in their religious rites: but all I could discover was evidence of an absurd and extravagant superstition. I deemed it expedient, therefore, to adjourn all further proceedings, in order to consult you. For it appears to be a matter highly deserving your consideration, more especially as great numbers must be involved in the danger of these prosecutions, which have already extended, and are still likely to extend, to persons of all ranks and ages, and even of both sexes. In fact, this contagious superstition is not confined to the cities only, but has spread its infection among the neighbouring villages and country. Nevertheless, it still seems possible to restrain its progress. The temples, at least, which were once almost deserted, begin now to be frequented; and the sacred rites, after a long intermission, are again revived; while there is a general demand for the victims, which till lately found very few purchasers. From all this it is easy to conjecture what numbers might be reclaimed if a general pardon were granted to those who shall repent of their error.

Emperor Trajan to Pliny

You have adopted the right course, my dearest Secundus, in investigating the charges against the Christians who were brought before you. It is not possible to lay down any general rule for all such cases. Do not go out of your way to look for them. If indeed they should be brought before you, and the crime is proved, they must be punished; with the restriction, however, that where the party denies he is a Christian, and shall make it evident that he is not, by invoking our gods, let him (notwithstanding any former suspicion) be pardoned upon his repentance. Anonymous informations ought not to be received in any sort of prosecution. It is introducing a very dangerous precedent, and is quite foreign to the spirit of our age.

Letter of the Smyrnaeans on the Martyrdom of Polycarp

156

Document Text

The church of God which sojourneth at Smyrna to the Church of God which sojourneth in Philomelium and to all the brotherhoods of the holy and universal Church sojourning in every place; mercy and peace and love from God the Father and our Lord Jesus Christ be multiplied.

We write unto you, brethren, an account of what befel those that suffered martyrdom and especially the blessed Polycarp, who stayed the persecution, having as it were set his seal upon it by his martyrdom. For nearly all the foregoing events came to pass that the Lord might show us once more an example of martyrdom which is conformable to the Gospel. For he lingered that he might be delivered up, even as the Lord did, to the end that we too might be imitators of him, *not looking* only *to that which concerneth ourselves, but also to that which concerneth our neighbours*. For it is the office of true and stedfast love, not only to desire that oneself be saved, but all the brethren also.

Blessed therefore and noble are all the martyrdoms which have taken place according to the will of God (for it behoveth us to be very scrupulous and to assign to God the power over all things). For who could fail to admire their nobleness and patient endurance and loyalty to the Master? seeing that when they were so torn by lashes that the mechanism of their flesh was visible even as far as the inward veins and arteries, they endured patiently, so that the very bystanders had pity and wept; while they themselves reached such a pitch of bravery that none of them uttered a cry or a groan, thus showing to us all that at that hour the martyrs of Christ being tortured were absent from the flesh, or rather that the Lord was standing by and conversing with them. And giving heed unto the grace of Christ they despised the tortures of this world, purchasing at the cost of one hour a release from eternal punishment And they found the fire of their inhuman torturers cold: for they set before their eyes the escape from the eternal fire which is never quenched; while with the eyes of their heart they gazed upon the good things which are reserved for those that endure patiently, things which neither ear hath heard nor eye hath seen, neither have they entered into the heart of man, but were shown by the Lord to them, for they were no longer men but angels already. And in like manner also those that were condemned to the wild beasts endured fearful punishments, being made to lie on sharp shells and buffeted with other forms of manifold tortures, that the devil might, if possible, by the persistence of the punishment bring them to a denial; for he tried many wiles against them.

But thanks be to God; for He verily prevailed against all. For the right noble Germanicus encouraged their timorousness through the constancy which was in him; and he fought with the wild beasts in a signal way. For when the proconsul wished to prevail upon him and bade him have pity on his youth, he used violence and dragged the wild beast towards him, desiring the more speedily to obtain a release from their unrighteous and lawless life. So after this all the multitude, marvelling at the bravery of the God-beloved and God-fearing people of the Christians, raised a cry, "Away with the atheists; let search be made for Polycarp."

But one man, Quintus by name, a Phrygian newly arrived from Phrygia, when he saw the wild beasts, turned coward. He it was who had forced himself and some others to come forward of their own free will. This man the proconsul by much entreaty persuaded to swear the oath and to offer incense. For this cause therefore, brethren, we praise not those who deliver themselves up, since the Gospel doth not so teach us.

Now the glorious Polycarp at the first, when he heard it, so far from being dismayed, was desirous of remaining in town; but the greater part persuaded him to withdraw. So he withdrew to a farm not far distant from the city; and there he stayed with a few companions, doing nothing else night and day but praying for all men and for the churches throughout the world; for this was his constant habit And while praying he falleth into a trance three days before his apprehension; and he saw his pillow burning with fire. And he turned and said unto those that were with him: "It must needs be that I shall be burned alive."

And as those that were in search of him persisted, he departed to another farm; and forthwith they that were in search of him came up; and not finding him, they seized two slave lads, one of whom confessed under torture; for it was impossible for him to lie concealed, seeing that the very persons who betrayed him were people of his own household. And the captain of the police, who chanced to have the very name, being called Herod, was eager to bring him into the stadium, that he himself might fulfil his appointed lot, being made a partaker with Christ, while they—his betrayers—underwent the punishment of Judas himself.

So taking the lad with them, on the Friday about the supper hour, the gendarmes and horsemen went forth with their accustomed arms, hastening as against a robber. And coming up in a body late in the evening, they found the man himself in bed in an upper chamber in a certain cottage; and though he might have departed thence to another place, he would not, saying, The will of God be done. So when he heard that they were come, he went down and conversed with them, the bystanders marvelling at his age and his constancy, and wondering how there should be so much eagerness for the apprehension of an old man like him. Thereupon forthwith he gave orders that a table should be spread for them to eat and drink at that hour, as much as they desired. And he persuaded them to grant him an hour that he might pray unmolested; and on their consenting, he stood up and prayed, being so full of the grace of God, that for two hours he could not hold his peace, and those that heard were amazed, and many repented that they had come against such a venerable old man.

But when at length he brought his prayer to an end, after remembering all who at any time had come in his way, small and great, high and low, and all the universal Church throughout the world, the hour of departure being come, they seated him on an ass and brought him into the city, it being a high sabbath. And he was met by Herod the captain of police and his father Nicetes, who also removed him to their carriage and tried to prevail upon him, seating themselves by his side and saying, "Why what harm is there in saying, Caesar is Lord, and offering incense," with more to this effect, "and saving thyself?" But he at first gave them no answer. When however they persisted, he said, "I am not going to do what ye counsel me." Then they, failing to persuade him, uttered threatening words and made him dismount with speed, so that he bruised his shin, as he got down from the carriage. And without even turning round, he went on his way promptly and with speed, as if nothing had happened to him, being taken to the stadium; there being such a tumult in the stadium that no man's voice could be so much as heard.

But as Polycarp entered into the stadium, a voice came to him from heaven; "Be strong, Polycarp, and play the man." And no one saw the speaker, but those of our people who were present heard the voice. And at length, when he was brought up, there was a great tumult, for they heard that Polycarp had been apprehended. When then he was brought before him, the proconsul enquired whether he were the man. And on his confessing that he was, he tried to persuade him to a denial saying, "Have respect to thine age," and other things in accordance therewith, as it is their wont to say; "Swear by the genius of Caesar; repent and say, Away with the atheists." Then Polycarp with solemn countenance looked upon the whole multitude of lawless heathen that were in the stadium, and waved his hand to them; and groaning and looking up to heaven he said, "Away with the atheists." But when the magistrate pressed him hard and said, "Swear the oath, and I will release thee; revile the Christ," Polycarp said, "Fourscore and six years have I been His servant, and He hath done me no wrong. How then can I blaspheme my King who saved me?"

But on his persisting again and saying, "Swear by the genius of Caesar," he answered, "If thou supposest vainly that I will swear by the genius of Caesar, as thou sayest, and feignest that thou art ignorant who I am, hear thou plainly, I am a Christian. But if thou wouldest learn the doctrine of Christianity, assign a day and give me a hearing." The proconsul said, "Prevail upon the people." But Polycarp said, "As for thyself, I should have held thee worthy of discourse; for we have been taught to render, as is meet, to princes and authorities appointed by God such honour as does us no harm; but as for these, I do not hold them worthy, that I should defend myself before them."

Whereupon the proconsul said, "I have wild beasts here and I will throw thee to them, except thou repent." But he said, "Call for them: for the repentance from better to worse is a change not permitted to us; but it is a noble thing to change from untowardness to righteousness." Then he said to him again, "I will cause thee to be consumed by fire, if thou despisest the wild beasts, unless thou repent." But Polycarp said, "Thou threatenest that fire which burneth for a season and after a little while is quenched: for thou art ignorant of the fire of the future judgment and eternal punishment, which is reserved for the ungodly. But why delayest thou? Come, do what thou wilt."

Saying these things and more besides, he was inspired with courage and joy, and his countenance was filled with grace, so that not only did it not drop in dismay at the things which were said to him, but on the contrary the proconsul was astounded and sent his own herald to proclaim three times in the midst of the stadium, "Polycarp hath confessed himself to be a Christian." When this was proclaimed by the herald, the whole multitude both of Gentiles and of Jews who dwelt in Smyrna cried out with ungovernable wrath and with a loud shout, "This is the teacher of Asia, the father of the Christians, the puller down of our gods, who teacheth numbers not to sacrifice nor worship." Saying these things, they shouted aloud and asked the Asiarch Philip to let a lion loose upon Polycarp. But he said that it was not lawful for him, since he had brought the sports to a close. Then they thought fit to shout out with one accord that Polycarp should be burned alive. For it must needs be that the matter of the vision should be fulfilled, which was shown him concerning his pillow, when he saw it on fire while praying, and turning round he said prophetically to the faithful who were with him, "I must needs be burned alive."

These things then happened with so great speed, quicker than words could tell, the crowds forthwith collecting from the workshops and baths timber and faggots, and the Jews more especially assisting in this with zeal, as is their wont. But when the pile was made ready, divesting himself of all his upper garments and loosing his girdle, he endeavoured also to take off his shoes, though not in the habit of doing this before, because all the faithful at all times vied eagerly who should soonest touch his flesh. For he had been treated with all honour for his holy life even before his gray hairs came. Forthwith then the instruments that were prepared for the pile were placed about him; and as they were going likewise to nail him to the stake, he said, "Leave me as I am; for He that hath granted me to endure the fire will grant me also to remain at the pile unmoved, even without the security which ye seek from the nails."

So they did not nail him, but tied him. Then he, placing his hands behind him and being bound to the stake, like a noble ram out of a great flock for an offering, a burnt sacrifice made ready and acceptable to God, looking up to heaven said, "O Lord God Almighty, the Father of Thy beloved and blessed Son Jesus Christ, through whom we have received the knowledge of Thee, the God of angels and powers and of all creation and of the whole race of the righteous, who live in Thy presence; I bless Thee for that Thou hast granted me this day and hour, that I might receive a portion amongst the number of martyrs in the cup of [Thy] Christ unto resurrection of eternal life, both of soul and of body, in the incorruptibility of the Holy Spirit May I be received among these in Thy presence this day, as a rich and acceptable sacrifice, as Thou didst prepare and reveal it beforehand, and hast accomplished it, Thou that art the faithful and true God. For this cause, yea and for all things, I praise Thee, I bless Thee, I glorify Thee, through the eternal and heavenly High-priest, Jesus Christ, Thy beloved Son, through whom with Him and the Holy Spirit be glory both now (and ever] and for the ages to come. Amen."

When he had offered up the Amen and finished his prayer, the firemen lighted the fire. And, a mighty flame flashing forth, we to whom it was given to see, saw a marvel, yea and we were preserved that we might relate to the rest what happened. The fire, making the appearance of a vault, like the sail of a vessel filled by the wind, made a wall round about the body of the martyr; and it was there in the midst, not like flesh burning, but like [a loaf in the oven or like] gold and silver refined in a furnace. For we perceived such a fragrant smell, as if it were the wafted odour of frankincense or some other precious spice.

So at length the lawless men, seeing that his body could not be consumed by the fire, ordered an executioner to go up to him and stab him with a dagger. And when he had done this, there came forth [a dove and] a quantity of blood, so that it extinguished the fire; and all the multitude marvelled that there should be so great a difference between the unbelievers and the elect. In the number of these was this man, the glorious martyr Polycarp, who was found an apostolic and prophetic teacher in our own time, a bishop of the holy Church which is in Smyrna. For every word which he uttered from his mouth was accomplished and will be accomplished.

But the jealous and envious Evil One, the adversary of the family of the righteous, having seen the greatness of his martyrdom and his blameless life from the beginning, and how he was crowned with the crown of immortality and had won a reward which none could gainsay, managed that not even his poor body should be taken away by us, although many desired to do this and to touch his holy flesh. So he put forward Nicetes, the father of Herod and brother of Alce, to plead with the magistrate not to give up his body, "lest," so it was said, "they should abandon the crucified one and begin to worship this man"—this being done at the instigation and urgent entreaty of the Jews, who also watched when we were about to take it from the fire, not knowing that it will be impossible for us either to forsake at any time the Christ who suffered for the salvation of the whole world of those that are saved—suffered though faultless for sinners—nor to worship any other. For Him, being the Son of God, we adore, but the martyrs as disciples and imitators of the Lord we cherish as they deserve for their matchless affection towards their own King and Teacher. May it be our lot also to be found partakers and fellow disciples with them.

The centurion therefore, seeing the opposition raised on the part of the Jews, set him in the midst and burnt him after their custom. And so we afterwards took up his bones which are more valuable than precious stones and finer than refined gold, and laid them in a suitable place; where the Lord will permit us to gather ourselves together, as we are able, in gladness and joy, and to celebrate the birth-day of his martyrdom for the commemoration of those that have already fought in the contest, and for the training and preparation of those that shall do so hereafter.

So it befel the blessed Polycarp, who having with those from Philadelphia suffered martyrdom in Smyrna—twelve in all—is especially remembered more than the others by all men, so that he is talked of even by the heathen in every place: for he showed himself not only a notable teacher, but also a distinguished martyr, whose martyrdom all desire to imitate, seeing that it was after the pattern of the Gospel of Christ. Having by his endurance overcome the unrighteous ruler in the conflict and so received the crown of immortality, he rejoiceth in company with the Apostles and all righteous men, and glorifieth the Almighty God and Father, and blesseth our Lord Jesus Christ, the saviour of our souls and helmsman of our bodies and shepherd of the universal Church which is throughout the world.

Ye indeed required that the things which happened should be shown unto you at greater length: but we for the present have certified you as it were in a summary through our brother Marcianus. When then ye have informed yourselves of these things, send the letter about likewise to the brethren which are farther off, that they also may glorify the Lord, who maketh election from His own servants. Now unto Him that is able to bring us all by His grace and bounty unto His eternal kingdom, through His only-begotten Son Jesus Christ, be glory, honour, power, and greatness for ever. Salute all the saints. They that are with us salute you, and Euarestus, who wrote the letter, with his whole house.

Now the blessed Polycarp was martyred on the second day of the first part of the month Xanthicus, on the seventh before the kalends of March, on a great sabbath, at the eighth hour. He was apprehended by Herodes, when Philip of Tralles was high-priest, in the proconsulship of Statius Quadratus, but in the reign of the Eternal King Jesus Christ To whom be the glory, honour, greatness, and eternal throne, from generation to generation. Amen.

We bid you God speed, brethren, while ye walk by the word of Jesus Christ which is according to the Gospel; with whom be glory to God for the salvation of His holy elect; even as the blessed Polycarp suffered martyrdom, in whose footsteps may it be our lot to be found in the kingdom of Jesus Christ

This account Gaius copied from the papers of Irenaeus, a disciple of Polycarp. The same also lived with Irenaeus.

And I Socrates wrote it down in Corinth from the copy of Gaius. Grace be with all men.

And I Pionius again wrote it down from the aforementioned copy, having searched it out (for the blessed Polycarp showed me in a revelation, as I will declare in the sequel), gathering it together when it was now well nigh worn out by age, that the Lord Jesus Christ may gather me also with His elect into His heavenly kingdom; to whom be the glory with the Father and the Holy Spirit for ever and ever. Amen.

Epistle to Diognetus

ca. 200

Document Text

1. Since I see, most excellent Diognetus, that thou art exceedingly anxious to understand the religion of the Christians, and that thy enquiries respecting them are distinctly and carefully made, as to what God they trust and how they worship Him, that they all disregard the world and despise death, and take no account of those who are regarded as gods by the Greeks, neither observe the superstition of the Jews, and as to the nature of the affection which they entertain one to another, and of this new development or interest, which has entered into men's lives now and not before: I gladly welcome this zeal in thee, and I ask of God, Who supplieth both the speaking and the hearing to us, that it may be granted to myself to speak in such a way that thou mayest be made better by the hearing, and to thee that thou mayest so listen that I the speaker may not be disappointed.

2. Come then, clear thyself of all the prepossessions which occupy thy mind, and throw off the habit which leadeth thee astray, and become a new man, as it were, from the beginning, as one who would listen to a new story, even as thou thyself didst confess. See not only with thine eyes, but with thine intellect also, of what substance or of what form they chance to be whom ye call and regard as gods. Is not one of them stone, like that which we tread under foot, and another bronze, no better than the vessels which are forged for our use, and another wood, which has already become rotten, and another silver, which needs a man to guard it lest it be stolen, and another iron, which is corroded with rust, and another earthenware, not a whit more comely than that which is supplied for the most dishonourable service? Are not all these of perishable matter? Are they not forged by iron and fire? Did not the sculptor make one, and the brass-founder another, and the silversmith another, and the potter another? Before they were moulded into this shape by the crafts of these several artificers, was it not possible for each one of them to have been changed in form and made to resemble these several utensils? Might not the vessels which are now made out of the same material, if they met with the same artificers, be made like unto such as these? Could not these things which are now worshipped by you, by human hands again be made vessels like the rest? Are not they all deaf and blind, are they not soul-less, senseless, motionless? Do they not all rot and decay? These things ye call gods, to these ye are slaves, these ye worship; and ye end by becoming altogether like unto them. Therefore ye hate the Christians, because they do not consider these to be gods. For do not ye yourselves, who now regard and worship them, much more despise them? Do ye not much rather mock and insult them, worshipping those that are of stone and earthenware unguarded, but shutting up those that are of silver and gold by night, and setting guards over them by day, to prevent their being stolen? And as for the honours which

ye think to offer to them, if they are sensible of them, ye rather punish them thereby, whereas, if they are insensible, ye reproach them by propitiating them with the blood and fat of victims. Let one of yourselves undergo this treatment, let him submit to these things being done to him. Nay, not so much as a single individual will willingly submit to such punishment, for he has sensibility and reason; but a stone submits, because it is insensible. Therefore ye convict his sensibility. Well, I could say much besides concerning the Christians not being enslaved to such gods as these; but if any one should think what has been said insufficient, I hold it superfluous to say more.

3. In the next place, I fancy that thou art chiefly anxious to hear about their not practising their religion in the same way as the Jews. The Jews then, so far as they abstain from the mode of worship described above, do well in claiming to reverence one God of the universe and to regard Him as Master; but so far as they offer Him this worship in methods similar to those already mentioned, they are altogether at fault. For whereas the Greeks, by offering these things to senseless and deaf images, make an exhibition of stupidity, the Jews considering that they are presenting them to God, as if He were in need of them, ought in all reason to count it folly and not religious worship. For He that made the heaven and the earth and all things that are therein, and furnisheth us all with what we need, cannot Himself need any of these things which He Himself supplieth to them that imagine they are giving them to Him. But those who think to perform sacrifices to Him with blood and fat and whole burnt offerings, and to honour Him with such honours, seem to me in no way different from those who show the same respect towards deaf images; for the one class think fit to make offerings to things unable to participate in the honour, the other class to One Who is in need of nothing.

4. But again their scruples concerning meats, and their superstition relating to the sabbath and the vanity of their circumcision and the dissimulation of their fasting and new moons, I do [not] suppose you need to learn from me, are ridiculous and unworthy of any consideration. For of the things created by God for the use of man to receive some as created well, but to decline others as useless and superfluous, is not this impious? And again to lie against God, as if He forbad us to do any good thing on the sabbath day, is not this profane? Again, to vaunt the mutilation of the flesh as a token of election as though for this reason they were particularly beloved by God, is not this ridiculous? And to watch the stars and the moon and to keep the observance of months and of days, and to distinguish the arrangements of God and the changes of the seasons according to their own impulses, making some into festivals and others into times of mourning, who would regard this as an exhibition of godliness and not much more of folly? That the Christians are right therefore in holding aloof from the common silliness and error of the Jews and from their excessive fussiness and pride, I consider that thou hast been sufficiently instructed; but as regards the mystery of their own religion, expect not that thou canst be instructed by man.

5. For Christians are not distinguished from the rest of mankind either in locality or in

speech or in customs. For they dwell not somewhere in cities of their own, neither do they use some different language, nor practise an extraordinary kind of life. Nor again do they possess any invention discovered by any intelligence or study of ingenious men, nor are they masters of any human dogma as some are. But while they dwell in cities of Greeks and barbarians as the lot of each is cast, and follow the native customs in dress and food and the other arrangements of life, yet the constitution of their own citizenship, which they set forth, is marvellous, and confessedly contradicts expectation. They dwell in their own countries, but only as sojourners; they bear their share in all things as citizens, and they endure all hardships as strangers. Every foreign country is a fatherland to them, and every fatherland is foreign. They marry like all other men and they beget children; but they do not cast away their offspring. They have their meals in common, but not their wives. They find themselves in the flesh, and yet they live not after the flesh. Their existence is on earth, but their citizenship is in heaven. They obey the established laws, and they surpass the laws in their own lives. They love all men, and they are persecuted by all. They are ignored, and yet they are condemned. They are put to death, and yet they are endued with life. They are in beggary, and yet they make many rich. They are in want of all things, and yet they abound in all things. They are dishonoured, and yet they are glorified in their dishonour. They are evil spoken of, and yet they are vindicated. They are reviled, and they bless; they are insulted, and they respect. Doing good they are punished as evil-doers; being punished they rejoice, as if they were thereby quickened by life. War is waged against them as aliens by the Jews, and persecution is carried on against them by the Greeks, and yet those that hate them cannot tell the reason of their hostility.

6. In a word, what the soul is in a body, this the Christians are in the world. The soul is spread through all the members of the body, and Christians through the divers cities of the world. The soul hath its abode in the body, and yet it is not of the body. So Christians have their abode in the world, and yet they are not of the world. The soul which is invisible is guarded in the body which is visible: so Christians are recognised as being in the world, and yet their religion remaineth invisible. The flesh hateth the soul and wageth war with it, though it receiveth no wrong, because it is forbidden to indulge in pleasures; so the world hateth Christians, though it receiveth no wrong from them, because they set themselves against its pleasures. The soul loveth the flesh which hateth it, and the members: so Christians love those that hate them. The soul is enclosed in the body, and yet itself holdeth the body together; so Christians are kept in the world as in a prison-house, and yet they themselves hold the world together. The soul though itself immortal dwelleth in a mortal tabernacle; so Christians sojourn amidst perishable things, while they look for the imperishability which is in the heavens. The soul when hardly treated in the matter of meats and drinks is improved; and so Christians when punished increase more and more daily. So great is the office for which God hath appointed them, and which it is not lawful for them to decline.

7. For it is no earthly discovery, as I said, which was committed to them, neither do they care to guard so carefully any mortal invention, nor have they entrusted to them

the dispensation of human mysteries. But truly the Almighty Creator of the Universe, the Invisible God Himself from heaven planted among men the truth and the holy teaching which surpasseth the wit of man, and fixed it firmly in their hearts, not as any man might imagine, by sending (to mankind) a subaltern, or angel, or ruler, or one of those that direct the affairs of earth, or one of those who have been entrusted with the dispensations in heaven, but the very Artificer and Creator of the Universe Himself, by Whom He made the heavens, by Whom He enclosed the sea in its proper bounds, Whose mysteries all the elements faithfully observe, from Whom [the sun] hath received even the measure of the courses of the day to keep them, Whom the moon obeys as He bids her shine by night, Whom the stars obey as they follow the course of the moon, by Whom all things are ordered and bounded and placed in subjection, the heavens and the things that are in the heavens, the earth and the things that are in the earth, the sea and the things that are in the sea, fire, air, abyss, the things that are in the heights, the things that are in the depths, the things that are between the two. Him He sent unto them. Was He sent, think you, as any man might suppose, to establish a sovereignty, to inspire fear and terror? Not so. But in gentleness [and] meekness has He sent Him, as a king might send his son who is a king. He sent Him, as sending God; He sent Him, as [a man] unto men; He sent Him, as Saviour, as using persuasion, not force: for force is no attribute of God. He sent Him, as summoning, not as persecuting; He sent Him, as loving, not as judging. For He will send Him in judgment, and who shall endure His presence? . . . [Dost thou not see] them thrown to wild beasts that so they may deny the Lord, and yet not overcome? Dost thou not see that the more of them are punished, just so many others abound? These look not like the works of a man; they are the power of God; they are proofs of His presence.

8. For what man at all had any knowledge what God was, before He came? Or dost thou accept the empty and nonsensical statements of those pretentious philosophers: of whom some said that God was fire (they call that God, whereunto they themselves shall go), and others water, and others some other of the elements which were created by God? And yet if any of these statements is worthy of acceptance, any one other created thing might just as well be made out to be God. Nay, all this is the quackery and deceit of the magicians; and no man has either seen or recognised Him, but He revealed Himself. And He revealed (Himself) by faith, whereby alone it is given to see God. For God, the Master and Creator of the Universe, Who made all things and arranged them in order, was found to be not only friendly to men, but also long-suffering. And such indeed He was always, and is, and will be, kindly and good and dispassionate and true, and He alone is good. And having conceived a great and unutterable scheme He communicated it to His Son alone. For so long as He kept and guarded His wise design as a mystery, He seemed to neglect us and to be careless about us. But when He revealed it through His beloved Son, and manifested the purpose which He had prepared from the beginning, He gave us all these gifts at once, participation in His benefits, and sight and understanding of (mysteries) which none of us ever would have expected.

9. Having thus planned everything already in His mind with His Son, He permitted us during the former time to be borne along by disorderly impulses as we desired, led astray by pleasures and lusts, not at all because He took delight in our sins, but because He bore with us, not because He approved of the past season of iniquity, but because He was creating the present season of righteousness, that, being convicted in the past time by our own deeds as unworthy of life, we might now be made deserving by the goodness of God, and having made clear our inability to enter into the kingdom of God of ourselves, might be enabled by the ability of God. And when our iniquity had been fully accomplished, and it had been made perfectly manifest that punishment and death were expected as its recompense, and the season came which God had ordained, when henceforth He should manifest His goodness and power (O the exceeding great kindness and love of God), He hated us not, neither rejected us, nor bore us malice, but was long-suffering and patient, and in pity for us took upon Himself our sins, and Himself parted with His own Son as a ransom for us, the holy for the lawless, the guileless for the evil, *the just for the unjust*, the incorruptible for the corruptible, the immortal for the mortal. For what else but His righteousness would have covered our sins? In whom was it possible for us lawless and ungodly men to have been justified, save only in the Son of God? O the sweet exchange, O the inscrutable creation, O the unexpected benefits; that the iniquity of many should be concealed in One Righteous Man, and the righteousness of One should justify many that are iniquitous! Having then in the former time demonstrated the inability of our nature to obtain life, and having now revealed a Saviour able to save even creatures which have no ability, He willed that for both reasons we should believe in His goodness and should regard Him as nurse, father, teacher, counsellor, physician, mind, light, honour, glory, strength and life.

10. This faith if thou also desirest, apprehend first full knowledge of the Father. *For God loved* men for whose sake He made the world, to whom He subjected all things that are in the earth, to whom He gave reason and mind, whom alone He permitted to look up to heaven, whom He created after His own image, to whom *He sent His only begotten Son*, to whom He promised the kingdom which is in heaven, and will give it to those that have loved Him. And when thou hast attained to this full knowledge, with what joy thinkest thou that thou wilt be filled, or how wilt thou love Him that so loved thee before? And loving Him thou wilt be an imitator of His goodness. And marvel not that a man can be an imitator of God. He can, if God willeth it. For happiness consisteth not in lordship over one's neighbours, nor in desiring to have more than weaker men, nor in possessing wealth and using force to inferiors; neither can any one imitate God in these matters; nay, these lie outside His greatness. But whosoever taketh upon himself the burden of his neighbour, whosoever desireth to benefit one that is worse off in that in which he himself is superior, whosoever by supplying to those that are in want possessions which he received from God becomes a God to those who receive them from him, he is an imitator of God. Then, though thou art placed on earth, thou shalt behold that God liveth in heaven; then shalt thou begin to declare the mysteries of God; then shalt thou both love and admire those that are punished because they will not deny God; then shalt thou condemn the deceit and error of the world; when

thou shalt perceive the true life which is in heaven, when thou shalt despise the apparent death which is here on earth, when thou shalt fear the real death, which is reserved for those that shall be condemned to the eternal fire that shall punish those delivered over to it unto the end. Then shalt thou admire those who endure for righteousness' sake the fire that is for a season, and shalt count them blessed when thou perceivest that fire. . . .

11. Mine are no strange discourses nor perverse questionings, but having been a disciple of Apostles I come forward as a teacher of the Gentiles, ministering worthily to them, as they present themselves disciples of the truth, the lessons which have been handed down. For who that has been rightly taught and has entered into friendship with the Word does not seek to learn distinctly the lessons revealed openly by the Word to the disciples; to whom the Word appeared and declared them, speaking plainly, not perceived by the unbelieving, but relating them to disciples who being reckoned faithful by Him were taught the mysteries of the Father? For which cause He sent forth the Word, that He might appear unto the world, Who being dishonoured by the people, and preached by the Apostles, was believed in by the Gentiles. This Word, Who was from the beginning, Who appeared as new and yet was proved to be old, and is engendered always young in the hearts of saints, He, I say, Who is eternal, Who to-day was accounted a Son, through Whom the Church is enriched and grace is unfolded and multiplied among the saints, grace which confers understanding, which reveals mysteries, which announces seasons, which rejoices over the faithful, which is bestowed upon those who seek her, even those by whom the pledges of faith are not broken, nor the boundaries of the fathers overstepped. Whereupon the fear of the law is sung, and the grace of the prophets is recognised, and the faith of the gospels is established, and the tradition of the apostles is preserved, and the joy of the Church exults. If thou grieve not this grace, thou shalt understand the discourses which the Word holds by the mouth of those whom He desires when He wishes. For in all things, that by the will of the commanding Word we were moved to utter with much pains, we become sharers with you, through love of the things revealed unto us.

12. Confronted with these truths and listening to them with attention, ye shall know how much God bestoweth on those that love (Him) rightly, who become a Paradise of delight, a tree bearing all manner of fruits and flourishing, growing up in themselves and adorned with various fruits. For in this garden a tree of knowledge and a tree of life hath been planted; yet the tree of knowledge does not kill, but disobedience kills; for the scriptures state clearly how God from the beginning planted a tree [of knowledge and a tree] of life in the midst of Paradise, revealing life through knowledge; and because our first parents used it not genuinely they were made naked by the deceit of the serpent. For neither is there life without knowledge, nor sound knowledge without true life; therefore the one (tree) is planted near the other. Discerning the force of this and blaming the knowledge which is exercised apart from the truth of the injunction which leads to life, the apostle says, *Knowledge puffeth up, but charity edifieth*. For the man who supposes that he knows anything without the true knowledge which is

testified by the life, is ignorant, he is deceived by the serpent, because he loved not life; whereas he who with fear recognises and desires life plants in hope expecting fruit. Let your heart be knowledge, and your life true reason, duly comprehended. Whereof if thou bear the tree and pluck the fruit, thou shalt ever gather the harvest which God looks for, which serpent toucheth not, nor deceit infecteth, neither is Eve corrupted, but is believed on as a virgin, and salvation is set forth, and the apostles are filled with understanding, and the passover of the Lord goes forward, and the congregations are gathered together, and [all things] are arranged in order, and as He teacheth the saints the Word is gladdened, through Whom the Father is glorified, to Whom be glory for ever and ever. Amen.

Laws Ending Persecution of Christians in the Roman Empire

311 and 313

Document Text

Editor's Note: The text of the two edicts is translated from Lactantius. The paragraph numbers are those given to the text of Lactantius. Additional material present in the text surviving in Eusebius is added in square brackets thus: [. . .]. The more significant of Eusebius's variations are indicated in square brackets preceded by a shilling stroke thus: [. . .]

Edict of Galerius (311)

[Emperor Caesar Galerius Valerius Maximianos, Unconquered Augustus, Pontifex Maximus, Germanicus Maximus, Egyptiacus Maximus, Thebaicus Maximus, Sarmaticus Maximus five times, Persicus Maximus twice, Carpicus Maximus six times, Armenicus Maximus, Medicus Maximus, Adiabenicus Maximus, in the 20th tenure of Tribunician Power, in the 19th year as Emperor, the 8th as Consul, Father of the Fatherland, Proconsul; and Emperor Caesar Flavius Valerius Constantinus, Pious, Fortunate, Unconquered Augustus, Pontifex Maximus, Holder of Tribunician Power, in the 5th year as Emperor, Consul, Father of the Fatherland, Proconsul; and Emperor Caesar Valerius Licinianus Licinius, Pious, Fortunate, Pontifex Maximus, in the 4th tenure of Tribunician Power, in the 3rd year as Emperor, Consul, Father of the Fatherland, Proconsul, to their provincials, Greeting !] (1) Among other measures which we are always laying down for the benefit and usefulness of the public good, we had indeed previously wished to amend all things in accordance with the ancient laws and the public *disciplina* of the Romans and to make provision that even the Christians who had abandoned the way of the life (*secta*) of their ancestors should return to their right minds.

(2) For such great willfulness had by some means invaded those same Christians and such great stupidity had occupied them that they would not follow those practices which their own ancestors had perhaps been the first to institute, but they have made laws for themselves which they might observe in accordance with their own will and as it seemed pleasant to them and they have gathered various people together in various places.

(3) At length when our command along these lines had been issued, many were subjected to danger and many also were struck down [/were afflicted by various deaths].

(4) Since many, however, persevered in their determination [/senselessness] and we saw that they did not offer to the Gods the worship and religious duty they owed them nor reverence the God of the Christians, taking into consideration the observance of our most mild clemency and of our sempiternal custom, by which we are accustomed to indulge all men with prompt pardon, we have determined that our indulgence should be extended to these men also, so that they may once more be Christians and may construct their meeting places [/houses in which they used to meet], provided they do nothing contrary to *disciplina*.

(5) We shall signify through another letter to governors what they should do. In consequence, in accordance with this our indulgence they will be [/are] obliged to pray to their God for our safety and that of the state, and for their own, so that from every side the state may be preserved unharmed and that they may be able to live free from care in their homes.

Letter of Licinius (313)

[As we have for a long time been considering that liberty of worship is not to be denied, but that the capacity to take care of divine matters should be given to the reason and wish of each man, in accordance with his own resolution, we have urged the Christians that they should observe the faith of their way of life and worship. But considering that many and various conditions appear clearly to have been imposed upon that rescript in which this same capacity was accorded to them, it is, all things considered, possible that certain of them within a short time were repelled from this observance.]

(2) When under fortunate auspices both I Constantine Augustus and also I Licinius Augustus had come together at Milan and were holding in discussion all affairs which have to do with advantages and the public security [/usefulness], we believed that, among other matters which we saw would be beneficial for many men, those which ought to be put in order first of all were those by which the reverence of divinity is sustained, so that we should give both to Christians and everyone the free power of following the religion which each wished, so that whatever there is of divinity in the heavenly place should be able to be placated and propitious to us and to all those who are established under our power. (3) We have therefore believed [/decreed] with salutary and correct reasoning that this policy should be entered upon, that we should consider that the opportunity [/capacity] should be denied to no one who pays attention either to Christian observance or to that religion which he might feel was most suited to himself, so that the most high divinity, whose religion we obey with free minds, may be able to offer to us his accustomed favour and benevolence.

(4) Therefore it is appropriate that Your Dedicatedness should know that it has pleased us that all stipulations about the name of the Christians which were contained in

documents previously given to your office should be entirely set aside, and that those things which seemed thoroughly sinister and alien to our clemency should be removed, and that now freely and in simplicity each one of those who exercise the same wish to observe the religion of the Christians may hasten to observe that same thing, setting aside any anxiety or molestation of them.

(5) We have considered these things should be fully signified to Your Solicitude so that by them you might know that we have given to these same Christians free and absolute opportunity to cultivate their religion.

(6) Since you thoroughly see that this has been granted to them by us, Your Dedicatedness understands that for others also open and free capacity for their religion or observance is granted in accordance with the peacefulness of our times, so that each should have free permission in worshipping what he has chosen. This has been done by us so that nothing should seem to be taken away by us either in respect of honour or in respect of religion.

(7) In addition we have decided that this should be decreed concerning the body corporate (*persona*) of the Christians: that if some people in an earlier time seem to have bought, either from our fisc or from anyone else, the same places where they had previously been accustomed to meet, concerning which also a certain procedure (*forma*) had before now been defined (*comprehensa*) in letters given to your office, they should restore the same places to the Christians without payment and without any request for a price, setting aside all obstruction and ambiguity.

(8) Those also who obtained them as a gift, shall similarly return the same to the Christians as fast as possible. But those who have bought or who have received as a gift, if they should seek something from our benevolence, let them make a request of the Vicarius, so that there may be relief (*consulatur*) for them from him through our clemency. All these things should be handed over to the body of the Christians immediately through your mediation and without delay.

(9) And because the same Christians are found to have had not only those places at which they were accustomed to meet, but also other property belonging by right to their body, that is to the churches, not to individual persons, you shall order all these things by the law which we have defined above to be returned to the same Christians, that is to their body corporate and to their assemblies, without any ambiguity or controversy whatsoever, observing however the above-mentioned proviso, that those who restore the same without charge, as we have said, may hope for indemnity from our benevolence.

(10) In all these affairs you will be obliged to offer to the aforesaid body corporate of the Christians your most effective co-operation, so that our command may be complet-

ed as fast as possible, in order that through our *clementia* there may be solace for the public peace in this matter.

(11) In this way it will come about that divine favour towards us, which we have experienced in such great things, will, as we have defined above, persist prosperously through all time on our achievements together with our public happiness.

(12) In order that the principle of this ordinance and of our benevolence may be able to come to the knowledge of all, it is appropriate that you post up this document everywhere and that you bring it thoroughly to the knowledge of all, with your proclamation prefixed to it, in order that the ordinance of this our benevolence should not be hidden.

Julian the Apostate: Letter to Arsacius

362

Document Text

The Hellenic religion does not yet prosper as I desire, and it is the fault of those who profess it; for the worship of the gods is on a splendid and magnificent scale, surpassing every prayer and every hope. May Adrasteia pardon my words, for indeed no one, a little while ago, would have ventured even to pray for a change of such a sort or so complete within so short a time. Why, then, do we think that this is enough, why do we not observe that it is their benevolence to strangers, their care for the graves of the dead and the pretended holiness of their lives that have done most to increase atheism? I believe that we ought really and truly to practise every one of these virtues. And it is not enough for you alone to practise them, but so must all the priests in Galatia, without exception. Either shame or persuade them into righteousness or else remove them from their priestly office, if they do not, together with their wives, children and servants, attend the worship of the gods but allow their servants or sons or wives to show impiety towards the gods and honour atheism more than piety. In the second place, admonish them that no priest may enter a theatre or drink in a tavern or control any craft or trade that is base and not respectable. Honour those who obey you, but those who disobey, expel from office. In every city establish frequent hostels in order that strangers may profit by our benevolence; I do not mean for our own people only, but for others also who are in need of money. I have but now made a plan by which you may be well provided for this; for I have given directions that 30,000 modii of corn shall be assigned every year for the whole of Galatia, and 60,000 pints of wine. I order that one-fifth of this be used for the poor who serve the priests, and the remainder be distributed by us to strangers and beggars. For it is disgraceful that, when no Jew ever has to beg, and the impious Galilaeans support not only their own poor but ours as well, all men see that our people lack aid from us. Teach those of the Hellenic faith to contribute to public service of this sort, and the Hellenic villages to offer their first fruits to the gods; and accustom those who love the Hellenic religion to these good works by teaching them that this was our practice of old. At any rate Homer makes Eumaeus say: "Stranger, it is not lawful for me, not even though a baser man than you should come, to dishonour a stranger. For from Zeus come all strangers and beggars. And a gift, though small, is precious.' Then let us not, by allowing others to outdo us in good works, disgrace by such remissness, or rather, utterly abandon, the reverence due to the gods. If I hear that you are carrying out these orders I shall be filled with joy.

As for the government officials, do not interview them often at their homes, but write to them frequently. And when they enter the city no priest must go to meet them, but only meet them within the vestibule when they visit the temples of the gods. Let no soldier march before them into the temple, but any who will may follow them; for the moment that one of them passes over the threshold of the sacred precinct he becomes a private citizen. For you yourself, as you are aware, have authority over what is within, since this is the bidding of the divine ordinance. Those who obey it are in very truth god-fearing, while those who oppose it with arrogance are vainglorious and empty-headed.

I am ready to assist Pessinus if her people succeed in winning the favour of the Mother of the Gods. But, if they neglect her, they are not only not free from blame, but, not to speak harshly, let them beware of reaping my enmity also. "For it is not lawful for me to cherish or to pity men who are the enemies of the immortal gods." Therefore persuade them, if they claim my patronage, that the whole community must become suppliants of the Mother of the Gods.

Pope Gelasius I: Letter to Emperor Anastasius

494

Document Text

There are two powers, august Emperor, by which this world is chiefly ruled, namely, the sacred authority of the priests and the royal power. Of these that of the priests is the more weighty, since they have to render an account for even the kings of men in the divine judgment. You are also aware, dear son, that while you are permitted honorably to rule over human kind, yet in things divine you bow your head humbly before the leaders of the clergy and await from their hands the means of your salvation. In the reception and proper disposition of the heavenly mysteries you recognize that you should be subordinate rather than superior to the religious order, and that in these matters you depend on their judgment rather than wish to force them to follow your will.

If the ministers of religion, recognizing the supremacy granted you from heaven in matters affecting the public order, obey your laws, lest otherwise they might obstruct the course of secular affairs by irrelevant considerations, with what readiness should you not yield them obedience to whom is assigned the dispensing of the sacred mysteries of religion. Accordingly, just as there is no slight danger in the case of the priests if they refrain from speaking when the service of the divinity requires, so there is no little risk for those who disdain—which God forbid—when they should obey. And if it is fitting that the hearts of the faithful should submit to all priests in general who properly administer divine affairs, how much the more is obedience due to the bishop of that see which the Most High ordained to be above all others, and which is consequently dutifully honored by the devotion of the whole Church.

Bernard Atton, Viscount of Carcassonne: Charter of Homage and Fealty

1110

Document Text

In the name of the Lord, I, Bernard Atton, Viscount of Carcassonne, in the presence of my sons, Roger and Trencavel, and of Peter Roger of Barbazan, and William Hugo, and Raymond Mantellini, and Peter de Vitry, nobles, and of many other honorable men, who have come to the monastery of St. Mary of Grasse, to the honor of the festival of the august St. Mary; since lord Leo, abbot of the said monastery, has asked me, in the presence of all those above mentioned, to acknowledge to him the fealty and homage for the castles, manors, and places which the patrons, my ancestors, held from him and his predecessors and from the said monastery as a fief, and which I ought to hold as they held, I have made to the lord abbot Leo acknowledgment and homage as I ought to do.

Therefore, let all present and to come know that I the said Bernard Atton, lord and viscount of Carcassonne, acknowledge verily to thee my lord Leo, by the grace of God abbot of St. Mary of Grasse, and to thy successors that I hold and ought to hold as a fief in Carcassonne the following: that is to say, the castles of Confoles, of Leocque, of Capendes (which is otherwise known as St. Martin of Sussagues); and the manors of Mairac, of Albars and of Musso; also, in the valley of Aquitaine, Rieux, Traverina, Herault, Archas, Servians, Villatritoes, Tansiraus, Presler, Cornelles. Moreover, I acknowledge that I hold from thee and from the said monastery as a fief the castle of Termes in Narbonne; and in Minerve the castle of Ventaion, and the manors of Cassanolles, and of Ferral and Aiohars; and in Le Rogès, the little village of Longville; for each and all of which I make homage and fealty with hands and with mouth to thee my said lord abbot Leo and to thy successors, and I swear upon these four gospels of God that I will always be a faithful vassal to thee and to thy successors and to the St. Mary of Grasse in all things in which a vassal is required to be faithful to his lord, and I will defend thee, my lord, and all thy successors, and the said monastery and the monks present and to come and the castles and manors and all your men and their possessions against all malefactors and invaders, at my request and that of my successors at my own cost; and I will give to thee power over all the castles and manors above described, in peace and in war, whenever they shall be claimed by thee or by thy successors.

Moreover I acknowledge that, as a recognition of the above fiefs, I and my successors ought to come to the said monastery, at our own expense, as often as a new abbot shall have been made, and there do homage and return to him the power over all the fiefs described above. And when the abbot shall mount his horse I and my heirs, viscounts of Carcassonne, and our successors ought to hold the stirrup for the honor of the dominion of St. Mary of Grasse; and to him and all who come with him, to as many as two hundred beasts, we should make the abbot's purveyance in the borough of St. Michael of Carcassonne, the first time he enters Carcassonne, with the best fish and meat and with eggs and cheese, honorably according to his will, and pay the expense of the shoeing of the horses, and for straw and fodder as the season shall require.

And if I or my sons or their successors do not observe to thee or to thy successors each and all the things declared above, and should come against these things, we wish that all the aforesaid fiefs should by that very fact be handed over to thee and to the said monastery of St. Mary of Grasse and to thy successors.

I, therefore, the aforesaid lord Leo, by the grace of God abbot of Mary of Grasse, receive the homage and fealty for all the fiefs of castles and manors and places which are described above; in the way and with the agreements and understandings written above and likewise I concede to thee and thy heirs and their successors, the viscounts of Carcassonne, all the castles and manors and places aforesaid, as a fief, along with this present charter, divided through the alphabet. And I promise to thee and thy heirs and successors, viscounts of Carcassonne, under the religion of my order, that I will be good and faithful lord concerning all those things described above.

Moreover, I, the aforesaid viscount, acknowledge that the little villages of Cannetis, Maironis, Villamagna, Aiglino, Villadasas, Villafrancos, Villadenz, Villaudriz, St. Genese, Conguste and Mata, with the farm-house of Mathus and the chateaux of Villalauro and Claromont, with the little villages of St. Stephen of Surlac, and of Upper and Lower Agrifolio, ought to belong to the said monastery, and whoever holds anything there holds from the same monastery, as we have seen and have heard read in the privileges and charters of the monastery, and as was there written.

Made in the year of the Incarnation of the Lord 1110, in the reign of Louis. Seal of Bernard Atton, viscount of Carcassonne, seal of Raymond Mantellini, seal of Peter Roger of Barbazon, seal of Roger, son of the said viscount of Carcassonne, seal of Peter de Vitry, seal of Trencavel, son of the said viscount of Carcassonne, seal of William Hugo, seal of lord abbot Leo, who has accepted this acknowledgment of the homage of the said viscount

And I, the monk John, have written this charter at the command of the said lord Bernard Atton, viscount of Carcassonne and of his sons, on the day and year given above, in the presence and witness of all those named above.

Henry IV of Germany and Pope Gregory VII: Letter and Ban

1076

Document Text

Henry IV's Letter to Gregory VII

Henry, king not through usurpation, but through the holy ordination of God, to Hildebrand, at present not pope but false monk. Such greeting as this hast thou merited through thy disturbances, inasmuch as there is no grade in the church which thou hast omitted to make a partaker not of honour but of confusion, not of benediction but of malediction. For, to mention few and especial cases out of many, not only hast thou not feared to lay hands upon the rulers of the holy church, the anointed of the Lord—the archbishops, namely, bishops and priests—but thou hast trodden them under foot like slaves ignorant of what their master is doing. Thou hast won favour from the common herd by crushing them; thou hast looked upon all of them as knowing nothing, upon thy sole self, moreover, as knowing all things. This knowledge, however, thou hast used not for edification but for destruction; so that with reason we believe that St. Gregory, whose name thou hast usurped for thyself, was prophesying concerning thee when he said: "The pride of him who is in power increases the more the greater the number of those subject to him; and he thinks that he himself can do more than all." And we, indeed, have endured all this, being eager to guard the honour of the apostolic see; thou, however, hast understood our humility to be fear, and hast not, accordingly, shunned to rise up against the royal power conferred upon us by God, daring to threaten to divest us of it. As if we had received our kingdom from thee! As if the kingdom and the empire were in thine and not in God's hand! And this although our Lord Jesus Christ did call us to the kingdom, did not, however, call thee to the priesthood. For thou hast ascended by the following steps. By wiles, namely, which the profession of monk abhors, thou hast achieved money; by money, favour; by the sword, the throne of peace. And from the throne of peace thou hast disturbed peace, inasmuch as thou hast armed subjects against those in authority over them; inasmuch as thou, who wert not called, hast taught that our bishops called of God are to be despised; inasmuch as thou hast usurped for laymen the ministry over their priests, allowing them to depose or condemn those whom they themselves had received as teachers from the hand of God through the laying on of hands of the bishops. On me also who, although unworthy to be among the anointed, have nevertheless been anointed to the kingdom, thou hast lain thy hand; me who—as the tradition of the holy Fathers teaches, declaring that I am not to be deposed for any crime unless, which God forbid, I should have strayed from the faith—am subject to the judgment of God alone. For the wisdom of the holy Fathers committed even Julian the apostate not to themselves, but to God alone, to be judged and to be deposed. For himself the true pope, Peter, also exclaims: "Fear God. Honour the king." But thou, who dost not fear God, dost dishonour in me his appointed one. Wherefore St. Paul, when he has not spared an angel of heaven if he shall have preached otherwise, has not excepted thee also who dost teach otherwise upon earth. For he says: "If any one, either I or an angel from heaven, should preach a gospel other than that which has been preached to you, he shall be damned." Thou, therefore, damned by this curse and by the judgment of all our bishops and by our own, descend and relinquish the apostolic chair which thou hast usurped. Let another ascend the throne of St. Peter, who shall not practise violence under the cloak of religion, but shall teach the sound doctrine of St. Peter. I, Henry, king by the grace of God, do say unto thee, together with all our bishops: Descend, descend, to be damned throughout the ages.

Gregory VII's First Deposition and Banning of Henry IV

O St. Peter, chief of the apostles, incline to us, I beg, thy holy ears, and hear me thy servant whom thou hast nourished from infancy, and whom, until this day, thou hast freed from the hand of the wicked, who have hated and do hate me for thy faithfulness to thee. Thou, and my mistress the mother of God, and thy brother St. Paul, are witnesses for me among all the saints that thy holy Roman church drew me to its helm against my will; that I had no thought of ascending thy chair through force, and that I would rather have ended my life as a pilgrim than, by secular means, to have seized thy throne for the sake of earthly glory. And therefore I believe it to be through thy grace, and not through my own deeds, that it has pleased and does please thee that the Christian people, who have been especially committed to thee, should obey me. And especially to me, as thy representative and by thy favour, has the power been granted by God of binding and loosing in heaven and on earth. On the strength of this belief, therefore, for the honour and security of thy church, in the name of Almighty God, Father, Son, and Holy Ghost, I withdraw, through thy power and authority, from Henry the king, son of Henry the emperor, who has risen against thy church with unheard of insolence, the rule over the whole kingdom of the Germans and over Italy. And I absolve all Christians from the bonds of the oath which they have made or shall make to him; and I forbid any one to serve him as king. For it is fitting that he who strives to lessen the honour of thy church should himself lose the honour which belongs to him. And since he has scorned to obey as a Christian, and has not returned to God whom he had deserted—holding intercourse with the excommunicated; practising manifold iniquities; spurning my commands which, as thou dost bear witness, I issued to him for his own salvation; separating himself from thy church, and striving to rend it;—I bind him in thy stead with the chain of the anathema. And, leaning on thee, I so bind him that the people may know and have proof that thou art Peter, and above thy rock the Son of the living God hath built His church, and the gates of hell shall not prevail against it.

Magna Carta

1215

Document Text

[Preamble] Edward by the grace of God, King of England, Lord of Ireland, and Duke of Guyan, to all Archbishops, Bishops, etc. We have seen the Great Charter of the Lord Henry, sometimes King of England, our father, of the Liberties of England, in these words: Henry by the grace of God, King of England, Lord of Ireland, Duke of Normandy and Guyan, and Earl of Anjou, to all Archbishops, Bishops, Abbots, Priors, Earls, Barons, Sheriffs, Provosts, Officers, and to all Bailiffs and other our faithful Subjects, which shall see this present Charter, Greeting. Know ye that we, unto the honour of Almighty God, and for the salvation of the souls of our progenitors and successors, Kings of England, to the advancement of holy Church, and amendment of our Realm, of our meer and free will, have given and granted to all Archbishops, Bishops, Abbots, Priors, Earls, Barons, and to all freemen of this our realm, these liberties following, to be kept in our kingdom of England for ever.

[1] First, We have granted to God, and by this our present Charter have confirmed, for us and our Heirs for ever, That the Church of England shall be free, and shall have her whole rights and liberties inviolable. We have granted also, and given to all the freemen of our realm, for us and our Heirs for ever, these liberties underwritten, to have and to hold to them and their Heirs, of us and our Heirs for ever.

[2] If any of our Earls or Barons, or any other, which holdeth of Us in chief by Knights service, shall die and at the time of his death his heir be of full age, and oweth us Relief, he shall have his inheritance by the old Relief; that is to say, the heir or heirs of an Earl, for a whole Earldom, by one hundred pound; the heir or heirs of a Baron, for a whole Barony, by one hundred marks; the heir or heirs of a Knight, for one whole Knights fee, one hundred shillings at the most; and he that hath less, shall give less, according to the custom of the fees.

[3] But if the Heir of any such be within age, his Lord shall not have the ward of him, nor of his land, before that he hath taken him homage. And after that such an heir hath been in ward (when he is come of full age) that is to say, to the age of one and twenty years, he shall have his inheritance without Relief, and without Fine; so that if such an heir, being within age, be made Knight, yet nevertheless his land shall remain in the keeping of his Lord unto the term aforesaid.

[4] The keeper of the land of such an heir, being within age, shall not take of the lands of the heir, but reasonable issues, reasonable customs, and reasonable services, and

that without destruction and waste of his men and goods. And if we commit the custody of any such land to the Sheriff, or to any other, which is answerable unto us for the issues of the same land, and he make destruction or waste of those things that he hath in custody, we will take of him amends and recompence therefore, and the land shall be committed to two lawful and discreet men of that fee, which shall answer unto us for the issues of the same land, or unto him whom we will assign. And if we give or sell to any man the custody of any such land, and he therein do make destruction or waste, he shall lose the same custody; and it shall be assigned to two lawful and discreet men of that fee, which also in like manner shall be answerable to us, as afore is said.

[5] The keeper, so long as he hath the custody of the land of such an heir, shall keep up the houses, parks, warrens, ponds, mills, and other things pertaining to the same land, with the issues of the said land; and he shall deliver to the Heir, when he cometh to his full age, all his land stored with ploughs, and all other things, at the least as he received it. All these things shall be observed in the custodies of the Archbishopricks, Bishopricks, Abbeys, Priories, Churchs, and Dignities vacant, which appertain to us; except this, that such custody shall not be sold.

[6] Heirs shall be married without Disparagement.

[7] A Widow, after the death of her husband, incontinent, and without any Difficulty, shall have her marriage and her inheritance, and shall give nothing for her dower, her marriage, or her inheritance, which her husband and she held the day of the death of her husband, and she shall tarry in the chief house of her husband by forty days after the death of her husband, within which days her dower shall be assigned her (if it were not assigned her before) or that the house be a castle; and if she depart from the castle, then a competent house shall be forthwith provided for her, in the which she may honestly dwell, until her dower be to her assigned, as it is aforesaid; and she shall have in the meantime her reasonable estovers of the common; and for her dower shall be assigned unto her the third part of all the lands of her husband, which were his during coverture, except she were endowed of less at the Church-door. No widow shall be distrained to marry herself: nevertheless she shall find surety, that she shall not marry without our licence and assent (if she hold of us) nor without the assent of the Lord, if she hold of another.

[8] We or our Bailiffs shall not seize any land or rent for any debt, as long as the present Goods and Chattels of the debtor do suffice to pay the debt, and the debtor himself be ready to satisfy therefore. Neither shall the pledges of the debtor be distrained, as long as the principal debtor is sufficient for the payment of the debt. And if the principal debtor fail in the payment of the debt, having nothing wherewith to pay, or will not pay where he is able, the pledges shall answer for the debt. And if they will, they shall have the lands and rents of the debtor, until they be satisfied of that which they before paid for him, except that the debtor can show himself to be acquitted against the said sureties.

[9] The city of London shall have all the old liberties and customs, which it hath been used to have. Moreover we will and grant, that all other Cities, Boroughs, Towns, and the Barons of the Five Ports, and all other Ports, shall have all their liberties and free customs.

[10] No man shall be distrained to do more service for a Knights fee, nor any freehold, than therefore is due.

[11] Common Pleas shall not follow our Court, but shall be holden in some place certain.

[12] Assises of novel disseisin, and of Mortdancestor, shall not be taken but in the shires, and after this manner: If we be out of this Realm, our chief Justicer shall send our Justicers through every County once in the Year, which, with the Knights of the shires, shall take the said Assises in those counties; and those things that at the coming of our foresaid Justicers, being sent to take those Assises in the counties, cannot be determined, shall be ended by them in some other place in their circuit; and those things, which for difficulty of some articles cannot be determined by them, shall be referred to our Justicers of the Bench, and there shall be ended.

[13] Assises of Darrein Presentment shall be alway taken before our Justices of the Bench, and there shall be determined.

[14] A Freeman shall not be amerced for a small fault, but after the manner of the fault; and for a great fault after the greatness thereof, saving to him his contenement; and a Merchant likewise, saving to him his Merchandise; and any other's villain than ours shall be likewise amerced, saving his wainage, if he falls into our mercy. And none of the said amerciaments shall be assessed, but by the oath of honest and lawful men of the vicinage. Earls and Barons shall not be amerced but by their Peers, and after the manner of their offence. No man of the Church shall be amerced after the quantity of his spiritual Benefice, but after his Lay-tenement, and after the quantity of his offence.

[15] No Town or Freeman shall be distrained to make Bridges nor Banks, but such as of old time and of right have been accustomed to make them in the time of King Henry our Grandfather.

[16] No Banks shall be defended from henceforth, but such as were in defence in the time of King Henry our Grandfather, by the same places, and the same bounds, as they were wont to be in his time.

[17] No Sheriff, Constable, Escheator, Coroner, nor any other our Bailiffs, shall hold Pleas of our Crown.

[18] If any that holdeth of us Lay-fee do die, and our Sheriff or Bailiff do show our Letters Patents of our summon for Debt, which the dead man did owe to us; it shall be lawful to our Sheriff or Bailiff to attach or inroll all the goods and chattels of the dead, being found in the said fee, to the Value of the same Debt, by the sight and testimony of lawful men, so that nothing thereof shall be taken away, until we be clearly paid off the debt; and the residue shall remain to the Executors to perform the testament of the dead; and if nothing be owing unto us, all the chattels shall go to the use of the dead (saving to his wife and children their reasonable parts).

[19] No Constable, nor his Bailiff, shall take corn or other chattels of any man, if the man be not of the Town where the Castle is, but he shall forthwith pay for the same, unless that the will of the seller was to respite the payment; and if he be of the same Town, the price shall be paid unto him within forty days.

[20] No Constable shall distrain any Knight to give money for keeping of his Castle, if he himself will do it in his proper person, or cause it to be done by another sufficient man, if he may not do it himself for a reasonable cause. And if we lead or send him to an army, he shall be free from Castle-ward for the time that he shall be with us in fee in our host, for the which he hath done service in our wars.

[21] No Sheriff nor Bailiff of ours, or any other, shall take the Horses or Carts of any man to make carriage, except he pay the old price limited, that is to say, for carriage with two horse, x.d. a day; for three horse, xiv.d. a day. No demesne Cart of any Spiritual person or Knight, or any Lord, shall be taken by our Bailiffs; nor we, nor our Bailiffs, nor any other, shall take any man's wood for our Castles, or other our necessaries to be done, but by the licence of him whose wood it shall be.

[22] We will not hold the Lands of them that be convict of Felony but one year and one day, and then those Lands shall be delivered to the Lords of the fee.

[23] All Wears from henceforth shall be utterly put down by Thames and Medway, and through all England, but only by the Sea-coasts.

[24] The Writ that is called Praecipe in capite shall be from henceforth granted to no person of any freehold, whereby any freeman may lose his Court.

[25] One measure of Wine shall be through our Realm, and one measure of Ale, and one measure of Corn, that is to say, the Quarter of London; and one breadth of dyed Cloth, Russets, and Haberjects, that is to say, two Yards within the lists. And it shall be of Weights as it is of Measures.

[26] Nothing from henceforth shall be given for a Writ of Inquisition, nor taken of him that prayeth Inquisition of Life, or of Member, but it shall be granted freely, and not denied.

[27] If any do hold of us by Fee-ferm, or by Socage, or Burgage, and he holdeth Lands of another by Knights Service, we will not have the Custody of his Heir, nor of his Land, which is holden of the Fee of another, by reason of that Fee-ferm, Socage, or Burgage. Neither will we have the custody of such Fee-ferm, or Socage, or Burgage, except Knights Service be due unto us out of the same Fee-ferm. We will not have the custody of the Heir, or of any Land, by occasion of any Petit Serjeanty, that any man holdeth of us by Service to pay a Knife, an Arrow, or the like.

[28] No Bailiff from henceforth shall put any man to his open Law, nor to an Oath, upon his own bare saying, without faithful Witnesses brought in for the same.

[29] No Freeman shall be taken, or imprisoned, or be disseised of his Freehold, or Liberties, or free Customs, or be outlawed, or exiled, or any otherwise destroyed; nor will we pass upon him, nor condemn him, but by lawful Judgment of his Peers, or by the Law of the Land. We will sell to no man, we will not deny or defer to any man either Justice or Right.

[30] All Merchants (if they were not openly prohibited before) shall have their safe and sure Conduct to depart out of England, to come into England, to tarry in, and go through England, as well by Land as by Water, to buy and sell without any manner of evil Tolts, by the old and rightful Customs, except in Time of War. And if they be of a land making War against us, and such be found in our Realm at the beginning of the Wars, they shall be attached without harm of body or goods, until it be known unto us, or our Chief Justice, how our Merchants be intreated there in the land making War against us; and if our Merchants be well intreated there, theirs shall be likewise with us.

[31] If any man hold of any Eschete, as of the honour of Wallingford, Nottingham, Boloin, or of any other Eschetes which be in our hands, and are Baronies, and die, his Heir shall give none other Relief, nor do none other Service to us, than he should to the Baron, if it were in the Baron's hand. And we in the same wise shall hold it as the Baron held it; neither shall we have, by occasion of any such Barony or Eschete, any Eschete or keeping of any of our men, unless he that held the Barony or Eschete hold of us in chief.

[32] No Freeman from henceforth shall give or sell any more of his Land, but so that of the residue of the Lands the Lord of the Fee may have the Service due to him, which belongeth to the Fee.

[33] All Patrons of Abbies, which have the King's Charters of England of Advowson, or have old Tenure or Possession in the same, shall have the Custody of them when they fall void, as it hath been accustomed, and as it is afore declared.

[34] No Man shall be taken or imprisoned upon the Appeal of a Woman for the Death of any other, than of her husband.

[35] No County Court from henceforth shall be holden, but from Month to Month; and where greater time hath been used, there shall be greater: Nor any Sheriff, or his Bailiff, shall keep his Turn in the Hundred but twice in the Year; and nowhere but in due place, and accustomed; that is to say, once after Easter, and again after the Feast of St. Michael. And the View of Frankpledge shall be likewise at the Feast of St. Michael without occasion; so that every man may have his Liberties which he had, or used to have, in the time of King Henry our Grandfather, or which he hath purchased since: but the View of Frankpledge shall be so done, that our Peace may be kept; and that the Tything be wholly kept as it hath been accustomed; and that the Sheriff seek no Occasions, and that he be content with so much as the Sheriff was wont to have for his Viewmaking in the time of King Henry our Grandfather.

[36] It shall not be lawful from henceforth to any to give his Lands to any Religious House, and to take the same Land again to hold of the same House. Nor shall it be lawful to any House of Religion to take the Lands of any, and to lease the same to him of whom he received it. If any from henceforth give his Lands to any Religious House, and thereupon be convict, the Gift shall be utterly void, and the Land shall accrue to the Lord of the Fee.

[37] Escuage from henceforth shall be taken like as it was wont to be in the time of King Henry our Grandfather; reserving to all Archbishops, Bishops, Abbots, Priors, Templers, Hospitallers, Earls, Barons, and all persons, as well Spiritual as Temporal, all their free liberties and free Customs, which they have had in time passed. And all these Customs and Liberties aforesaid, which we have granted to be holden within this our Realm, as much as appertaineth to us and our Heirs, we shall observe; and all Men of this our Realm, as well Spiritual as Temporal (as much as in them is) shall observe the same against all persons in like wise. And for this our Gift and Grant of these Liberties, and of other contained in our Charter of Liberties of our Forest, the Archbishops, Bishops, Abbots, Priors, Earls, Barons, Knights, Freeholders, and other our Subjects, have given unto us the Fifteenth Part of all their Moveables. And we have granted unto them for us and our Heirs, that neither we, nor our Heirs shall procure or do anything whereby the Liberties in this Charter contained shall be infringed or broken; and if anything be procured by any person contrary to the premises, it shall be had of no force nor effect. These being Witnesses; Lord B. Archbishop of Canterbury, E. Bishop of London, J. Bishop of Bathe, P. of Winchester, H. of Lincoln, R. of Salisbury, W. of Rochester, W. of Worester, J. of Ely, H. of Hereford, R. of Chichester, W. of Exeter, Bishops; the Abbot of St. Edmunds, the Abbot of St. Albans, the Abbot of Bello, the Abbot of St. Augustines in Canterbury, the Abbot of Evesham, the Abbot of Westminster, the Abbot of Bourgh St. Peter, the Abbot of Reading, the Abbot of Abindon, the Abbot of Malmsbury, the Abbot of Winchcomb, the Abbot of Hyde, the Abbot of Certefey, the Abbot of Sherburn, the Abbot of Cerne, the Abbot of Abbotebir, the Abbot

of Middleton, the Abbot of Seleby, the Abbot of Cirencester; H. de Burgh Justice, H. Earl of Chester and Lincoln, W. Earl of Salisbury, W. Earl of Warren, G. de Clare Earl of Gloucester and Hereford, W. de Ferrars Earl of Derby, W. de Mandeville Earl of Essex, H. de Bygod Earl of Norfolk, W. Earl of Albermarle, H. Earl of Hereford, J. Constable of Chester, R. de Ros, R. Fitzwalter, R. de Vyponte, W. de Bruer, R. de Muntefichet, P. Fitzherbert, W. de Aubenie, F. Grefly, F. de Breus, J. de Monemue, J. Fitzallen, H. de Mortimer, W. de Beauchamp, W. de St. John, P. de Mauly, Brian de Lisle, Thomas de Multon, R. de Argenteyn, G. de Nevil, W. de Mauduit, J. de Balun, and others.

We, ratifying and approving these Gifts and Grants aforesaid, confirm and make strong all the same for us and our Heirs perpetually, and, by the Tenour of these Presents, do renew the same; willing and granting for us and our Heirs, that this Charter, and all and singular his Articles, for ever shall be stedfastly, firmly, and inviolably observed; although some Articles in the same Charter contained, yet hitherto peradventure have not been kept, we will, and by Authority Royal command, from henceforth firmly they be observed. In witness whereof we have caused these our Letters Patents to be made. T. Edward our Son at Westminster, the Twenty-eighth Day of March, in the Twenty-eighth Year of our Reign.

Martin Luther: Address to the Christian Nobility of the German Nation

1520

Document Text

The Three Walls of the Romanists

The Romanists have, with great adroitness, drawn three walls round themselves, with which they have hitherto protected themselves, so that no one could reform them, whereby all Christendom has fallen terribly.

Firstly, if pressed by the temporal power, they have affirmed and maintained that the temporal power has no jurisdiction over them, but, on the contrary, that the spiritual power is above the temporal.

Secondly, if it were proposed to admonish them with the Scriptures, they objected that no one may interpret the Scriptures but the Pope.

Thirdly, if they are threatened with a council, they pretend that no one may call a council but the Pope.

Thus they have secretly stolen our three rods, so that they may be unpunished, and intrenched themselves behind these three walls, to act with all the wickedness and malice, which we now witness. And whenever they have been compelled to call a council, they have made it of no avail by binding the princes beforehand with an oath to leave them as they were, and to give moreover to the Pope full power over the procedure of the council, so that it is all one whether we have many councils or no councils, in addition to which they deceive us with false pretences and tricks. So grievously do they tremble for their skin before a true, free council; and thus they have overawed kings and princes, that these believe they would be offending God, if they were not to obey them in all such knavish, deceitful artifices.

Now may God help us, and give us one of those trumpets that overthrew the walls of Jericho, so that we may blow down these walls of straw and paper, and that we may set free our Christian rods for the chastisement of sin, and expose the craft and deceit of the devil, so that we may amend ourselves by punishment and again obtain God's favour.

The First Wall: That the Temporal Power Has No Jurisdiction over the Spirituality

It has been devised that the Pope, bishops, priests, and monks are called the *spiritual estate*, princes, lords, artificers, and peasants are the *temporal estate*. This is an artful lie and hypocritical device, but let no one be made afraid by it, and that for this reason: that all Christians are truly of the spiritual estate, and there is no difference among them, save of office alone. As St. Paul says (1 Cor. xii.), we are all one body, though each member does its own work, to serve the others. This is because we have one baptism, one Gospel, one faith, and are all Christians alike; for baptism, Gospel, and faith, these alone make spiritual and Christian people.

...

Since, then, the temporal power is baptised as we are, and has the same faith and Gospel, we must allow it to be priest and bishop, and account its office an office that is proper and useful to the Christian community. For whatever issues from baptism may boast that it has been consecrated priest, bishop, and pope, although it does not beseem every one to exercise these offices. For, since we are all priests alike, no man may put himself forward or take upon himself, without our consent and election, to do that which we have all alike power to do. For, if a thing is common to all, no man may take it to himself without the wish and command of the community. And if it should happen that a man were appointed to one of these offices and deposed for abuses, he would be just what he was before. Therefore a priest should be nothing in Christendom but a functionary; as long as he holds his office, he has precedence of others; if he is deprived of it, he is a peasant or a citizen like the rest. Therefore a priest is verily no longer a priest after deposition. But now they have invented *characteres indelebiles*, and pretend that a priest after deprivation still differs from a simple layman. They even imagine that a priest can never be anything but a priest-that is, that he can never become a layman. All this is nothing but mere talk and ordinance of human invention.

...

Therefore the temporal Christian power must exercise its office without let or hindrance, without considering whom it may strike, whether pope, or bishop, or priest: whoever is guilty, let him suffer for it.

...

The Second Wall: That No One May Interpret the Scriptures but the Pope

The second wall is even more tottering and weak: that they alone pretend to be considered masters of the Scriptures; although they learn nothing of them all their life. They assume authority, and juggle before us with impudent words, saying that the Pope cannot err in matters of faith, whether he be evil or good, albeit they cannot prove it by a single letter. That is why the canon law contains so many heretical and unchristian, nay unnatural, laws; but of these we need not speak now. For whereas they imagine the Holy Ghost never leaves them, however unlearned and wicked they may be, they grow bold enough to decree whatever they like. But were this true, where were the need and use of the Holy Scriptures? Let us burn them, and content ourselves with the unlearned gentlemen at Rome, in whom the Holy Ghost dwells, who, however, can dwell in pious souls only. If I had not read it, I could never have believed that the devil should have put forth such follies at Rome and find a following.

...

The Third Wall: That No One May Call a council but the Pope

The third wall falls of itself, as soon as the first two have fallen; for if the Pope acts contrary to the Scriptures, we are bound to stand by the Scriptures, to punish and to constrain him, according to Christ's commandment, "Moreover, if thy brother shall trespass against thee, go and tell him his fault between thee and him alone; if he shall hear thee, thou hast gained thy brother. But if he will not hear thee, then take with thee one or two more, that in the mouth of two or three witnesses every word may be established. And if he shall neglect to hear them, tell it unto the Church; but if he neglect to hear the Church, let him be unto thee as a heathen man and a publican" (St. Matt. xviii. 15-17). Here each member is commanded to take care for the other; much more then should we do this, if it is a ruling member of the community that does evil, which by its evil-doing causes great harm and offence to the others. If then I am to accuse him before the Church, I must collect the Church together. Moreover, they can show nothing in the Scriptures giving the Pope sole power to call and confirm councils; they have nothing but their own laws; but these hold good only so long as they are not injurious to Christianity and the laws of God. Therefore, if the Pope deserves punishment, these laws cease to bind us, since Christendom would suffer, if he were not punished by a council. Thus we read (Acts xv.) that the council of the Apostles was not called by St. Peter, but by all the Apostles and the elders. But if the right to call it had lain with St. Peter alone, it would not have been a Christian council, but a heretical *conciliabulum*. Moreover, the most celebrated council of all—that of Nicaea—was neither called nor confirmed by the Bishop of Rome, but by the Emperor Constantine; and after him many other emperors have done the same, and yet the councils called by them were accounted most Christian. But if the Pope alone had the power, they must all have been heretical. Moreover, if I consider the councils that the Pope has called, I do not find that they produced any notable results.

Act of Supremacy

1534

Document Text

Albeit the king's Majesty justly and rightfully is and ought to be the supreme head of the Church of England, and so is recognized by the clergy of this realm in their convocations, yet nevertheless, for corroboration and confirmation thereof, and for increase of virtue in Christ's religion within this realm of England, and to repress and extirpate all errors, heresies, and other enormities and abuses heretofore used in the same, be it enacted, by authority of this present Parliament, that the king, our sovereign lord, his heirs and successors, kings of this realm, shall be taken, accepted, and reputed the only supreme head in earth of the Church of England, called Anglicans Ecclesia; and shall have and enjoy, annexed and united to the imperial crown of this realm, as well the title and style thereof, as all honors, dignities, preeminences, jurisdictions, privileges, authorities, immunities, profits, and commodities to the said dignity of the supreme head of the same Church belonging and appertaining; and that our said sovereign lord, his heirs and successors, kings of this realm, shall have full power and authority from time to time to visit, repress, redress, record, order, correct, restrain, and amend all such errors, heresies, abuses, offenses, contempts and enormities, whatsoever they be, which by any manner of spiritual authority or jurisdiction ought or may lawfully be reformed, repressed, ordered, redressed, corrected, restrained, or amended, most to the pleasure of Almighty God, the increase of virtue in Christ's religion, and for the conservation of the peace, unity, and tranquility of this realm; any usage, foreign land, foreign authority, prescription, or any other thing or things to the contrary hereof notwithstanding.

First Act of Succession

1534

Document Text

In their most humble wise shown unto your majesty your most humble and obedient subjects, the lords spiritual and temporal and the Commons in this present Parliament assembled, that since it is the natural inclination of every man, gladly and willingly to provide for the surety of both his title and succession, although it touch only his private cause; we therefore; most rightful and dreadful sovereign lord, reckon ourselves much more bound to beseech and instant your highness (although we doubt not of your princely heart and wisdom, mixed with a natural affection to the same) to foresee and provide for the perfect surety of both you, and of your most lawful succession and heirs, upon which dependeth all our joy and wealth, in whom also is united and knit the only mere true inheritance and title of this realm, without any contradiction;

Wherefore we your said most humble and obedient subjects, in this present Parliament assembled, calling to our remembrance the great divisions which in times past have been in this realm, by reason of several titles pretended to the imperial crown of the same, which sometimes, and for the most part ensued, by occasion of ambiguity and doubts, then not so perfectly declared, but that men might, upon forward intents, expound them to every man's sinister appetite and affection, after their sense, contrary to the right legality of the succession and posterity of the lawful kings and emperors of this realm; whereof hath ensued great effusion and destruction of man's blood, as well of a great number of the nobles, as of other the subjects, and especially inheritors in the same; and the greatest occasion thereof hath been because no perfect and substantial provision by law hath been made within this realm of itself, when doubts and questions have been moved and proponed, of the certainty and legality of the succession and posterity of the crown; by reason whereof the Bishop of Rome, and see apostolic, contrary to the great and inviolable grants of jurisdictions given by God immediately to emperors, kings and princes, in succession to their heirs, has presumed, in times past, to invest who should please them, to inherit in other men's kingdoms and dominions, which thing we, your most humble subjects, both spiritual and temporal, do most abhor and detest; and sometimes other foreign princes and potentates of sundry degrees, minding rather dissension and discord to continue in the realm, to the utter desolation thereof, than charity, equity, or unity, have many times supported wrong titles, whereby they might the more easily and facilely aspire to the superiority of the same; the continuance and sufferance whereof deeply considered and pondered, were too dangerous and perilous to be suffered any longer within this realm, and too much contrary to the unity, peace, and tranquillity of the same, being greatly reproachable and dishonourable to the whole realm:

In consideration whereof, your said most humble and obedient subjects, the nobles and Commons of this realm, calling further to their remembrance that the good unity, peace and wealth of this realm, and the succession of the subjects of the same, most especially and principally above all worldly things consists and rests in the certainty and surety of the procreation and posterity of your highness, in whose most royal person, at this present time, is no manner of doubt nor question; do therefore most humbly beseech your highness, that it may please your majesty, that it may be enacted by your highness, with the assent of the lords spiritual and temporal, and the Commons, in this present Parliament assembled, and by the authority of the same, that the marriage heretofore solemnized between your highness and the Lady Katherine, being before lawful wife to Prince Arthur, your elder brother, which by him was carnally known, as does duly appear by sufficient proof in a lawful process had and made before Thomas, by the sufferance of God, now archbishop of Canterbury and metropolitan and primate of all this realm, shall be, by authority of this present Parliament, definitively, clearly, and absolutely declared, deemed, and adjudged to be against the laws of Almighty God, and also accepted, reputed, and taken of no value nor effect, but utterly void and annulled, and the separation thereof, made by the said archbishop, shall be good and effectual to all intents and purposes; any licence, dispensation, or any other act or acts going afore, or ensuing the same, or to the contrary thereof, in any wise notwithstanding; and that every such licence, dispensation, act or acts, thing or things heretofore had, made, done, or to be done to the contrary thereof, shall be void and of none effect ; and that the said Lady Katherine shall be from henceforth called and reputed only dowager to Prince Arthur, and not queen of this realm; and that the lawful matrimony had and solemnized between your highness and your most dear and entirely beloved wife Queen Anne, shall be established, and taken for undoubtful, true, sincere, and perfect ever hereafter, according to the just judgment of the said Thomas, archbishop of Canterbury, metropolitan and primate of all this realm, whose grounds of judgment have been confirmed, as well by the whole clergy of this realm in both the Convocations, and by both the universities thereof, as by the universities of Bologna, Padua, Paris, Orleans, Toulouse, Anjou, and divers others, and also by the private writings of many right excellent well-learned men; which grounds so confirmed, and judgment of the said archbishop ensuing the same, together with your marriage solemnized between your highness and your said lawful wife Queen Anne, we your said subjects, both spiritual and temporal, do purely, plainly, constantly, and firmly accept, approve, and ratify for good and consonant to the laws of Almighty God, without error or default, most humbly beseeching your majesty, that it may be so established for ever by your most gracious and royal assent.

And furthermore, since many inconveniences have fallen, as well within this realm as in others, by reason of marrying within degrees of marriage prohibited by God's laws, that is to say, the son to marry the mother, or the stepmother, the brother the sister, the father his son's daughter, or his daughter's daughter, or the son to marry the daughter of his father procreate and born by his stepmother, or the son to marry his aunt, being his father's or mother's sister, or to marry his uncle's wife, or the father to marry his son's wife, or the brother to marry his brother's wife, or any man to marry his wife's daughter, or his wife's son's daughter, or his wife's daughter's daughter, or his wife's sister; which marriages, although they be plainly prohibited and detested by the laws of God, yet nevertheless at some times they have proceeded under colours of dispensations by man's power, which is but usurped, and of right ought not to be granted, admitted, nor allowed; for no man, of what estate, degree, or condition soever he be, has power to dispense with God's laws, as all the clergy of this realm in the said Convocations, and the most part of all the famous universities of Christendom, and we also, do affirm and think.

Be it therefore enacted by authority aforesaid, that no person or persons, subjects or residents of this realm, or in any your dominions, of what estate, degree, or dignity soever they be, shall from henceforth marry within the said degrees afore rehearsed, what pretence soever shall be made to the contrary thereof.

And in case any person or persons, of what estate, dignity, degree, or condition soever they be, has been heretofore married within this realm, or in any the king's dominions, within any the degrees above expressed, and by any the archbishops, bishops, or ministers of the Church of England, be separated from the bonds of such unlawful marriage, that every such separation shall be good, lawful, firm, and permanent for ever, and not by any power, authority, or means to be revoked or undone hereafter, and that the children proceeding and procreated under such unlawful marriage, shall not be lawful nor legitimate; any foreign laws, licences, dispensations, or other thing or things to the contrary thereof notwithstanding.

And in case there be any person or persons within this realm, or in any the king's dominions, already married within any the said degrees above specified, and not yet separated from the bonds of such unlawful marriage, that then every such person so unlawfully married shall be separate by the definitive sentence and judgments of the archbishops, bishops, and other ministers of the Church of England, and in other your dominions, within the limits of their jurisdictions and authorities, and by none other power or authority; and that all sentences and judgments given and to be given by any archbishop, bishop, or other minister of the Church of England, or in other the king's dominions, within the limits of their jurisdictions and authorities, shall be definitive, firm, good, and effectual, to all intents, and be observed and obeyed, without suing any provocations, appeals, prohibitions, or other process from the Court of Rome, to the derogation thereof, or contrary to the Act made since the beginning of this present Parliament, for restraint of such provocations, appeals, prohibitions, and other processes.

And also be it enacted by authority aforesaid, that all the issue had and procreated, or hereafter to be had and procreated, between your highness and your said most dear and entirely beloved wife Queen Anne, shall be your lawful children, and be inheritable, and inherit, according to the course of inheritance and laws of this realm, the imperial crown of the same, with all dignities, honours, pre-eminences, prerogatives, authorities, and jurisdictions to the same annexed or belonging, in as large and ample manner as your highness at this present time has the same as king of this realm; the inheritance thereof to be and remain to your said children and right heirs in manner and form as hereafter shall be declared, that is to say:

First the said imperial crown, and other the premises, shall be to your majesty, and to your heirs of your body lawfully begotten, that is to say: to the first son of your body, between your highness and your said lawful wife, Queen Anne, begotten, and to the heirs of the body of the same first son lawfully begotten, and for default of such heirs, then to the second son of your body and of the body of the said Queen Anne begotten, and to the heirs of the body of the said second son lawfully begotten, and so to every son of your body and of the body of the said Queen Anne begotten, and to the heirs of the body of every such son begotten, according to the course of inheritance in that behalf; and if it shall happen your said dear and entirely beloved wife Queen Anne to decease without issue male of the body of your highness to be begotten (which God defend), then the same imperial crown, and all other the premises, to be to your majesty, as is aforesaid, and to the son and heir male of your body lawfully begotten, and to the heirs of the body of the same son and heir male lawfully begotten; and for default of such issue, then to your second son of your body lawfully begotten, and to the heirs of the body of the same second son lawfully begotten, and so from son and heir male to son and heir male, and to the heirs of the several bodies of every such son and heir male to be begotten, according to the course of inheritance, in like manner and form as is above said.

And for default of such sons of your body begotten, and of heirs of the several bodies of every such sons lawfully begotten, that then the said imperial crown, and other the premises, shall be to the issue female between your majesty and your said most dear and entirely beloved wife, Queen Anne, begotten, that is to say: first to the eldest issue female, which is the Lady Elizabeth, now princess, and to the heirs of her body lawfully begotten, and for default of such issue, then to the second issue female, and to the heirs of her body lawfully begotten, and so from issue female to issue female, and to the heirs of their bodies one after another, by course of inheritance, according to their ages, as the crown of England has been accustomed, and ought to go, in cases where there be heirs females to the same; and for default of such issue, then the said imperial crown, and all other the premises, shall be in the right heirs of your highness for ever.

And be it further enacted by authority aforesaid, that on this side the first day of May next coming, proclamation shall be made in all shires within this realm, of the tenor and contents of this Act.

And if any person or persons, of what estate, dignity, or condition soever they be, subject or resident within this realm, or elsewhere within any the king's dominions, after the said first day of May, by writing or imprinting, or by any exterior act or deed, maliciously procure or do, or cause to be procured or done, any thing or things to the peril of your most royal person, or maliciously give occasion by writing, print, deed, or act, whereby your highness might be disturbed or interrupted of the crown of this realm, or by writing, print, deed, or act, procure or do, or cause to be procured or done, any thing or things to the prejudice, slander, disturbance, or derogation of the said lawful matrimony solemnized between your majesty and the said Queen Anne, or to the peril, slander, or disherison of any the issues and heirs of your highness, being limited by this Act to inherit and to be inheritable to the crown of this realm, in such form as is aforesaid, whereby any such issues or heirs of your highness might be destroyed, disturbed, or interrupted in body or title of inheritance to the crown of this realm, as to them is limited in this Act in form above rehearsed; that then every such person and persons, of what estate, degree, or condition they be of, subject or resident within this realm, and their aiders, counselors, maintainers, and abettors, and every of them, for every such offence shall be adjudged high traitors, and every such offence shall be adjudged high treason, and the offenders and their aiders, counsellors, maintainers, and abettors, and every of them, being lawfully convicted of such offence by presentment, verdict, confession, or process, according to the customs and laws of this realm, shall suffer pains of death, as in cases of high treason; and that also every such offender, being convicted as is aforesaid, shall lose and forfeit to your highness, and to your heirs, kings of this realm, all such manors, lands, tenements, rents, annuities, and hereditaments, which they had in possession as owners, or were sole seized of by or in any right, title, or means, or any other person or persons had to their use, of any estate of inheritance, at the day of such treasons and offences by them committed and done; and shall also lose and forfeit to your highness, and to your said heirs, as well all manner such estates of freehold and interests for years of lands and rents, as all their goods, chattels, and debts, which they had at the time of conviction or attainder of any such offence; saving always to every person and persons, and bodies politic, to their heirs, assigns, and successors, and every of them, other than such persons as shall be so convicted, and their heirs and successors, and all other claiming to their uses, all such right, title, use, interest, possession, condition, rents, fees, offices, annuities, and commons, which they or any of them shall happen to have in, to, or upon any such manors, lands, tenements, rents, annuities, or hereditaments, that shall so happen to be lost and forfeited by reason of attainder for any the treasons and offences above rehearsed, at any time before the said treasons and offences committed.

And be it further enacted by authority aforesaid, that if any person or persons, after the said first day of May, by any words, without writing, or any exterior deed or act, maliciously and obstinately shall publish, divulge, or utter any thing or things to the peril of your highness, or to the slander or prejudice of the said matrimony solemnized between your highness and the said Queen Anne, or to the slander or disherison of the issue and heirs of your body begotten and to be begotten of the said Queen Anne, or any other your lawful heirs, which shall be inheritable to the crown of this realm, as is before limited by this Act; that then every such offence shall be taken and adjudged for misprision of treason; and that every person and persons, of what estate, degree, or condition soever they be, subject or resident within this realm, or in any the king's dominions, so doing and offending, and being thereof lawfully convicted by presentment, verdict, process, or confession, shall suffer imprisonment of their bodies at the king's will, and shall lose as well all their goods, chattels, and debts, as all such interests and estates of freehold or for years, which any such offenders shall have of or in any lands, rents, or hereditaments whatsoever, at the time of conviction and attainder of such offence.

And be it also enacted by the authority aforesaid, that no person nor persons offending in any of the treasons and misprisions contained and limited by this Act, shall in any wise have or enjoy the privilege and immunity of any manner of sanctuaries within this realm, or elsewhere within any of the king's dominions, but shall utterly lose and be excluded of the same; any use, custom, grant, prescription, confirmation, or any other thing or things to the contrary thereof in any wise notwithstanding.

And be it also enacted by authority aforesaid, that if your majesty should happen to decease before any such your issue and heir male which should inherit the crown of this realm, shall be of his age of eighteen years, or before such your issue and heir female which should inherit the crown of this realm, shall be married, or be of the age of sixteen years, which Almighty God defend, that then your said issue and heir male to the crown, so being within the said age of eighteen years, or your said issue and heir female to the crown, unmarried, or within the said age of sixteen years, shall be and remain unto such time as such issues and heirs shall come to their said several ages afore limited, at and in the governance of their natural mother, she living, with such others, counsellors of your realm, as your majesty in your lifetime shall depute and assign by your will, or otherwise, for the same, without contradiction of any person or persons to the contrary thereof.

And if any person and persons by writing, or exterior deed or act, procure or do, or cause to be procured or done any thing or things to the let or disturbance of the same; that then every such offence shall be high treason, and the offenders, being thereof convicted, shall suffer such pains of death and losses of inheritance, freeholds, interests for years, goods, chattels and debts, in such manner and form as is above specified in cases of treason afore mentioned.

And for the more sure establishment of the succession of your most royal majesty, according to the tenor and form of this Act, be it further enacted by authority aforesaid, that as well all the nobles of your realm spiritual and temporal, as all other your subjects now living and being, or that hereafter shall be, at their full ages, by the commandment of your majesty or of your heirs, at all times hereafter from time to time, when it shall please your highness or your heirs to appoint, shall make a corporal oath in the presence of your highness or your heirs, or before such others as your majesty or your heirs will depute for the same, that they shall truly, firmly, and constantly, without fraud or guile, observe, fulfil, maintain, defend, and keep, to their cunning, wit, and uttermost of their powers, the whole effects and contents of this present Act. And that all manner your subjects, as well spiritual as temporal, suing livery, restitutions, or ouster le main out of the hands of your highness or of your heirs, or doing any fealty to your highness or to your heirs, by reason of tenure of their lands, shall swear a like corporal oath, that they and every of them, without fraud or guile, to their cunning, wit, and uttermost of their powers, shall truly, firmly, and constantly observe, fulfil, maintain, defend, and keep the effects and contents contained and specified in this Act, or in any part thereof; and that they, nor any of them, shall hereafter have any liveries, ouster le main, or restitution out of your hands, nor out of the hands of your heirs, till they have made the said corporal oath in form above rehearsed.

And if any person or persons, being commanded by authority of this Act to take the said oath afore limited, obstinately refuse that to do, in contempt of this Act, that then every such person so doing, to be taken and accepted for offender in misprision of high treason; and that every such refusal shall be deemed and adjudged misprision of high treason; and the offender therein to suffer such pains and imprisonment, losses and forfeitures, and also lose privileges of sanctuaries, in like manner and form as is above mentioned for the misprisions of treasons afore limited by this Act.

Provided always, that the article in this Act contained concerning prohibitions of marriages within the degrees afore mentioned in this Act, shall always be taken, interpreted, and expounded of such marriages, where marriages were solemnized and carnal knowledge was had.

Second Act of Succession

1534

Document Text

Where at the last session or this present Parliament, in the Act then made for the establishment of the succession of the heirs of the king's highness in the imperial crown of this realm, it is contained, amongst other things, that all and singular the king's subjects, as well the nobles spiritual and temporal as other, should make and take a corporal oath, whensoever it should please the king's majesty, or his heirs, to appoint, that they should truly, firmly, and constantly, without fraud or guile, observe, fulfil, maintain, defend, and keep, to their cunning, wit, and uttermost of their powers, the whole effects and contents of the said Act, as in the same Act, among other things, more plainly appeareth.

And at the day of the last prorogation of this present Parliament, as well the nobles spiritual and temporal as other the Commons of this present Parliament then assembled in the high house of Parliament, most lovingly accepted and took such oath as then was devised in writing for maintenance and defence of the said Act, and meant and intended at that time that every other the King's subjects should be bound to accept and take the same, upon the pains contained in the said Act, the tenor of which oath hereafter ensueth:

Ye shall swear to bear faith, truth, and obedience alonely to the king's majesty, and to his heirs of his body of his most dear and entirely beloved lawful wife Queen Anne, begotten and to be begotten, and further to the heirs of our said sovereign lord according to the limitation in the statute made for surety of his succession in the crown of this realm, mentioned and contained, and not to any other within this realm, nor foreign authority or potentate: and in case any oath be made, or has been made, by you, to any person or persons, that then ye [are] to repute the same as vain and annihilate; and that, to your cunning, wit, and uttermost of your power, without guile, fraud, or other undue means, you shall observe, keep, maintain, and defend the said Act of Succession, and all the whole effects and contents thereof, and all other Acts and statutes made in confirmation, or for execution of the same, or of anything therein contained; and this ye shall do against all manner of persons, of what estate, dignity, degree, or condition soever they be, and in no wise do or attempt, nor to your power suffer to be done or attempted, directly or indirectly, any thing or things privily or apartly to the let, hindrance, damage, or derogation thereof, or of any part of the same, by any manner of means, or for any manner of pretence; so help you God, all saints, and the holy Evangelists.

And forosmuch as it is convenient for the sure maintenance and defence of the same Act that the said oath should not only be authorized by authority of Parliament, but also be interpreted and expounded by the whole assent of this present Parliament, that it was meant and intended by the king's majesty, the Lords and Commons of the Parliament, at the said day of the said last prorogation, that every subject should be bounden to take the same oath, according to the tenor and effect thereof, upon the pains and penalties contained in the said Act:

Therefore be it enacted by authority of this present Parliament that the said oath above rehearsed shall be interpreted, expounded, reputed, accepted, and adjudged the very oath that the king's highness, the Lords spiritual and temporal, and the Commons of this present Parliament meant and intended that every subject of this realm should be obliged and bounden to take and accept, for maintenance and defence of the same Act, upon the pains contained in the said Act, and that every of the king's subjects, upon the said pains, shall be obliged to accept and take the said oath.

And be it further enacted by authority aforesaid that the commissioners that hereafter shall be appointed to receive such oath of the king's subjects, or two of them at the least, shall have power and authority to certify into the king's Bench, by writing under their seals, every refusal that hereafter shall be made afore them of the same oath by any person or persons coming before them to take the same oath; and that every such certificate to be made by such commissioners, as is aforesaid, shall be taken as strong and as available in the law as an indictment of twelve men lawfully found of the said refusal; so that the person and persons, against whom any such certificate shall be made, shall be compelled to answer thereunto as if they were indicted; and that such process, judgment, execution, and every other thing shall be had, used, and ministered, of and upon every such certificate against the offenders, as if they had been lawfully indicted of such offences by the due course and order of the common laws of this realm.

Treasons Act

1534

Document Text

Forasmuch as it is most necessary, both for common policy and duty of subjects, above all things to prohibit, provide, restrain, and extinct all manner of shameful slanders, perils, or imminent danger or dangers, which might grow, happen, or rise to their sovereign lord the king, the queen, or their heirs, which when they be heard, seen, or understood, cannot be but odible, and also abhorred of all those sorts that he true and loving subjects, if in any point they may do, or shall touch the king, his queen, their heirs or successors, upon which dependeth the whole unity and universal weal of this realm, without providing wherefore too great a scope of unreasonable liberty should be given to all cankered and traitorous hearts, willers and workers of the same; and also the king's loving subjects should not declare unto their sovereign lord now being, which unto them has been, and is most entirely both beloved and esteemed, their undoubted sincerity and truth.

Be it therefore enacted by the assent and consent of our sovereign lord the king, and the Lords spiritual and temporal, and Commons in this present Parliament assembled, and by the authority of the same, that if any person or persons, after the first day of February next coming, do maliciously wish, will, or desire, by words or writing, or by craft imagine, invent, practise, or attempt any bodily harm to be done or committed to the king's most royal person, the queen's, or their heirs apparent, or to deprive them or any of them of their dignity, title, or name of their royal estates, or slanderously and maliciously publish and pronounce, by express writing or words, that the king our sovereign lord should be heretic, schismatic, tyrant, infidel or usurper of the crown, or rebelliously do detain, keep, or withhold from our said sovereign lord, his heirs or successors, any of his or their castles, fortresses, fortalices, or holds within this realm, or in any other the king's dominions or marches, or rebelliously detain, keep, or withhold from the king's said highness, his heirs or successors, any of his or their ships, ordnances, artillery, or other munitions or fortifications of war, and do not humbly render and give up to our said sovereign lord, his heirs or successors, or to such persons as shall be deputed by them, such castles, fortresses, fortalices, holds, ships, ordnances, artillery, and other munitions and fortifications of war, rebelliously kept or detained, within six days next after they shall be commanded by our said sovereign lord, his heirs or successors, by open proclamation under the great seal:

That then every such person and persons so offending in any the premises, after the said first day of February, their aiders, counsellors, consenters, and abettors, being thereof lawfully convicted according to the laws and customs of this realm, shall be adjudged traitors, and that every such offence in any the premises, that shall he committed or done after the said first day of February, shall be reputed, accepted, and adjudged high treason, and the offenders therein and their aiders, consenters, counsellors, and abettors, being lawfully convicted of any such offence as is aforesaid, shall have and suffer such pains of death and other penalties, as is limited and accustomed in cases of high treason.

And to the intent that all treasons should be the more dread, hated and detested to be done by any person or persons, and also because it is a great boldness and an occasion to ill-disposed persons, to adventure and embrace their malicious intents and enterprises, which all true subjects ought to study to eschew: be it therefore enacted by the authority aforesaid, that none offender in any kinds of high treasons whatsoever they be, their aiders, consenters, counsellers, nor abettors, shall be admitted to have the benefit or privilege of any manner of sanctuary, considering that matters of treasons touch so nigh both the surety of the king our sovereign lord's person, and his heirs and successors.

And over that, be it enacted by authority aforesaid, that if any of the king's subjects, denizens or other, do commit or practise out of the limits of this realm, in any outward parts, any such offences, which by this Act are made, or heretofore have been made treason, that then such treasons, whatsoever they be, or wheresoever they shall happen so to be done or committed, shall be inquired and presented by the oaths of twelve good and lawful men, upon good and probable evidence and witness, in such shire and county or this realm, and before such persons as it shall please the king's highness to appoint by commission under his great seal, in like manner and form as treasons committed within this realm have been used to be inquired of and presented; and that upon every indictment and presentment found and made of any such treasons, and certified into the King's Bench, like process and other circumstance shall be there had and made against the offenders, as if the same treasons, so presented, had been lawfully found to be done and committed within the limits of this realm. And that all process of outlawry hereafter to be made and had within this realm against any offenders in treason, being resident or inhabited out of the limits of this realm, or in any of the parts of beyond the sea, at the time of the outlawry pronounced against them, shall be as good and as effectual in the law to all intents and purposes, as if such offenders had been resident and dwelling within this realm at the time of such process awarded, and outlawry pronounced.

And be it further enacted by authority aforesaid, that every offender and offenders, being hereafter lawfully convicted of any manner of high treasons, by presentment, confession, verdict or process of outlawry, according to the due course and custom of the common laws of this realm, shall lose and forfeit to the king's highness, his heirs and successors, all such lands, tenements, and hereditaments, which any such offender or offenders shall have of any estate of inheritance in use or possession, by any right, title, or means, within this realm of England, or elsewhere, within any of the king's dominions, at the time of any such treason committed, or any time after; saving to every person and persons, their heirs and successors (other than the offenders in any treasons, their heirs and successors, and such person and persons as claim to any their uses), all such rights, titles, interests, possessions, leases, rents, offices, and other profits, which they shall have at the day of committing such treasons, or any time afore, in as large and ample manner as if this Act had never been had nor made.

The Trial of Thomas More

1535

Document Text

Bill being preferred in Parliament, *November* 1534. to attaint *Elizabeth Barton*, and several others of High-Treason, Bishop *Fisher* and Sir *Thomas Moore* were also brought into it for Misprision of Treason, for the refusing of the Oath of Succession— Says my Lord *Herbert*. The fame Author avows the Bill did so pass; but Sir *Thomas's* Great-Grandson, in his Life, shews the contrary, and that notwithstanding the Archbishop of *Canterbury*, the Lord Chancellor, Duke of *Norfolk*, and Secretary *Cromwell*, by the King's Command, went to him and pressed him to a Compliance; yet the Chancellor influenced the King so far, that the matter of Misprison was dropt.

Sir *Thomas* was also examined at other times by the Lord Chancellor, Dukes of *Norfolk* and *Suffolk*, Mr. Secretary, and others of the Privy-Council, who press'd him, with all the Arguments they could think of, to own the King's Supremacy in direct and open Terms, or plainly to deny it; but he being loth to aggravate the King's Displeasure, would say no more than that the Statute was like a two-edged Sword, for if he spoke against it, he should be the Cause of the Death of his Bod ; and if he assented to it, he should purchase the Death of his Soul. Those Examinations being over, *Richard Rich*, newly made Sollicitor General, and afterwards Lord *Rich*, with Sir *Richard Southwell*, and Mr. *Palmer*, Secretary *Cromwell's* Man, were sent by the King to take away his Books. *Rich* pretending Friendship to him, and protesting he had no Commission to talk with him about the former Affair of the Supremacy, he put a Case to him thus: If it were enacted by Parliament that *Richard Rich* should be King, and that it should be Treason in any body to deny it, what Offence it were to contravene that Act? Sir *Thomas* Moore answered, That he should offend if he said so, because he was bound by the Act; but, that this was *casus levis*. Whereupon Sir *Thomas* said, he would propose a higher Case: Suppose it were enacted by Parliament, *Quod Deus non sit Deus*, and that it were Treason to contravene, whether it were not an Offence to say it according to the said Act,? *Rich* reply'd, yea; but said withal, I will propose a middle Case, because this is too high: The King, you know, is constituted supreme Head of the Church upon Earth; why should not you, *Master More*, accept him for such? as you would me, if I were made King by the aforesaid Supposition. *More* answered, the Case was not the same, because, said he, a Parliament can make a King, and depose him; and that every Parliament Man may give his Consent hereunto, but that a Subject cannot be bound so in the Case of Supremacy. *Quia consensum ab eo ad Parliamentum praebere non potest* (so says my Lord *Herbert*) it is in my Copy if it be not mistaken, & *quanquam Rex sic acceptus sit in* Angha, *plurima tamen Partes exterae idem non affirmant*.

[Trial]

Sir *Thomas* having continued a Prisoner in the *Tower* somewhere more than a Twelvemonth, for he was committed about the middle of *April* 1534, and was brought to his Trial on the 7th of *May*, 1535. he went into the Court leaning on his Staff, because he was much weakened by his Imprisonment, but appeared with a cheerful and composed Countenance. The Persons constituted to try him, were,

Sir Thomas Audley, Lord Chancellor,

Sir Richard Leicester,

Thomas Duke of Norfolk,

Sir John Port,

Sir John Fitz-James,

Sir John Spelman,

Lord Chief Justice, Sir John Baldwin

Sir Walter Luke

Sir Anthony Fitz-Herbert.

The Indictment was Very long, but where to procure a Copy of it, I could never learn; it's said in general, it contain'd all the Crimes that could be laid to the charge of any notorious Malefactor; and Sir *Thomas* professed it was so long, that he could scarce remember the third part of what was objected therein against him. It was read aloud by the Attorney-General; and Sir *Thomas*'s mortal Sin seem'd plainly to be his refusing the Oath of Succession, already mention'd.

To prove this, his double Examination in the *Tower* was all edged against him, the first before Secretary *Cromwell, Thomas Beade, John-Tregonnel, &c.* to whom he professed he had given over all Thoughts of Titles either to Popes or Princes, tho the whole World should be given him, he being fully determined only to serve God. The second time before the Lord Chancellor, the Duke of *Suffolk*, Earl of *Wiltshire,* and others, before whom he compared that Oath to a two-edged Sword, as before observed.

Presently after the Indictment was read, the Lord Chancellor, and the Duke of *Norfolk* spoke to him to this effect:

You see now how grievously you have offended his Majesty; yet he is so very merciful, that if you will lay aside your Obstinacy, and change your Opinion, we hope you may obtain Pardon and Favour in his sight. But Sir *Thomas* stoutly reply'd, Most Noble Lords, I have great reason to return thanks to your Honours for this your great Civility, but I beseech Almighty God, that I may continue in the Mind I am in, thro' his Grace, unto Death.

Then having Intimation given that he might say what he thought fit in his own Defence, he began thus: When I consider the length of my Accusation, and what heinous Matters are laid to my charge, I am struck with Fear, left my Memory and Understanding, which are both impaired, together with my bodily Health, thro' a long Indisposition contracted by my Imprisonment, should now fail me so far, as to make me incapable of making such ready Answers in my Defence, as otherwise I might have done.

The Court being sensible of his Weakness, ordered a Chair to be brought in, wherein he might feat himself, which he did accordingly, and then went on thus. This my Indictment, if I mistake not, consists of four principal Heads, each of which I purpose, God willing, to answer in order. As to the first Crime objected against me, that I have been an Enemy out of stubbornness of Mind to the King's second Marriage; I confess, I always told his Majesty my Opinion of it, according to the Dictates of my Conscience, which I neither ever would, nor ought to have concealed: for which I am so far from thinking my self guilty of High-Treason, that on the contrary, being required to give my Opinion by so great a Prince in an Affair of so much importance, upon which the Peace of the Kingdom depended; I should have basely flatter'd him, and my own Conscience, had not I spoke the Truth as I thought: Then indeed I might justly have been esteemed a molt wicked Subject, and a perfidious Traitor to God. If I have offended the King herein; if it can be an Offence to tell one's Mind freely, when his Sovereign puts the Question to him; I suppose I have been sufficiently punish'd already for the Fault, by the great Afflictions I have endured, by the loss of my Estate, and *my* tedious Imprisonment, which has continued already near fifteen Months.

The second Charge against me is, That I have violated the Act made in the last Parliament: that is, being a Prisoner, and twice examined, I would not, out of a malignant, perfidious, obstinate and traitorous Mind, tell them my Opinion, whether the King was Supreme Head of the Church or not; but confessed then, that I had nothing to do with that Act, as to the Justice or Injustice of it, because I had no Benefice in the Church: yet then I protested, that I had never said nor done any thing against it; neither can any one Word or Action of mine be alleged, or produced, to make me culpable. Nay, this I own was then my Answer to their Honours, that I would think of nothing else hereafter, but of the bitter Passions of our Blessed Saviour, and of my Exit out of this miserable World. I wish no body any harm, and if this does not keep me alive, I desire not to live; by all which I know, I would not transgress any Law, or become guilty of any treasonable Crime: for this Statute, nor no other Law in the World can punish any Man for his Silence, feeing they can do no more than punish Words or Deeds; 'tis God only that is the Judge of the Secrets of our Hearts.

Attorney. Sir *Thomas*, tho we have not one Word or Deed of yours to object against you, yet we have your Silence, which is an evident sign of the Malice of your Heart: because no dutiful Subject, being lawfully ask'd this Question, will refuse to answer.

Sir *Thomas More.* Sir, my Silence is no sign of any Malice in my Heart, which the King himself must Own by my Conduct upon divers Occasions; neither doth it convince any Man of the Breach of the Law: for It is a Maxim amongst the Civilians and Canonists, *Qui tacet consentire videtur*, he that holds his peace; seems to give his Consent. And as to what you say, that no good Subject will refuse to give a direct Answer; I did really think it to be the Duty of every good Subject, except he be such a Subject as will be a bad Christian, rather to obey God than Man; to be more cautious to offend his Conscience, than of any thing else in the whole World ; especially if his Conscience be not the Occasion of same Sedition and great Injury to his Prince and Country : for I do here sincerely protest, that I never revealed it to any Man alive.

I come now to the third principal Article in my Indictment, by which I am accused of malicious Attempts, traitorous Endeavours, and perfidious Practices against that Statute, as the Words therein do alledge, because I wrote, while in the *Tower,* divers Packets of Letters to Bishop *Fisher*; whereby I exhorted him to violate the same Law and encouraged him in the like Obstinacy. I do insist that these Letters, be produced and read in Court, by which I may be either acquitted or convinced of a Lye; but because you say the Bishop burnt them all, I will here tell you the whole truth of the matter. Some of my Letters related only to our private Affairs, as about our old Friendship and Acquaintance: One of them was in answer to his, wherein he desired me to let him know what Answers I made upon my Examinations concerning the Oath of Supremacy; and what I wrote to him upon it was this, That I had already settled my Conscience, and let him satisfy his according to his own Mind. God is my Witness, and as I hope he will save my Soul, I gave him no other Answer; and this I presume is no Breach of the Laws.

As to the principal Crime objected against me, that I should say upon my Examination in the *Tower,* That this Law was like a two-edged Sword; for in consenting to it, I should endanger my Soul, and in rejecting it should lose my Life: it's evidently concluded, as you say, from this Answer, because *Fisher* made the like, that he was in the fame Conspiracy. To this I reply, That my Answer there was conditional, if there were both danger either in allowing or disallowing that Act; and therefore, like a two-edged Sword, it seem'd a hard thing should be put upon me; who had never hitherto contradicted it either in Word or Deed. These were my Words; what the Bishop answered, I know not: if his Answer was like mine, it did not proceed from any Conspiracy of ours, but from the Similitude of our Learning and Understanding. To conclude, I do sincerely avouch, that I never spoke a Word against this Law so any Man living, tho perhaps the King's Majesty has been told the contrary, There was little or no reply made to this full Answer by Mr. Attorney, or any body else; the word Malice was what was principally insisted on, and in the mouths of the whole Court; tho for proof of it no body could produce either Words or Actions: nevertheless, to set the best gloss that could be upon the Matter, Mr. *Rich* was called to give Evidence in open Court upon Oath, which he immediately did, affirming what we have already related concerning a Conference between him and Sir *Thomas* in the *Tower*, To which Sir *Thomas* made answer, If I were a Man, my Lords, that had no regard to my Oath, I had had no occasion to be here at this time, as is well known to every body, as a Criminal; and if this Oath, Mr. *Rich*, which you have taken be true, then I pray I may never see God's Face, which, were it otherwise, is an Imprecation I would not be guilty of to gain the whole World.

More having recited in the Face of the Court all the Discourse they had together in the *Tower*, as it truly and sincerely was, he added: In good Faith, Mr. *Rich*, I am more concerned for your Perjury, than my own Danger; and I must tell you, that neither my self nor any body else to my knowledge, ever took you to be a Man of such Reputation, that I or any other would have any thing to do with you in a Matter of Importance. You know that I have been acquainted with your manner of Life and Conversation long time, even from your Youth to the present Juncture, for we lived in the same Parish; and you very well know, I am sorry I am forced to speak it, you always lay under the Odium of a very lying Tongue, of a great Gamester, and of no good Name and Character either there or in the *Temple*, where you was educated. Can it therefore seem likely to your Lordships, that I should in so weighty an Affair as this, act so unadvisedly, as to trust Mr. *Rich*, a Man I had always so mean an Opinion of, in reference to his Truth and Honesty, so very much before my Sovereign Lord the King, to whom I am so deeply indebted for his manifold Favours, or any of his noble and grave Counselors, that I should only impart to Mr. *Rich* the Secrets of my Conscience in respect to the King's Supremacy, the particular Secrets, and only Point about which I have been so long pressed to explain my self? which I never did, nor never would reveal; when the Act was once made, either to the King himself, or any of his Privy-Counselors, as is well known to your Honours, who have been sent upon no other account at several times by his Majesty to me in the *Tower*. I refer it to your Judgments, my Lords, whether this can seem credible to any of your Lordships.

But supposing what Mr. *Rich* has swore should be true, seeing the Words were spoke in familiar and private Conversation, and that there was nothing at all asserted, but only Cases put without any offensive Circumstances; it cannot in justice be said, that they were spoke maliciously, and where there is no Malice, there is no Offence. Besides, my Lords, I cannot think so many reverend Bishops, so many honourable Personages, and so many virtuous and learned Men, of whom the Parliament consisted in the enacting of that Law, ever meant to have any Man punish'd with Death, in whom no Malice could be found, taking the Word *Malitia* for *Malevoentia*; for if *Malitia* be taken in a general Signification for any Crime, there is no Man can be free: Therefore this Word *Maliciously* is so far significant in this Statute, as the Word *Forcible* is in that of *Forcible*

Entry; for in that Case is any enter peaceably and puts his Adversary out forcibly, it is no Offence, but is he enters forcibly; he shall be punished by that Statute.

Besides, all the unspeakable Goodness of his Majesty towards me, who has been so many ways my singular good and gracious Lord, who has so dearly loved and trusted me, even from my first Entrance into his Royal Service, vouchsafing to honor me with the Dignity of being one of his Privy-Council, and has most generously promoted me to Offices of great Reputation and Honor, and lastly to that of Lord High-Chancellor, which Honor he never did to any Layman before, the same being the highest Dignity in his famous Kingdom, and next to the King's Royal Person, so far beyond my Merits and Qualifications; honoring and exalting me by his Incomparable Benignity, for these twentyYears and upwards, heaping continual Saviors upon me; and now at last, at my own humble Request, giving me liberty to dedicate the Remainder of my Life to the Service of God for the better saving of my Soul, has been pleased to discharge and free me from that weighty Dignity; before which he had still heaped more and more Honors upon me: I say, all this his Majesty's Bounty, so long and so plentifully conferred upon me, is enough, in my opinion, to invalidate the scandalous Accusation so injuriously surmised and urged by this Man against me.

This touched the Reputation of Mr. *Rich* to the very quick, and was a Slur that could not be effaced, without the utmost difficulty; and the only way to do it, was, is possible, to produce substantial and creditable Witnesses to attest the contrary: and therefore he caused Sir *Richard Southwell*, and Mr. *Palmer*, who were in the same Room with Sir *Thomas* and Mr. *Rich* when they conferred together, to be sworn as to the Words that passed between them. Whereupon Mr. *Palmer* deposed, *what he was so busy in thrusting Sir Thomas's Books into a Sack, that he took no notice of their Talk*, And Sir R, *Southwell* likewise swore, *that because his Business was only to take care of conveying his Books away, he gave no ear to their Discourse.*

[Verdict and Sentence]

Sir *Thomas* having urged other Reasons in his own Defense, to the discrediting of Mr. *Rich*'s Evidence; the Judge proceeded to give the Charge to the Jury. Whether Sir *Thomas* had challenged any of the Panel, when they were returned to serve, does not appear; but the twelve Persons on whose Verdict his Life now depended; were these:

Sir Thomas Palmer, KNT.

Falper Leake, Gent.

Sir Thomas Peirt, Knt.

William Browne, Gent.

George Lovell, Esq;

Thomas Billington, Gent.

Thomas Burbage, Esq;

John Parnel, Gent.

Geoffry Chamber, Gent.

Richard Bellame, Gent.

Edward Stockmore, Gent.

George Stoakes, Gent.

Now the Jury having withdrawn, scarce were out a quarter of an Hour before they returned with their Verdict, by which they found the Prisoner guilty; upon which the Lord Chancellor, as chief in the Commission for this Trial, immediately began to proceed to Judgment: which Sir *Thomas* observing, he said to him, My Lord, when I was concerned in the Law, the Practice in. I am sure there are far more, who all the while such Cases was to ask the Prisoner before Sentence, whether he had any thing to offer why Judgment should not be pronounced against him. The Lord Chancellor hereupon stopping his Sentence, wherein he had already proceeded in part, asked Sir *Thomas*, *What he was able to say to the contrary.* Who presently made Answer in these words: For as much as, my Lords, this Indictment is grounded upon an Act of Parliament, directly repugnant ,to the Laws of God and his Holy Church, the Supreme Government of which, or of any part thereof, no Temporal Person may by any Law presume to take upon him, being what right belongs to the See of *Rome*, which by special Prerogative was granted by the Mouth of our Savior Christ himself to St. *Peter*, and the Bishops of *Rome* his Successors only, whilst he lived, and was personally present here on Earth: it is therefore, amongst Catholic Christians, insufficient in Law, to charge any Christian to obey it. And in order to the proof of his Assertion, he declared among other things, that whereas this Kingdom alone being but one Member, and a small part of the Church, was not to make a particular Law disagreeing with the general Law of Christ's universal Catholic Church, no more than the City of *London*, being but one Member in respect to the whole Kingdom, might enact a Law against an Act of Parliament, to be binding to the whole Realm: so he shewed farther, That Law was ,even contrary to the Laws and Statutes of the Kingdom yet unrepealed, as might evidently be seen by *Magna Charta*, wherein are these Words; *Ecclesia Anglicana libera sit, & habet omnia jura integra, & libertates suas illcesas*: And it is contrary also to that sacred Oath which the

King's Majesty himself, and every other Christian Prince, always take with great Solemnity, at their Coronations. So great was Sir *Thomas*'s Zeal, that he further alleged, that it was worse in the Kingdom of *England* to restıse Obedience to the See of *Rome*, than for any Child to do to his natural Parent: for, as St. *Paul* said to the Corinthians, I have regenerated you, my Children, in Christ; so might that worthy Pope of *Rome*, St. *Gregory the Great*, say of us *Englishmen*, *Ye are my Children, because I have given you everlasting Salvation*: for by St. *Augustine* and his followers, his immediate Messengers, England first received the Christian faith, which is a far higher and better Inheritance than any carnal Sather can leave to his Children; for a. Son is only by generation, we are by Regeneration made the spiritual Children of Christ and the Pope.

Here the Lord Chancellor took him up and said; that seeing all the Bishops, Universities, and the most learned Men in the Kingdom had agreed to that Act, it was much wondered that he alone should so stiffly stickle, and so vehemently argue there against it.

HIS Answer was, That Is the Number of Bishops and Universities were so material as his Lordship seemed to make it; then, my Lord, I see no reason why that thing should make any Change in my Conscience: for I doubt not, but of the learned and virtuous Men now alive, I do not speak only of this Realm, but of all Christendom, there are ten to one of my mind in this matter; nut if I should take notice of those learned Doctors and virtuous Fathers that are already dead, many of whom are Saints in Heaven, I am sure there are far more, who all the while they lived thought in this CafÃ© as I do now. And therefore, my Lord, I do not think my self bound to conform my Conscience to the Counsel of one Kingdom, against the general Consent of all Christendom.

Here it seems the Lord Chancellor, not willing to take the whole Load of this Condemnation upon himself, asked In open Court the Advice of Sir *John Fitz-James*, the Lord Chief Justice of *England*, Whether the Indictment was valid, or no? Who wisely answered thus: *My Lords all, By St.* Gillian (for that was always his Oath) *I must needs confess, that if the Act of Parliament be not of unlawful, then the indictment is not in my Conscience invalid.* Some have wrote, That the Lord Chancellor should hereupon say, Quid adhuc desideramus testimonium, reus est mortis, and then presently proceeded to give Sentence to this effect:

That he should be carried back to the Tower of London, *by the Help of* William Kingston, *Sheriff, and from thence drawn on a Hurdle through the City of* London *to Tyburn, there to be hanged till he should be half dead; that then he should be cut down alive, his Privy Parts cut off, his Belly ripped, his Bowels burnt, his four Quarters sit up over four Gates of the City: and his Head upon* London-Bridge.

This was the Judgment pronounced upon this great Man, who had deserved so well both of the King and Kingdom, and for which *Paulus Jovius* calls King *Henry* VIII another *Phalaris*.

This severe Sentence was afterwards, by the Kings Pardon, changed to beheading, because he had borne the greatest Office in the Kingdom; of which mercy of the King's, word being brought to. Sir *Thomas* he merrily said, God forbid the King should use any more such Mercy to any of my Friends, and God bless all my Posterity from such Pardons.

When he had received Sentence of Death he spoke thus with a resolute and sedate Aspect: Well, seeing I am condemned, God knows ,how justly, I will freely speak for the disburdening my Conscience, what I think of this Law. When I perceived it was the King's Pleasure to sift out from whence the Pope's Authority was derived; I confess I studied seven years together to find out the truth of it, and I could not meet with the Works of any one Doctor, approved by the Church, , that avouch a Layman was, or ever could be the Head of the Church.

Chancellor. Would you be esteemed wiser, or to have a sincerer Conscience than all the Bishops, learned Doctors, Nobility and Commons of this Realm?

More. I am able to produce against, one Bishop which you can produce on your side, a hundred holy and Catholic Bishops for my Opinion; and against one Realm, the Consent of *Christendom* for a thousand years.

Norfolk: Sir *Thomas*, you shew your obstinate and malicious Mind.

More. Noble Sir, it's no Malice or Obstinacy that makes me say this, but the just necessity of the Cause obliges me to it for the Discharge of my Conscience ; and call God to witness, that nothing but this has excited me to it.

After this the Judges kindly offering him their favorable Audience if he had any thing else to say; but that as the blessed Apostle St. *Paul*, as we read in the *Acts* of the Apostles, was present, and consenting to the Protomartyr *Stephen*, keeping their Clothes that stoned him to death, and yet they are both now holy Saints in heaven, and there shall continue Friends to Eternity; so I verily trust, and shall therefore heartily pray, that albeit your Lordships have been on Earth my Judges to Condemnation, yet that we , may hereafter meet joyfully together in Heaven to our everlasting Salvation: and God preserve you, especially my Sovereign Lord the King, and grant him faithful Counselors.

Sir *Thomas*, after his Condemnation, was conducted from the Bar to the *Tower,* an Axe being carried before him, with the Edge towards him.

[Execution]

Sir *Thomas* More having remained a Prisoner in the *Tower* about a Week after his Sentence, on the 6th of *July* early in the Morning, his old Friend Sir *Thomas Pope* came to him with a Message from the King and Council, to acquaint him, That his Execution was appointed to be before nine that Morning. Whereupon Sir Thomas said, He thanked him heartily for his good News. I have been, says he, much obliged to his Majesty for the Benefits and Honors he has most bountifully conferred upon me; yet I am more bound to his Grace, I do assure you, for confining me in this Place, where I have had convenient Place and Opportunity to put me in mind of my last End. I am most of all bound to him, that his Majesty is pleased to rid me out of the Miseries of this Wretched World. Then Sir *Thomas Pope* acquainted him, it was the King's Pleasure he should not use many Words at the Place of Execution. *Sir,* said he, *you do well to acquaint me with the King's Pleasure; for I had otherwise designed to have made a Speech to the People; but it matters not, and I am ready to conform myself to his Highness's Pleasure. And I beseech you, Sir; you would become a Suitor to his Majesty, that my Daughter* Margaret *may attend my funeral.* To which *Pope* replied, that the King was willing his Wise and Children, and other Friends should be present. Sir *Thomas Pope* being about to take his Leave, could not restrain from Tears. Whereupon Sir *Thomas More* said, *Let not your Spirits be cast down, for I hope we shall see one another in a better Place, where we shall be free to live and love in Eternal Bliss.* And to divert *Pope's* Grief, he took up his Urinal and shook it, saying merrily, *I see no Danger—but that this Man may live longer, if the King pleases.*

About Nine he was brought out of the *Tower*; his Beard was long, his face pale and thin, and carrying a Red Cross in his Hand, he often lift up his Eyes to Heaven; a Woman meeting him with a cup of Wine, he refused it saying, *Christ at his Passion drank no wine, but Gall and Vinegar.* Another Woman came crying and demanded some Papers she said she had left in his Hands, when he was Lord Chancellor, to whom he said, *Good woman, have Patience but for an Hour and the King will rid me of the Care I have for those Papers, and every thing else.* Another Woman followed him, crying, He had done her much Wrong when he was Lord Chancellor, to whom he said, *I very well remember the Cause, and is I were to decide it now, I should make the same Decree.*

When he came to the Scaffold, it seemed ready to fall, whereupon he said merrily to the Lieutenant, *Pray, Sir, see me safe up; and as to my coming down, let me shift for myself.* Being about to speak to the People, he was interrupted by the Sheriff, and thereupon he only desired the People to pray for him, and bear Witness he died in the Faith of the Catholic Church, a faithful Servant both to God and the King. Then kneeling, he repeated the *Miserere Psalm* with much Devotion; and, rising up the Executioner asked him Forgiveness. He kissed him, and said, *Pick up thy Spirits, Man, and be not afraid to do thine Office; my Neck is very short, take heed therefore thou strike not awry for having thine Honesty.* Laying his Head upon the Block, he bid the Executioner stay till he had put his Beard aside, for that had committed no Treason. Thus he suffered with much Cheerfulness; his Head was taken off at one Blow, and was placed upon *London-Bridge*, where, having continued for some Months, and being about to be thrown into the

Thames to make room for others, his Daughter *Margaret* bought it, inclosed it in a Leaden Box, and kept *it* for a Relique.

James Otis: The Rights of the British Colonies Asserted and Proved

1764

Document Text

...Let no Man think I am about to commence advocate for *despotism*, because I affirm that government is founded on the necessity of our natures; and that an original supreme Sovereign, absolute, and uncontroulable, *earthly* power *must* exist in and preside over every society; from whose final decisions there can be no appeal but directly to Heaven. It is therefore *originally* and *ultimately* in the people. I say this supreme absolute power is *originally* and *ultimately* in the people; and they never did in fact *freely*, nor can they *rightfully* make an absolute, unlimited renunciation of this divine right. It is ever in the nature of the thing given in *trust*, and on a condition, the performance of which no mortal can dispense with; namely, that the person or persons on whom the sovereignty is conferred by the people, shall *incessantly* consult *their* good. Tyranny of all kinds is to be abhorred, whether it be in the hands of one, or of the few, or of the many. And though "in the last age a generation of men sprung up that would flatter Princes with an opinion that *they* have a *divine right* to absolute power;" yet "slavery is so vile and miserable an estate of man, and so directly opposite to the generous temper and courage of our nation, that it is hard to be conceived that an *Englishman*, much less a *gentleman*, should plead for it:" Especially at a time when the finest writers of the most polite nations on the continent of *Europe*, are enraptured with the beauties of the civil constitution of *Great Britain*; and envy her, no less for the *freedom* of her sons, than for her immense *wealth* and *military* glory.

But let the *origin* of government be placed where it may, the *end* of it is manifestly the good of *the whole. Salus populi suprema lex esto, is* of the law of nature, and part of that grand charter given the human race (though too many of them are afraid to assert it) by the only monarch in the universe, who has a clear and indisputable right to *absolute* power; because he is the *only* ONE who is *omniscient* as well as *omnipotent*....

The British constitution in theory and in the present administration of it, in general comes nearest the idea of perfection, of any that has been reduced to practice, and if the principles of it are adhered to, it will, according to the infallible prediction of *Harrington*, always keep the *Britons* uppermost in *Europe*, 'till their *only* rival nation shall either embrace that perfect model of a commonwealth given us by that author, or come as near it as *Great Britain is*. Then indeed, and not till then, will that rival and our nation either be eternal confederates, or contend in greater earnest than they have ever yet done, till one of them shall sink under the power of the other, and rise no more....

Every British Subject born on the continent of America, or in any other of the British dominions, is by the law of God and nature, by the common law, and by act of parliament, (exclusive of all charters from the crown) entitled to all the natural, essential, inherent and inseparable rights of our fellow subjects in Great-Britain.

1st. *That the supreme and subordinate powers of legislation should be free and sacred in the hands where the community have once rightfully placed them.*

2dly. *The supreme national legislative cannot be altered justly till the commonwealth is dissolved, nor a subordinate legislative taken away without forfeiture or other good cause.* Nor then can the subjects in the subordinate government be reduced to a state of slavery, and subject to the despotic rule of others. A state has no right to make slaves of the conquered. Even when the subordinate right of legislature is forfeited, and so declared, this cannot effect the natural persons either of those who were invested with it, or the inhabitants, so far as to deprive them of the rights of subjects and of men. The colonists will have an equitable right, notwithstanding any such forfeiture of charter, to be represented in parliament, or to have some new subordinate legislature among themselves. It would be best if they had both. Deprived, however, of their common rights as subjects, they cannot lawfully be, while they remain such. Representation in Parliament from the several colonies, since they are become so large and numerous, as to be called on not only to maintain provincial government, civil and military, among themselves, for this they have chearfully done, but to contribute towards the support of a national standing army, by reason of the heavy national debt, when they themselves owe a large one, contracted in the common cause, cannot be thought an unreasonable thing, nor if asked, could it be called an immodest request) *Qui sentit commodum sentire debet et onus*, has been thought a maxim of equity. But that a man should bear a burthen for other people, as well as himself, without a return, never long found a place in any law-book or decrees, but those of the most despotic princes. Besides the equity of an American representation in parliament, a thousand advantages would result from it. It would be the most effectual means of giving those of both countries a thorough knowledge of each others interests; as well as that of the whole, which are inseparable.

Were this representation allowed; instead of the scandalous memorials and depositions that have been sometimes, in days of old, privately cooked up in an inquisitorial manner, by persons of bad minds and wicked views, and sent from America to the several boards, persons of the first reputation among their countrymen, might be on the spot, from the several colonies, truly to represent them. Future ministers need not, like some of their predecessors, have recourse for information in American affairs, to every vagabond stroller, that has run or rid post *through* America, from his creditors, or to people of no kind of reputation from the colonies; some of whom, at the time of administering their sage advice, have been as ignorant of the state of this country, as of the regions in Jupiter and Saturn.

No representation of the colonies in parliament alone, would, however, be equivalent to a subordinate legislative among themselves; nor so well answer the ends of increasing their prosperity and the commerce of Great Britain. It would be impossible for the parliament to judge so well of their abilities to bear taxes, impositions on trade, and other duties and burthens, or of the local laws that might be really needful, as a legislative here.

3dly. *No legislative, supreme or subordinate, has a right to make itself arbitrary.*

Patrick Henry: Resolutions in Opposition to the Stamp Act

1765

Document Text

RESOLVES of the House of Burgesses in Virginia, *June* 1765.

That the first Adventurers & Settlers of this his Majesty's Colony and Dominion of *Virginia*, brought with them, and transmitted to their Posterity, and all other his Majesty's Subjects since inhabiting in this his Majesty's Colony, all the Liberties, Privileges, Franchises, and Immunities, that at any Time been held, enjoyed, and possessed, by the people of *Great Britain*.

That by Two Royal Charters, granted by King *James* the First, the Colonists aforesaid are Declared Entitled, to all Liberties, Privileges and Immunities, of Denizens and Natural Subjects (to all Intents and Purposes) as if they had been Abiding and Born within the Realm of *England*.

That the Taxation of the People by Themselves, or by Persons Chosen by Themselves to Represent them, who can only know what Taxes the People are able to bear, or the easiest Method of Raising them, and must themselves be affected by every Tax laid upon the People, is the only Security against a Burthensome Taxation; and the distinguishing Characteristic of *British* FREEDOM; and, without which, the ancient Constitution cannot exist.

That his Majesty's Liege People of this most Ancient and Loyal Colony, have, without Interruption, the inestimable Right of being Governed by such Laws, respecting their internal Policy and Taxation, as are derived from their own Consent, with the Approbation of their Sovereign, or his Substitute; which Right hath never been Forfeited, or Yielded up; but hath been constantly recognized by the Kings and People of *Great Britain*.

Resolved therefore, That the General Assembly of this Colony, with the consent of his Majesty, or his Substitute, HAVE the Sole Right and Authority to lay Taxes and Impositions upon Its Inhabitants: And, That every Attempt to vest such Authority in any other Person or Persons whatsoever, has a Manifest Tendency to Destroy AMERICAN FREEDOM.

That his Majesty's Liege People, Inhabitants of this Colony, are not bound to yield

Obedience to any Law or Ordinance whatsoever, designed to impose any Taxation upon them, other than the Laws or Ordinances of the General Assembly as aforesaid.

That any Person who shall, by Speaking, or Writing, assert or maintain, That any Person or Persons, other than the General Assembly of this Colony, with such Consent as aforesaid, have any Right or Authority to lay or impose any Tax whatever on the Inhabitants therof, shall be Deemed, AN ENEMY TO THIS HIS MAJESTY'S COLONY.

John Dickinson: Letters from a Farmer in Pennsylvania

1767–1768

Document Text

Letter I

My dear Countrymen,

I am a *Farmer*, settled, after a variety of fortunes, near the banks of the river *Delaware*, in the province of *Pennsylvania*. I received a liberal education, and have been engaged in the busy scenes of life; but am now convinced, that a man may be as happy without bustle, as with it. My farm is small; my servants are few, and good; I have a little money at interest; I wish for no more; my employment in my own affairs is easy; and with a contented grateful mind, undisturbed by worldly hopes or fears, relating to myself, I am completing the number of days allotted to me by divine goodness.

Being generally master of my time, I spend a good deal of it in a library, which I think the most valuable part of my small estate; and being acquainted with two or three gentlemen of abilities and learning, who honor me with their friendship, I have acquired, I believe, a greater knowledge in history, and the laws and constitution of my country, than is generally attained by men of my class, many of them not being so fortunate as I have been in the opportunities of getting information.

From my infancy I was taught to love *humanity* and *liberty*. Enquiry and experience have since confirmed my reverence for the lessons then given me, by convincing me more fully of their truth and excellence. Benevolence toward mankind, excites wishes for their welfare, and such wishes endear the means of fulfilling them. *These* can be found in liberty only, and therefore her sacred cause ought to be espoused by every man on every occasion, to the utmost of his power. As a charitable, but poor person does not withhold his *mite*, because he cannot relieve *all* the distresses of the miserable, so should not any honest man suppress his sentiments concerning freedom, however small their influence is likely to be. Perhaps he "may touch some wheel," that will have an effect greater than he could reasonably expect.

These being my sentiments, I am encouraged to offer to you, my countrymen, my thoughts on some late transactions, that appear to me to be of the utmost importance to you. Conscious of my own defects, I have waited some time, in expectation of seeing the subject treated by persons much better qualified for the task; but being therein disappointed, and apprehensive that longer delays will be injurious, I venture at length to request the attention of the public, praying, that these lines may be *read* with the same zeal for the happiness of *British America*, with which they were *wrote*.

With a good deal of surprise I have observed, that little notice has been taken of an act of parliament, as injurious in its principle to the liberties of these colonies, as the *Stamp Act* was: I mean the act for suspending the legislation of *New York*.

The assembly of that government complied with a former act of parliament, requiring certain provisions to be made for the troops in *America*, in every particular, I think, except the articles of salt, pepper and vinegar. In my opinion they acted imprudently, considering all circumstances, in not complying so far as would have given satisfaction, as several colonies did: But my dislike of their conduct in that instance, has not blinded me so much, that I cannot plainly perceive, that they have been punished in a manner pernicious to *American* freedom, and justly alarming to all the colonies.

If the *British* parliament has legal authority to issue an order, that we shall furnish a single article for the troops here, and to compel obedience to *that* order, they have the same right to issue an order for us to supply those troops with arms, clothes, and every necessary; and to compel obedience to *that* order also; in short, to lay *any burthens* they please upon us. What is this but *taxing* us at a *certain sum*, and leaving to us only the *manner* of raising it? How is this mode more tolerable than the *Stamp Act*? Would that act have appeared more pleasing to *Americans*, if being ordered thereby to raise the sum total of the taxes, the mighty privilege had been left to them, of saying how much should be paid for an instrument of writing on paper, and how much for another on parchment?

An act of parliament, commanding us to do a certain thing, if it has any validity, is a *tax* upon us for the expense that accrues in complying with it; and for this reason, I believe, every colony on the continent, that chose to give a mark of their respect for *Great Britain*, in complying with the act relating to the troops, cautiously avoided the mention of that act, lest their conduct should be attributed to its supposed obligation.

The matter being thus stated, the assembly of *New York* either had, or had not, a right to refuse submission to that act. If they had, and I imagine no *American* will say they had not, then the parliament had *no right* to compel them to execute it. If they had not *this right*, they had *no right* to punish them for not executing it; and therefore *no right* to suspend their legislation, which is a punishment. In fact, if the people of *New York* cannot be legally taxed but by their own representatives, they cannot be legally deprived of the privilege of legislation, only for insisting on that exclusive privilege of taxation. If they may be legally deprived in such a case, of the privilege of legislation, why may they not, with equal reason, be deprived of every other privilege? Or why may not every colony be treated in the same manner, when any of them shall dare to deny their assent to any impositions, that shall be directed? Or what signifies the repeal of the *Stamp Act*, if these colonies are to lose their *other* privileges, by not tamely surrendering *that* of taxation?

There is one consideration arising from this suspension, which is not generally attended to, but shows its importance very clearly. It was not *necessary* that this suspension should be caused by an act of parliament. The crown might have restrained the governor of *New York*, even from calling the assembly together, by its prerogative in the royal governments. This step, I suppose, would have been taken, if the conduct of the assembly of *New York* had been regarded as an act of disobedience *to the crown alone*; but it is regarded as an act of "disobedience to the authority of the British Legislature." This gives the suspension a consequence vastly more affecting. It is a parliamentary assertion of the *supreme authority* of the *British* legislature over these colonies, in *the point of taxation*, and is intended to Compel *New York* into a submission to that authority. It seems therefore to me as much a violation of the liberties of the people of that province, and consequently of all these colonies, as if the parliament had sent a number of regiments to be quartered upon them till they should comply. For it is evident, that the suspension is meant as a *compulsion*; and the *method* of compelling is totally indifferent. It is indeed probable, that the sight of redcoats, and the hearing of drums, would have been most alarming; because people are generally more influenced by their eyes and ears, than by their reason. But whoever seriously considers the matter, must perceive that a dreadful stroke is aimed at the liberty of these colonies. I say, of these colonies; for the cause of *one* is the cause of *all*. If the parliament may lawfully deprive *New York* of any of *her* rights, it may deprive any, or all the other colonies of *their* rights; and nothing can possibly so much encourage such attempts, as a mutual inattention to the interests of each other. *To divide, and thus to destroy*, is the first political maxim in attacking those, who are powerful by their union....

With concern I have observed, that *two* assemblies of this province have sat and adjourned, without taking any notice of this act. It may perhaps be asked, what would have been proper for them to do? I am by no means fond of inflammatory measures; I detest them. I should be sorry that anything should be done which might justly displease our sovereign, or our mother country: But a firm, modest exertion of a free spirit, should never be wanting on public occasions. It appears to me, that it would have been sufficient for the assembly to have ordered our agents to represent to the King's ministers their sense of the suspending act, and to pray for its repeal. Thus we should have borne our testimony against it; and might therefore reasonably expect that, on a like occasion, we might receive the same assistance from the other colonies.

Concordia res parvae crescunt.

Small things grow great by concord.

A Farmer

Letter III

My dear Countrymen,

I rejoice to find that my two former letters to you have been generally received with so much favor by such of you, whose sentiments I have had an opportunity of knowing. Could you look into my heart you would instantly perceive a zealous attachment to your interests, and a lively resentment of every insult and injury offered to you, to be the motives that have engaged me to address you.

I am no further concerned in anything affecting *America*, than any one of you; and when liberty leaves it, I can quit it much more conveniently than most of you: But while Divine Providence, that gave me existence in a land of freedom, permits my head to think, my lips to speak, and my hand to move, I shall so highly and gratefully value the blessing received as to take care that my silence and inactivity shall not give my implied assent to any act, degrading my brethren and myself from the birthright, wherewith heaven itself *"hath made us free."*

Sorry I am to learn that there are some few persons who shake their heads with solemn motion, and pretend to wonder, what can be the meaning of these letters. "*Great Britain*," they say, "is too powerful to contend with; she is determined to oppress us; it is in vain to speak of right on one side, when there is power on the other; when we are strong enough to resist we shall attempt it; but now we are not strong enough, and therefore we had better be quiet; it signifies nothing to convince us that our rights are invaded when we cannot defend them; and if we should get into riots and tumults about the late act, it will only draw down heavier displeasure upon us."

What can such men design? What do their grave observations amount to, but this— "that these colonies, totally regardless of their liberties, should commit them, with humble resignation, to *chance*, *time*, and the tender mercies of *ministers*."

Are these men ignorant that usurpations, which might have been successfully opposed at first, acquire strength by continuance, and thus become irresistible? Do they condemn the conduct of these colonies, concerning the *Stamp Act*? Or have they forgot its successful issue? Should the colonies at that time, instead of acting as they did, have trusted for relief to the fortuitous events of futurity? If it is needless "to speak of rights" now, it was as needless then. If the behavior of the colonies was prudent and glorious then, and successful too; it will be equally prudent and glorious to act in the same manner now, if our rights *are* equally invaded, and may be as successful. Therefore it becomes necessary to inquire whether "our rights are invaded." To talk of "defending" them, as if they could be no otherwise "defended" than by arms, is as much out of the way, as if a man having a choice of several roads to reach his journey's end, should prefer the worst, for no other reason, but because it *is* the worst.

As to "riots and tumults," the gentlemen who are so apprehensive of them, are much mistaken, if they think that grievances cannot be redressed without such assistance.

I will now tell the gentlemen, what is "the meaning of these letters." The meaning of them is, to convince the people of these colonies that they are at this moment exposed to the most imminent dangers; and to persuade them immediately, vigorously, and unanimously, to exert themselves in the most firm, but most peaceable manner, for obtaining relief.

The cause of *liberty* is a cause of too much dignity to be sullied by turbulence and tumult. It ought to be maintained in a manner suitable to her nature. Those who engage in it, should breathe a sedate, yet fervent spirit, animating them to actions of prudence, justice, modesty, bravery, humanity and magnanimity.

To such a wonderful degree were the ancient *Spartans*, as brave and free a people as ever existed, inspired by this happy temperature of soul, that rejecting even in their battles the use of trumpets and other instruments for exciting heat and rage, they marched up to scenes of havoc, and horror, with the sound of flutes, to the tunes of which their steps kept pace—"exhibiting," as *Plutarch* says, "at once a terrible and delightful fight, and proceeding with a deliberate valor, full of hope and good assurance, as if some divinity had sensibly assisted them."

I hope, my dear countrymen, that you will, in every colony, be upon your guard against those who may at any time endeavor to stir you up, under pretenses of patriotism, to any measures disrespectful to our Sovereign, and our mother country. Hot, rash, disorderly proceedings, injure the reputation of the people as to wisdom, valor, and virtue, without procuring them the least benefit. I pray GOD that he may be pleased to inspire you and your posterity, to the latest ages, with a spirit of which I have an idea, that I find a difficulty to express. To express it in the best manner I can, I mean a spirit that shall so guide you that it will be impossible to determine whether an *American's* character is most distinguishable for his loyalty to his Sovereign, his duty to his mother country, his love of freedom, or his affection for his native soil.

Every government at some time or other falls into wrong measures. These may proceed from mistake or passion. But every such measure does not dissolve the obligation between the governors and the governed. The mistake may be corrected; the passion may subside. It is the duty of the governed to endeavor to rectify the mistake, and to appease the passion. They have not at first any other right, than to represent their grievances, and to pray for redress, unless an emergency is so pressing as not to allow time for receiving an answer to their applications, which rarely happens. If their applications are disregarded, then that kind of *opposition* becomes justifiable which can be made without breaking the laws or disturbing the public peace. This conflicts in the *prevention of the oppressors reaping advantage from their oppressions*, and not in their punishment. For experience may teach them what reason did not; and harsh methods cannot be proper until milder ones have failed.

If at length it becomes Undoubted that an inveterate resolution is formed to annihilate the liberties of the governed, the *English* history affords frequent examples of resistance by force. What particular circumstances will in any future case justify such resistance can never be ascertained till they happen. Perhaps it may be allowable to say generally, that it never can be justifiable until the people are Fully Convinced that any further submission will be destructive to their happiness.

When the appeal is made to the sword, highly probable is it, that the punishment will exceed the offense; and the calamities attending on war outweigh those preceding it. These considerations of justice and prudence, will always have great influence with good and wise men.

To these reflections on this subject, it remains to be added, and ought for ever to be remembered, that resistance, in the case of colonies against their mother country, is extremely different from the resistance of a people against their prince. A nation may change their king, or race of kings, and, retaining their ancient form of government, be gainers by changing. Thus *Great Britain*, under the illustrious house of *Brunswick*, a house that seems to flourish for the happiness of mankind, has found a felicity unknown in the reigns of the *Stuarts*. But if once we are separated from our mother country, what new form of government shall we adopt, or where shall we find another *Britain* to supply our loss? Torn from the body, to which we are united by religion, liberty, laws, affections, relation, language and commerce, we must bleed at every vein.

In truth—the prosperity of these provinces is founded in their dependence on *Great Britain*; and when she returns to her "old good humor, and her old good nature," as Lord *Clarendon* expresses it, I hope they will always think it their duty and interest, as it most certainly will be, to promote her welfare by all the means in their power.

We cannot act with too much caution in our disputes. Anger produces anger; and differences, that might be accommodated by kind and respectful behavior, may, by imprudence, be enlarged to an incurable rage. In quarrels between countries, as well as in those between individuals, when they have risen to a certain height, the first cause of dissension is no longer remembered, the minds of the parties being wholly engaged in recollecting and resenting the mutual expressions of their dislike. When feuds have reached that fatal point, all considerations of reason and equity vanish; and a blind fury governs, or rather confounds all things. A people no longer regards their interest, but the gratification of their wrath. The sway of the *Cleons and Clodiuses*, the designing and detectable flatterers of the *prevailing passion*, becomes confirmed. Wise and good men in vain oppose the storm, and may think themselves fortunate, if, in attempting to preserve their ungrateful fellow citizens, they do not ruin themselves. Their *prudence* will be called *baseness*; their *moderation* will be called guilt; and if their virtue does not lead them to destruction, as that of many other great and excellent persons has done, they may survive to receive from their expiring country the mournful glory of her acknowledgment, that their counsels, if regarded, would have saved her.

The constitutional modes of obtaining relief are those which I wish to see pursued on the present occasion; that is, by petitions of our assemblies, or where they are not permitted to meet, of the people, to the powers that can afford us relief.

We have an excellent prince, in whose good dispositions toward us we may confide. We have a generous, sensible and humane nation, to whom we may apply. They may be deceived. They may, by artful men, be provoked to anger against us. I cannot believe they will be cruel and unjust; or that their anger will be implacable. Let us behave like dutiful children who have received unmerited blows from a beloved parent. Let us complain to our parent; but let our complaints speak at the same time the language of affliction and veneration.

If, however, it shall happen, by an unfortunate course of affairs, that our applications to his Majesty and the parliament for redress, prove ineffectual, let us then take *another step*, by withholding from *Great Britain* all the advantages she has been used to receive from us. Then let us try, if our ingenuity, industry, and frugality, will not give weight to our remonstrances. Let us all be united with one spirit, in one cause. Let us invent—let us work—let us save—let us, continually, keep up our claim, and incessantly repeat our complaints—But, above all, let us implore the protection of that infinitely good and gracious being, "by whom kings reign, and princes decree justice."

Nil desperandum.

Nothing is to be despaired of.

A Farmer

Proclamation of 1763

1763

Document Text

By the King. A Proclamation. *George R.*

Whereas We have taken into Our Royal Consideration the extensive and valuable Acquisitions in America, secured to our Crown by the late *Definitive Treaty of Peace,* concluded at Paris, the 10th Day of February last; and being desirous that all Our loving Subjects, as well of our Kingdom as of our Colonies in America, may avail themselves with all convenient Speed, of the great Benefits and Advantages which must accrue therefrom to their Commerce, Manufactures, and Navigation, We have thought fit, with the Advice of our Privy Council, to issue this our Royal Proclamation, hereby to publish and declare to all our loving Subjects, that we have, with the Advice of our Said Privy Council, granted our Letters Patent, under our Great Seal of Great Britain, to erect, within the Countries and Islands ceded and confirmed to Us by the said Treaty, Four distinct and separate Governments, styled and called by the names of Quebec, East Florida, West Florida and Grenada, and limited and bounded as follows, viz.

First—The Government of Quebec bounded on the Labrador Coast by the River St. John, and from thence by a Line drawn from the Head of that River through the Lake St. John, to the South end of the Lake Nipissim; from whence the said Line, crossing the River St. Lawrence, and the Lake Champlain, in 45 Degrees of North Latitude, passes along the High Lands which divide the Rivers that empty themselves into the said River St. Lawrence from those which fall into the Sea; and also along the North Coast of the Baye des Chaleurs, and the Coast of the Gulph of St. Lawrence to Cape Rosieres, and from thence crossing the Mouth of the River St. Lawrence by the West End of the Island of Anticosti, terminates at the aforesaid River of St. John.

Secondly—The Government of East Florida. bounded to the Westward by the Gulph of Mexico and the Apalachicola River; to the Northward by a Line drawn from that part of the said River where the Chatahouchee and Flint Rivers meet, to the source of St. Mary's River, and by the course of the said River to the Atlantic Ocean; and to the Eastward and Southward by the Atlantic Ocean and the Gulph of Florida, including all Islands within Six Leagues of the Sea Coast.

Thirdly—The Government of West Florida, bounded to the Southward by the Gulph of Mexico, including all Islands within Six Leagues of the Coast, from the River Apalachicola to Lake Pontchartrain; to the Westward by the said Lake, the Lake Maurepas, and the River Mississippi; to the Northward by a Line drawn due East from that part of the River Mississippi which lies in 31 Degrees North Latitude, to the River Apalachicola or Chatahouchee; and to the Eastward by the said River.

Fourthly—The Government of Grenada, comprehending the Island of that name, together with the Grenadines, and the Islands of Dominico, St. Vincent's and Tobago, And to the end that the open and free Fishery of our Subjects may be extended to and carried on upon the Coast of Labrador, and the adjacent Islands, We have thought fit, with the advice of our said Privy Council to put all that Coast, from the River St. John's to Hudson's Streights, together with the Islands of Anticosti and Madelaine, and all other smaller Islands lying upon the said Coast, under the care and Inspection of our Governor of Newfoundland.

We have also, with the advice of our Privy Council, thought fit to annex the Islands of St. John's and Cape Breton, or Isle Royale, with the lesser Islands adjacent thereto, to our Government of Nova Scotia.

We have also, with the advice of our Privy Council aforesaid, annexed to our Province of Georgia all the Lands lying between the Rivers Alatamaha and St. Mary's.

And whereas it will greatly contribute to the speedy settling of our said new Governments, that our loving Subjects should be informed of our Paternal care, for the security of the Liberties and Properties of those who are and shall become Inhabitants thereof, We have thought fit to publish and declare, by this Our Proclamation, that We have, in the Letters Patent under our Great Seal of Great Britain, by which the said Governments are constituted, given express Power and Direction to our Governors of our Said Colonies respectively, that so soon as the state and circumstances of the said Colonies will admit thereof, they shall, with the Advice and Consent of the Members of our Council, summon and call General Assemblies within the said Governments respectively, in such Manner and Form as is used and directed in those Colonies and Provinces in America which are under our immediate Government: And We have also given Power to the said Governors, with the consent of our Said Councils, and the Representatives of the people, so to be summoned as aforesaid, to make, constitute, and ordain Laws, Statutes and Ordinances for the public peace, welfare and good government of our said colonies, and of the people and inhabitants thereof, as near as may be agreeable to the Laws of England, and under such regulations and restrictions as are used in other colonies; and in the mean time, and until such assemblies can be called as aforesaid, all persons inhabiting in, or resorting to our said colonies may confide in our royal protection for the enjoyment of the benefit of the Laws of our Realm of England; for which purpose, we have given power under our Great Seal to the Governors of our said colonies respectively, to erect and constitute, with the advice of our said Councils respectively, courts of Judicature and public justice within our said colonies, for the hearing and determining all causes, as well criminal as civil, according to Law and Equity, and, as near as may be, agreeable to the Laws of England, with liberty to all persons, who may think themselves aggrieved by the sentence of such courts, in all civil cafes, to appeal, under the usual limitations and restrictions, to us, in our Privy Council.

We have also thought fit, with the advice of our Privy Council as aforesaid, to give unto the Governors and Councils of our said Three new Colonies, upon the Continent full Power and Authority to settle and agree with the Inhabitants of our said new Colonies or with any other Persons who shall resort thereto, for such Lands. Tenements and Hereditaments, as are now or hereafter shall be in our Power to dispose of; and them to grant to any such Person or Persons upon such Terms, and under such moderate Quit-Rents, Services and Acknowledgments, as have been appointed and settled in our other Colonies, and under such other Conditions as shall appear to us to be necessary and expedient for the Advantage of the Grantees, and the Improvement and settlement of our said Colonies.

And Whereas, We are desirous, upon all occasions, to testify our Royal Sense and Approbation of the Conduct and bravery of the Officers and Soldiers of our Armies, and to reward the same, We do hereby command and impower our Governors of our said Three new Colonies, and all other our Governors of our several Provinces on the Continent of North America, to grant without Fee or Reward, to such reduced Officers as have served in North America during the late War, and to such Private Soldiers as have been or shall be disbanded in America, and are actually residing there, and shall personally apply for the same, the following Quantities of Lands, subject, at the Expiration of Ten Years, to the same Quit-Rents as other Lands are subject to in the Province within which they are granted, as also subject to the same Conditions of Cultivation and Improvement; viz.

—To every Person having the Rank of a Field Officer—5,000 Acres.

—To every Captain—3,000 Acres.

—To every Subaltern or Staff Officer—2,000 Acres.

—To every Non-Commission Officer—200 Acres.

—To every Private Man—50 Acres.

We do likewise authorize and require the Governors and Commanders in Chief of all our said Colonies upon the Continent of North America to grant the like Quantities of Land, and upon the same conditions, to such reduced Officers of our Navy of like Rank as served on board our Ships of War in North America at the times of the Reduction of Louisbourg and Quebec in the late War, and who shall personally apply to our respective Governors for such Grants.

And whereas it is just and reasonable, and essential to our Interest, and the Security of our Colonies, that the several Nations or Tribes of Indians with whom We are connected, and who live under our Protection, should not be molested or disturbed in the Possession of such Parts of Our Dominions and Territories as, not having been ceded to or purchased by Us, are reserved to them, or any of them, as their Hunting Grounds.—We do therefore, with the Advice of our Privy Council, declare it to be our Royal Will and Pleasure, that no Governor or Commander in Chief in any of our Colonies of Quebec, East Florida, or West Florida, do presume, upon any Pretence whatever, to grant Warrants of Survey, or pass any Patents for Lands beyond the Bounds of their respective Governments, as described in their Commissions: as also that no Governor or Commander in Chief in any of our other Colonies or Plantations in America do presume for the present, and until our further Pleasure be known, to grant Warrants of Survey or pass any Patent for lands beyond the heads of sources of any of the rivers which fall into the Atlantic Ocean from the West or North West; or upon any lands whatever, which not having been ceded to, or purchased by us, as aforesaid, are reserved to the said Indians, or any of them.

And We do further declare it to be Our Royal Will and Pleasure, for the present as aforesaid, to reserve under our Sovereignty, Protection, and Dominion, for the use of the said Indians, all the Lands and Territories not included within the Limits of Our said Three new Governments, or within the Limits of the Territory granted to the Hudson's Bay Company, as also all the Lands and Territories lying to the Westward of the Sources of the Rivers which fall into the Sea from the West and North West as aforesaid.

And We do hereby strictly forbid, on Pain of our Displeasure, all our loving Subjects from making any Purchases or Settlements whatever, or taking Possession of any of the Lands above reserved, without our especial leave and Licence for that Purpose first obtained.

And We do further strictly enjoin and require all Persons whatever who have either wilfully or inadvertently seated themselves upon any Lands within the Countries above described, or upon any other Lands which, not having been ceded to or purchased by Us, are still reserved to the said Indians as aforesaid, forthwith to remove themselves from such Settlements.

And whereas great Frauds and Abuses have been committed in purchasing Lands of the Indians, to the great Prejudice of our Interests, and to the great Dissatisfaction of the said Indians: In order, therefore, to prevent such Irregularities for the future, and to the end that the Indians may be convinced of our Justice and determined Resolution to remove all reasonable Cause of Discontent, We do, with the Advice of our Privy Council strictly enjoin and require, that no private Person do presume to make any purchase from the said Indians of any Lands reserved to the said Indians, within those parts of our Colonies where, We have thought proper to allow Settlement: but that, if at any Time any of the Said Indians should be inclined to dispose of the said Lands, the same shall be Purchased only for Us, in our Name, at some public Meeting or Assembly of the said Indians, to be held for that Purpose by the Governor or Commander in Chief of our Colony respectively within which they shall lie: And in case they shall lie within the limits of any proprietaries, conformable to such directions and instructions as we or they shall think proper to give for that purpose: and we do by the advice of our Privy Council, declare and enjoin, that the trade with the said Indians shall be free and open to all our subjects whatever; provided that every person who may incline to trade with the said Indians, do take out a licence for carrying on such trade, from the Governor or Commander in chief of any of our colonies respectively, where such person shall reside, and also give security to observe such regulations as we shall at any time think fit, by ourselves or commissaries, to be appointed for this purpose, to direct and appoint for the benefit of the said trade; and we do hereby authorize, enjoin and require the Governors and Commanders in chief of all our colonies respectively, as well those under our immediate government, as those under the government and direction of proprietaries, to grant such licences without fee or reward, taking especial care to insert therein a condition that such licence shall be void, and the security forfeited, in case the person to whom the same is granted shall refuse or neglect to observe such regulations as we shall think proper to prescribe as aforesaid.

And we do hereby authorize, enjoin, and require the Governors and Commanders in Chief of all our Colonies respectively, as well those under Our immediate Government as those under the Government and Direction of Proprietaries, to grant such Licences without Fee or Reward, taking especial Care to insert therein a Condition, that such Licence shall be void, and the Security forfeited in case the Person to whom the same is granted shall refuse or neglect to observe such Regulations as We shall think proper to prescribe as aforesaid.

And we do further expressly conjoin and require all Officers whatever, as well Military as those Employed in the Management and Direction of Indian Affairs, within the Territories reserved as aforesaid for the use of the said Indians, to seize and apprehend all Persons whatever, who standing charged with Treason, Misprisions of Treason, Murders, or other Felonies or Misdemeanors, shall fly from Justice and take Refuge in the said Territory, and to send them under a proper guard to the Colony where the Crime was committed of which they, stand accused, in order to take their Trial for the same.

Given at our Court, at St. James's the 7th. day of October, one thousand, seven hundred and sixty-three, in the third year of our reign.

GOD SAVE THE KING

Samuel Seabury (as "A. W. Farmer"): A View of the Controversy between Great Britain and Her Colonies

1774

Document Text

Sir,

You have done me the honour "to bestow some notice upon" a little pamphlet which I lately published, entitled, Free Thoughts on the Proceedings of the Continental Congress, in a Piece which you call, A full Vindication of the Measures of the Congress, from the Calumnies of their Enemies. My present business shall be to examine your Vindication, and see whether it fully exculpates the measures of the Congress, from the charges brought against them by the friends of order and good government. This task I shall endeavour to perform, with all that freedom of thought and expression, which, as an Englishman I have a right to; and which never shall be wrested from me, either by yourself or the Congress.

I freely own, that I wrote and published the Free Thoughts with a design to "diminish the influence, and prevent the effects of the decisions" of the Congress. You speak of the impotence of such attempts; of the general indignation with which they are treated; you say "that no material ill consequences (i.e. to your party) can be dreaded from them." Why then did you take the pains to write so long, so elaborate a pamphlet, to justify decisions against whose influence none but impotent attempts had been made?—to prevent ill consequences which were not to be dreaded?—You felt, Sir, the force of the stubborn facts exhibited to the view of the public in the Free Thoughts: You perceived the ground on which the decrees of the Congress were founded, to be hollow and ready to fall in: you was willing to prop it up at any rate. You knew, that at the bar of impartial reason, and common sense, the conduct of the Congress must be condemned. You was too much interested, too deeply engaged in party views and party heats, to bear this with patience. You had no remedy but artifice, sophistry, misrepresentation and abuse: These are your weapons, and these you wield like an old experienced practitioner....

I, who am a plain Farmer, though of some education, have no manner of inclination to dispute the prize of Wit and Ridicule, with the panegyrist of the late all-accomplished Congress. You, Sir, shall bear off the palm, unrivalled, unenvied by me....

You begin your vindication with such an air of importance, and such pomposity of expression, as I scarce ever met with before.—"It was hardly to be expected that any man could be so presumptuous, as openly to controvert the equity, wisdom and authority of the measures adopted by the Congress: an assembly truly respectable on every account!—whether we consider the characters of the men, who composed it; the number and dignity of their constituents, or the important ends for which they were appointed."—Mere explosions of the wind of vanity! Three grains of consideration would have prevented such a sentence from ever seeing the light.

It has ever been esteemed the privilege of Englishmen to canvass freely, the proceedings of every branch of the legislature; to examine into all public measures; to point out the errors that are committed in the administration of the government, and to censure without fear the conduct of all persons in public stations, whose conduct shall appear to deserve it. The exercise of this right has always been considered as one of the grand pillars which support our present happy constitution. . . . Nor is this privilege exercised with less freedom in America than England. . . .

The Congress, Sir, was founded in sedition; its decisions are supported by tyranny; and is it presumption to controvert its authority? . . .

I have no inclination to scrutinize the characters of men, who composed the Congress. It is not the dignity of their private characters, but their public conduct as Delegates that comes under my examination. The manner in which they were chosen was subversive of all law, and of the very constitution of the province. After they had met they were only a popular assembly, without check or controul, and therefore unqualified to make laws, or to pass ordinances. Upon supposition that they had been chosen by all the people with one voice, they could be only the servants of the people; and every individual must have had a right to animadvert on their conduct, and to have censured it where he thought it wrong. We think, Sir, that we have a double right to do so, seeing they were chosen by a party only, and have endeavoured to tyrannize over the whole people.

You seem to think it very wrong that the Delegates should be called to any account, because "we did not, especially in this province, circumscribe them by any fixed boundary, and therefore as they cannot be said to have exceeded the limits of their authority, their act must be esteemed the act of their constituents."—Above you had said that "their decrees are binding upon all, and demand a religious observance." A little below you make them their own judges, whether they have done right or not. And you represent it as no small degree of arrogance and self-sufficiency for any individual to oppose his private sentiments to their united counsels.

I have looked at this paragraph at least ten times, and every time with astonishment. It is so superlatively arrogant and impudent, that I confess myself at a loss what to say to it. And here, least I should grow angry and forget it, I must observe once for all, that I verily believe the New-York Delegates were some of the very best who attended the Congress.

I have been informed that they, for a long time, opposed the violent measures that were in agitation. I honour them for this opposition; and should almost have adored them, had they preserved their integrity to the end.—But evil communications corrupt good manners. Let no honest man hereafter trust himself at a Philadelphia Congress!

Not a hundredth part of the people of this province, Sir, had any vote in sending the Delegates, and do you imagine that they would take the trouble to circumscribe them, when they did not chuse to have any thing to do with them? The juntos indeed who sent them, acted the same foolish part in not circumscribing them, that they did in chusing them. But supposing all the people in the province had joined in sending them uncircumscribed: Were the Delegates at liberty to do as they pleased? To pursue the most violent measures? To stop up every avenue of accommodation with Great-Britain? And render our state ten times worse than they found it? . . .

Do you think, Sir, that because the Delegates were chosen by a party, that therefore they are accountable only to the party who chose them? You deceive yourself if you do. . . .

I wish you had explicitly declared to the public your ideas of the natural rights of mankind. Man in a state of nature may be considered as perfectly free from all restraints of law and government: And then the weak must submit to the strong. From such a state, I confess, I have a violent aversion. I think the form of government we lately enjoyed a much more eligible state to live in: And cannot help regretting our having lost it, by the equity, wisdom, and authority of the Congress, who have introduced in the room of it, confusion and violence; where all must submit to the power of a mob.

You have taken some pains to prove what would readily have been granted you—that liberty is a very good thing, and slavery a very bad thing. But then I must think that liberty under a King, Lords and Commons is as good as liberty under a republican Congress: And that slavery under a republican Congress is as bad, at least, as slavery under a King, Lords and Commons: And upon the whole, that liberty under the supreme authority and protection of Great-Britain, is infinitely preferable to slavery under an American Congress. I will also agree with you, "that Americans are intitled to freedom." I will go further: I will own and acknowledge that not only Americans, but Africans, Europeans, Asiaticks, all men, of all countries and degrees, of all sizes and complexions, have a right to as much freedom as is consistent with the security of civil society. . . .

But when you assert that "since Americans have not by any act of theirs impowered the British parliament to make laws for them, it follows they can have no just authority to do it," you advance a position subversive of that dependence which all colonies must, from their very nature, have on the mother country. . . .

Now the dependence of the colonies on the mother-country has ever been acknowledged. It is an impropriety of speech to talk of an independent colony. The words independency and colony, convey contradictory ideas: much like killing and sparing. As soon as a colony becomes independent on its parent state, it ceases to be any longer a colony; just as when you kill a sheep, you cease to spare him. The British colonies make a part of the British Empire....

If therefore the colony of New-York be a part of the British dominions, the colony of New-York is subject, and dependent on the supreme legislative authority of Great-Britain....

The position that we are bound by no laws to which we have not consented, either by ourselves, or our representatives, is a novel position, unsupported by any authoratative record of the British constitution, ancient or modern. It is republican in its very nature, and tends to the utter subversion of the English monarchy.

This position has arisen from an artful change of terms. To say that an Englishman is not bound by any laws, but those to which the representatives of the nation have given their consent, is to say what is true: But to say that an Englishman is bound by no laws but those to which he hath consented in person, or by his representative, is saying what never was true, and never can be true. A great part of the people in England have no vote in the choice of representatives, and therefore are governed by laws to which they never consented either by themselves or by their representatives.

The right of colonists to exercise a legislative power, is no natural right. They derive it not from nature, but from the indulgence or grant of the parent state, whose subjects they were when the colony was settled, and by whose permission and assistance they made the settlement....

And every man who endeavours to accelerate the independency of the colonies on the British parliament endeavours to accelerate the ruin of the British empire.

To talk of being liege subjects to King George, while we disavow the authority of parliament is another piece of whiggish nonsense. I love my King as well as any whig in America or England either, and am as ready to yield him all lawful submission... .If we obey the laws of the King, we obey the laws of the parliament. If we disown the authority of the parliament, we disown the authority of the King. There is no medium without ascribing powers to the King which the constitution knows nothing of:—without making him superior to the laws, and setting him above all restraint. These are some of the ridiculous absurdities of American whiggism....

You appeal to "our charters, the express conditions on which our progenitors relinquished their native countries, and came to settle in this," and our charters you say, "preclude every claim of ruling and taxing us without our assent." Did you examine all the charters of the different colonies, before you made this bold assertion? I fear you did not read one of them. . . .

The first charter granted by the crown of England, for the purpose of colonization, is that of King James the first to the two Virginia companies. This, as it is explained and enlarged by another charter, dated only three years after, has the following clauses:—
That the Governor and other magistrates and officers to be appointed by a Council residing in London, are vested with full and absolute power and authority to correct, punish and pardon, govern and rule all such the subjects of us, our heirs and successors, as shall from time to time adventure themselves in any voyage thither; . . . so always as the said statutes, ordinances and proceedings as near as conveniently may be, be agreeable to the laws, statutes, government and policy of this our realm of England. . . .

The territory granted by these charters to the two Virginia companies, extended from the latitude 34 to the latitude 45, which includes the whole country from the south boundary of Virginia to the frontiers of Nova-Scotia: and the first settlers in that part of the territory, now called New-England, settled under those very charters, having purchased the right so to do from one of these companies.

We find, also, that the New-England company's having levied money on the inhabitants, which their charter gave them no right to do, was one of the principal acts of delinquency alledged in the writ of *feri facias*, issued against their charter in the 36th year of Charles the second, and upon which judgment was given in the Court of King's-Bench against the Governor and company of that colony, and their charter, thereon, taken away. And in their new charter granted by King William and Queen Mary, the power to levy taxes is restrained to provincial and local purposes only, and to be exercised over such only as are inhabitants and proprietors of the said province. . . .

These extracts abundantly prove that the colony charters by no means imply an independence on the supreme legislative authority of Great-Britain: they prove also, that you, Sir, was too hasty when you asserted, that "our charters precluded every claim of ruling and taxing us without our assent." Great-Britain still retains the power of binding the colonies by such laws as she shall think necessary to secure and preserve the dependence of the colonies on the mother country;— to promote their particular welfare, or the welfare of the whole empire collectively. . . .

If it be said, that admitting the foregoing reasoning and authorities, yet the right of taxation will not follow, let it be considered, that in every government, legislation and taxation, or the right of raising a revenue, must be conjoined. If you divide them, you weaken, and finally destroy the government; for no government can long subsist without power to raise the supplies necessary for its defence and administration. . . .Government implies, not only a power of making and enforcing laws, but defence and protection. Now protection implies tribute. Those that share in the protection of any government, are in reason and duty, bound to maintain and support the government that protects them: Otherwise they destroy their own protection; or else they throw an unjust burthen on their fellow-subjects, which they ought to bear in common with them....

The authority of the British Parliament, that is, of the supreme sovereign authority of the British empire, over the colonies, and its right to raise a proportional part of its revenue, for the support of its government, in the colonies, being established; it is to be considered, what is the most reasonable and equitable method of doing it....

Good policy will require, that the heavier duties be laid upon articles of luxury, especially foreign ones: and that as little as possible be laid upon the raw materials for manufactures, and upon our own exports.

The right of the British parliament to regulate the trade of the whole empire has been fully acknowledged by some of the warmest advocates for American liberty....

When it is considered, that Great Britain is a maritime power; that the present flourishing state of her trade, and of the trade of her colonies, depends in a great measure, upon the protection which they receive from her navy; that her own security depends upon her navy; and that it is principally a naval protection that we receive from her, there will appear a peculiar propriety in laying the chief burden of supporting her navy upon her commerce, and in requesting us to bear a part of the expence, proportional to our ability, and to that protection and security which we receive from it....

Our assemblies, from the very nature of things, can have but a legated, subordinate, and local authority of legislation. Their power of making laws in conjunction with the other branches of the legislature, cannot extend beyond the limits of the province to which they belong. Their authority must be subordinate to the supreme sovereign authority of the nation, or there is imperium in imperio: two sovereign authorities in the same state; which is a contradiction. Every thing that relates to the internal policy and government of the province which they represent comes properly before them, whether they be matters of law or revenue. But all laws relative to the empire in general, or to all the colonies conjunctively, or which regulates the trade of any particular colony, in order to make it compatible with the general good of the whole empire, must be left to the parliament. There is no other authority which has a right to make such regulations, or weight sufficient to carry them into execution.

Our Assemblies are also the true, proper, legal guardians of our rights, privileges and liberties. If any laws of the British Parliament are thought oppressive; or if, in the administration of the British government, any unnecessary or unreasonable burthen be laid upon us, they are the proper persons to seek for redress: And they are the most likely to succeed. They have the legal and constitutional means in their hands. They are the real not the pretended representatives of the people. They are bodies known, and acknowledged by the public laws of the empire. Their representations will be attended to, and their remonstrances heard....

A great part of the people in England, a considerable number of people in this province, are bound by laws, and taxed without their consent, or the consent of their representatives: for representatives they have none, unless the absurd position of a virtual representation be admitted. These people may object to the present mode of government. They may say, that they have nothing that they can call their own. That if they may be taxed a penny without their consent, they may be taxed a pound; and so on. You will think it a sufficient security to these people, that the representatives of the nation or province cannot hurt them, without hurting themselves; because, they cannot tax them, without taxing themselves. This security however may not be so effectual as at first may be imagined. The rich are never taxed so much in proportion to their estates as the poor: And even an equal proportion of that tax which a rich man can easily pay, may be a heavy burthen to a poor man. But the same security that these people have against being ruined by the representatives of the nation, or province where they live; the same security have we against being ruined by the British parliament. They cannot hurt us without hurting themselves....

But the colonies have become so considerable by the increase of their inhabitants and commerce, and by the improvement of their lands, that they seem incapable of being governed in the same lax and precarious manner as formerly. They are arrived to that mature state of manhood which requires a different, and more exact policy of ruling, than was necessary in their infancy and childhood. They want, and are entitled to, a fixed determinate constitution of their own. A constitution which shall unite them firmly with Great-Britain, and with one another....

Every man who wishes well, either to America or Great-Britain, must wish to see a hearty and firm union subsisting between them, and between every part of the British empire. The first object of his desire will be to heal the unnatural breach that now subsists, and to accomplish a speedy reconciliation. All parties declare the utmost willingness to live in union with Great-Britain. They profess the utmost loyalty to the King; the warmest affection to their fellow-subjects in England, Ireland, and the West-Indies, and their readiness to do every thing to promote their welfare, that can reasonably be expected from them. Even those republicans, who with the destruction of every species and appearance of monarchy in the world, find it necessary to put on a fair face, and make the same declaration.

What steps, Sir, I beseech you, has the Congress taken to accomplish these good purposes? Have they fixed any determined point for us to aim at? they have, and the point marked out by them, is, absolute independence on Great-Britain;—a perfect discharge from all subordination to the supreme authority of the British empire.—Have they proposed any method of cementing our union with the mother country? Yes, but a queer one, viz. to break off all dealings and intercourse with her.—Have they done any thing to shew their love and affection to their fellow-subjects in England, Ireland, and the West-Indies?—Undoubtedly they have,—they have endeavoured to starve them all to death.—Is this "Equity?" Is this "Wisdom?"—Then murder is equity, and folly, wisdom.

I will here, Sir, venture to deliver my sentiments upon the line that ought to be drawn between the supremacy of Great-Britain, and the dependency of the Colonies. And I shall do it with the more boldness, because, I know it to be agreeable to the opinions of many of the warmest advocates for America, both in England and in the colonies, in the time of the stamp-act.—I imagine that if all internal taxation be vested in our own legislatures, and the right of regulating trade by duties, bounties, &c. be left in the power of the Parliament; and also the right of enacting all general laws for the good of all the colonies, that we shall have all the security for our rights, liberties and property, which human policy can give us: The dependence of the colonies on the mother country will be fixed on a firm foundation; the sovereign authority of Parliament, over all the dominions of the empire will be established, and the mother-country and all her colonies will be knit together, in ONE GRAND, FIRM, AND COMPACT BODY....

A. W. Farmer.

December 24, 1774.

Olive Branch Petition

1775

Document Text

To the King's Most Excellent Majesty.

Most Gracious Sovereign: We, your Majesty's faithful subjects of the Colonies of New-Hampthire, Massachusetts-Bay, Rhode-Island and Providence Plantations, Connecticut, New-York, New-Jersey, Pennsylvania, the Counties of Newcastle, Kent, and Sussex, on Delaware, Maryland, Virginia, North Carolina, and South Carolina, in behalf of ourselves and the inhabitants of these Colonies, who have deputed us to represent them in General Congress, entreat your Majesty's gracious attention to this our humble petition.

The union between our Mother Country and these Colonies, and the energy of mild and just Government, produced benefits so remarkably important, and afforded such an assurance of their permanency and increase, that the wonder and envy of other nations were excited, while they beheld Great Britain rising to a power the most extraordinary the world had ever known.

Her rivals, observing that there was no probability of this happy connexion being broken by civil dissensions, and apprehending its future effects if left any longer undisturbed, resolved to prevent her receiving such continual and formidable accessions of wealth and strength, by checking the growth of those settlements from which they were to be derived.

In the prosecution of this attempt, events so unfavourable to the design took place, that every friend to the interest of Great Britain and these Colonies, entertained pleasing and reasonable expectations of seeing an additional force and exertion immediately given to the operations of the union hitherto experienced, by an enlargement of the dominions of the Crown, and the removal of ancient and warlike enemies to a greater distance.

At the conclusion, therefore, of the late war, the most glorious and advantageous that ever had been carried on by British arms, your loyal Colonists having contributed to its success by such repeated and strenuous exertions as frequently procured them the distinguished approbation of your Majesty, of the late King, and of Parliament, doubted not but that they should be permitted, with the rest of the Empire, to share in the blessings of peace, and the emoluments of victory and conquest.

While these recent and honourable acknowledgments of their merits remained on record in the Journals and acts of that august Legislature, the Parliament, undefaced by the imputation or even the suspicion of any offence, they were alarmed by a new system of statutes and regulations adopted for the administration of the Colonies, that filled their minds with the most painful fears and jealousies; and, to their inexpressible astonishment, perceived the danger of a foreign quarrel quickly succeeded by domestick danger, in their judgment of a more dreadful kind.

Nor were these anxieties alleviated by any tendency in this system to promote the welfare of their Mother Country. For though its effects were more immediately felt by them, yet its influence appeared to be injurious to the commerce and prosperity of Great Britain.

We shall decline the ungrateful task of describing the irksome variety of artifices practised by many of your Majesty's Ministers, the delusive pretences, fruitless terrours, and unavailing severities, that have, from time to time, been dealt out by them, in their attempts to execute this impolitick plan, or of tracing through a series of years past the progress of the unhappy differences between Great Britain and these Colonies, that have flowed from this fatal source.

Your Majesty's Ministers, persevering in their measures, and proceeding to open hostilities for enforcing them, have compelled us to arm in our own defence, and have engaged us in a controversy so peculiarly abhorrent to the affections of your still faithful Colonists, that when we consider whom we must oppose in this contest, and if it continues, what may be the consequences, our own particular misfortunes are accounted by us only as parts of our distress. Knowing to what violent resentments and incurable animosities civil discords are apt to exasperate and inflame the contending parties, we think ourselves required by indispensable obligations to Almighty God, to your Majesty, to our fellow-subjects, and to ourselves, immediately to use all the means in our power, not incompatible with our safety, for stopping the further effusion of blood, and for averting the impending calamities that threaten the British Empire.

Thus called upon to address your Majesty on affairs of such moment to America, and probably to all your Dominions, we are earnestly desirous of performing this office with the utmost deference for your Majesty; and we therefore pray, that your Majesty's royal magnanimity and benevolence may make the most favourable constructions of our expressions on so uncommon an occasion. Could we represent in their full force the sentiments that agitate the minds of us your dutiful subjects, we are persuaded your Majesty would ascribe any seeming deviation from reverence in our language, and even in our conduct, not to any reprehensible intention, but to the impossibility of reconciling the usual appearances of respect with a just attention to our own preservation against those artful and cruel enemies who abuse your royal confidence and authority, for the purpose of effecting our destruction.

Attached to your Majesty's person, family, and Government, with all devotion that principle and affection can inspire; connected with Great Britain by the strongest ties that can unite societies, and deploring every event that tends in any degree to weaken them, we solemnly assure your Majesty, that we not only most ardently desire the former harmony between her and these Colonies may be restored, but that a concord may be established between them upon so firm a basis as to perpetuate its blessings, uninterrupted by any future dissensions, to succeeding generations in both countries, and to transmit your Majesty's name to posterity, adorned with that signal and lasting glory that has attended the memory of those illustrious personages, whose virtues and abilities have extricated states from dangerous convulsions, and, by securing happiness to others, have erected the most noble and durable monuments to their own fame.

We beg leave further to assure your Majesty, that notwithstanding the sufferings of your loyal Colonists during the course of this present controversy, our breasts retain too tender a regard for the kingdom from which we derive our origin, to request such a reconciliation as might, in any manner, be inconsistent with her dignity or her welfare. These, related as we are to her, honour and duty, as well as inclination, induce us to support and advance; and the apprehensions that now oppress our hearts with unspeakable grief, being once removed, your Majesty will find your faithful subjects on this Continent ready and willing at all times, as they have ever been, with their lives and fortunes, to assert and maintain the rights and interests of your Majesty, and of our Mother Country.

We therefore beseech your Majesty, that your royal authority and influence may be graciously interposed to procure us relief from our afflicting fears and jealousies, occasioned by the system before-mentioned, and to settle peace through every part of our Dominions, with all humility submitting to your Majesty's wise consideration, whether it may not be expedient, for facilitating those important purposes, that your Majesty be pleased to direct some mode, by which the united applications of your faithful Colonists to the Throne, in pursuance of their common counsels, may be improved into a happy and permanent reconciliation; and that, in the mean time, measures may be taken for preventing the further destruction of the lives of your Majesty's subjects; and that such statutes as more immediately distress any of your Majesty's Colonies, may be repealed.

For such arrangements as your Majesty's wisdom can form for collecting the united sense of your American people, we are convinced your Majesty would receive such satisfactory proofs of the disposition of the Colonists towards their Sovereign and Parent State, that the wished for opportunity would soon be restored to them, of evincing the sincerity of their professions, by every testimony of devotion becoming the most dutiful subjects, and the most affectionate Colonists.

That your Majesty may enjoy a long and prosperous reign, and that your descendants may govern your Dominions with honour to themselves and happiness to their subjects, is our sincere prayer.

Proclamation by the King for Suppressing Rebellion and Sedition

1775

Document Text

August 23, 1775

Whereas many of our subjects in divers parts of our Colonies and Plantations in North America, misled by dangerous and ill designing men, and forgetting the allegiance which they owe to the power that has protected and supported them; after various disorderly acts committed in disturbance of the public peace, to the obstruction of lawful commerce, and to the oppression of our loyal subjects carrying on the same; have at length proceeded to open and avowed rebellion, by arraying themselves in a hostile manner, to withstand the execution of the law, and traitorously preparing, ordering and levying war against us: And whereas, there is reason to apprehend that such rebellion hath been much promoted and encouraged by the traitorous correspondence, counsels and comfort of divers wicked and desperate persons within this realm:

To the end therefore, that none of our subjects may neglect or violate their duty through ignorance thereof, or through any doubt of the protection which the law will afford to their loyalty and zeal, we have thought fit, by and with the advice of our Privy Council, to issue our Royal Proclamation, hereby declaring, that not only all our Officers, civil and military, are obliged to exert their utmost endeavors to suppress such rebellion, and to bring the traitors to justice, but that all our subjects of this Realm, and the dominionsthereunto belonging, are bound by law to be aiding and assisting in the suppression of such rebellion, and to disclose and make known all traitorous conspiracies and attempts against us our crown and dignity; and we do accordingly strictly charge and command all our Officers, as well civil as military, and all others our obedient and loyal subjects, to use their utmost endeavors to withstand and suppress such rebellion, and to disclose and make known all treasons and traitorous conspiracies which they shall know to be against us, our crown and dignity; and for that purpose, that they transmit to one of our principal Secretaries of State, or other proper officer, due and full information of all persons who shall be found carrying on correspondence with, or in any manner or degree aiding or abetting the persons now in open arms and rebellion against our Government, within any of our Colonies and Plantations in North America, in order to bring to condign punishment the authors, perpetrators, and abetters of such traitorous designs.

Given at our Court at St. James's the twenty-third day of August, one thousand seven hundred and seventy-five, in the fifteenth year of our reign.

God save the King.

The Second Continental Congress Responds to King George III's Proclamation of Rebellion

1775

Document Text

We, the Delegates of the thirteen United Colonies in North America, have taken into our most serious consideration, a Proclamation issued from the Court of St. James's on the Twenty-Third day of August last. The name of Majesty is used to give it a sanction and influence; and, on that account, it becomes a matter of importance to wipe off, in the name of the people of these United Colonies, the aspersions which it is calculated to throw upon our cause; and to prevent, as far as possible, the undeserved punishments, which it is designed to prepare, for our friends. We are accused of "forgetting the allegiance which we owe to the power that has protected and sustained us." Why all this ambiguity and obscurity in what ought to be so plain and obvious, as that he who runs may read it? What allegiance is it that we forget? Allegiance to Parliament? We never owed—we never owned it. Allegiance to our King? Our words have ever avowed it,—our conduct has ever been consistent with it. We condemn, and with arms in our hands,—a resource which Freemen will never part with,—we oppose the claim and exercise of unconstitutional powers, to which neither the Crown nor Parliament were ever entitled. By the British Constitution, our best inheritance, rights, as well as duties, descend upon us: We cannot violate the latter by defending the former: We should act in diametrical opposition to both, if we permitted the claims of the British Parliament to be established, and the measures pursued in consequence of those claims to be carried into execution among us. Our sagacious ancestors provided mounds against the inundation of tyranny and lawless power on one side, as well as against that of faction and licentiousness on the other. On which side has the breach been made? Is it objected against us by the most inveterate and the most uncandid of our enemies, that we have opposed any of the just prerogatives of the Crown, or any legal exertion of those prerogatives? Why then are we accused of forgetting our allegiance? We have performed our duty: We have resisted in those cases, in which the right to resist is stipulated as expressly on our part, as the right to govern is, in other cases, stipulated on the part of the Crown. The breach of allegiance is removed from our resistance as far as tyranny is removed from legal government. It is alledged, that "we have proceeded to an open and avowed rebellion." In what does this rebellion consist. It is thus described—"Arraying ourselves in hostile manner, to withstand the execution of the law, and traiterously preparing, ordering, and levying war against the King." We know of no laws binding upon us, but such as have been transmitted to us by our ancestors, and such as have been consented to by ourselves, or our representatives elected for that purpose. What laws, stampt with these characters, have we withstood? We have indeed defended them; and we will risque every thing, do every thing, and suffer every thing in their defence. To support our laws, and our liberties established by our laws, we have prepared, ordered, and levied war: But is this traiterously, or against the King? We view him as the Constitution represents him. That tells us he can do no wrong. The cruel and illegal attacks, which we oppose, have no foundation in the royal authority. We will not, on our part, lose the distinction between the King and his Ministers: happy would it have been for some former, had it been always preserved on that part of the Crown.

Besides all this, we observe, on this part of the proclamation, that "rebellion" is a term undefined and unknown in the law; it might have been expected that a proclamation, which by the British constitution has no other operation than merely that of enforcing what is already law, would have had a known legal basis to have rested upon. A correspondence between the inhabitants of Great Britain and their brethren in America, produced, in better times, much satisfaction to individuals, and much advantage to the public. By what criterion shall one, who is unwilling to break off this correspondence, and is, at the same time, anxious not to expose himself to the dreadful consequences threatened in this proclamation—by what criterion shall he regulate his conduct? He is admonished not to carry on correspondence with the persons now in rebellion in the colonies. How shall he ascertain who are in rebellion, and who are not? He consults the law to learn the nature of the supposed crime: the law is silent upon the subject. This, in a country where it has been often said, and formerly with justice, that the government is by law, and not by men, might render him perfectly easy. But proclamations have been sometimes dangerous engines in the hands of those in power; Information is commanded to be given to one of the Secretaries of states, of all persons "who shall be found carrying on correspondence with the persons in rebellion, in order to bring to condign punishment the authors, perpetrators, or abettors, of such dangerous designs." Let us suppose, for a moment, that some persons in the colonies are in rebellion, and that those who carry on correspondence with them, might learn by some rule, which Britons are bound to know, how to discriminate them; Does it follow that all correspondence with them deserves to be punished? It might have been intended to apprize them of their danger, and to reclaim them from their crimes. By what law does a correspondence with a criminal transfer or communicate his guilt? We know that those who aid and adhere to the King's enemies, and those who correspond with them in order to enable enable them to carry their designs into effect, are criminal in the eye of the law. But the law goes no farther. Can proclamations, according to the principles of reason and justice, and the constitution, go farther than the law?

But, perhaps the principles of reason and justice, and the constitution will not prevail: Experience suggests to us the doubt: If they should not, we must resort to arguments drawn from very different source. We, therefore, in the name of the people of these United Colonies, and by authority, according to the purest maxims of representation, derived from them, declare, that whatever punishment shall be inflicted upon any persons in the power of our enemies for favouring, aiding, or abetting the cause of American liberty, shall be retaliated in the same kind, and the same degree upon those in our power, who have favoured, aided, or abetted, or shall favour, aid, or abet the system of ministerial oppression. The essential difference between our cause, and that of our enemies, might justify a severer punishment: The law of retaliation will unquestionably warrant one equally severe.

We mean not, however, by this declaration, to occasion or to multiply punishments; Our sole view is to prevent them. In this unhappy and unnatural controversy, in which Britons fight against Britons, and the descendants of Britons, let the calamities immediately incident to a civil war suffice. We hope additions will not from wantonness be made to them on one side: We shall regret the necessity, if laid under the necessity, of making them on the other.

Nzinga Mbemba: Appeal to the King of Portugal

1526

Document Text

July 6, 1526

To the very powerful and excellent prince Dom João, our brother.

On the 20th of June just past, we received word that a trading ship from your highness had just come to our port of Sonyo. We were greatly pleased by that arrival for it had been many days since a ship had come to our kingdom, for by it we would get news of your highness, which many times we had desired to know, . . . and likewise as there was a great and dire need for wine and flour for the holy sacrament; and of this we had had no great hope for we have the same need frequently. And that, sir, arises from the great negligence of your highness's officials toward us and toward shipping us those things. . . .

Sir, your highness should know how our kingdom is being lost in so many ways that we will need to provide the needed cure, since this is caused by the excessive license given by your agents and officials to the men and merchants who come to this kingdom to set up shops with goods and many things which have been prohibited by us, and which they spread throughout our kingdoms and domains in such abundance that many of our vassals, whose submission we could once rely on, now act independently so as to get the things in greater abundance than we ourselves; whom we had formerly held content and submissive and under our vassalage and jurisdiction, so it is doing a great harm not only to the service of God, but also to the security and peace of our kingdoms and state.

And we cannot reckon how great the damage is, since every day the mentioned merchants are taking our people, sons of the land and the sons of our noblemen and vassals and our relatives, because the thieves and men of bad conscience grab them so as to have the things and wares of this kingdom that they crave; they grab them and bring them to be sold. In such a manner, sir, has been the corruption and deprivation that our land is becoming completely depopulated, and your highness should not deem this good nor in your service. And to avoid this we need from these kingdoms [of yours] no more than priests and a few people to teach in schools, and no other goods except wine and flour for the holy sacrament, which is why we beg of your highness to help and assist us in this matter. Order your agents to send here neither merchants nor wares, because it is our will that in these kingdoms there should not be any dealings in slaves nor outlet for them, for the reasons stated above. Again we beg your highness's agreement, since otherwise we cannot cure such manifest harm. May Our Lord in His mercy have your highness always under His protection and may you always do the things of His holy service. I kiss your hands many times.

From our city of Kongo....

The King, Dom Afonso

October 18, 1526

Very high and very powerful prince King of Portugal, our brother,

Sir, your highness has been so good as to promise us that anything we need we should ask for in our letters, and that everything will be provided. And so that there may be peace and health of our kingdoms, by God's will, in our lifetime. And as there are among us old folks and people who have lived for many days, many and different diseases happen so often that we are pushed to the ultimate extremes. And the same happens to our children, relatives, and people, because this country lacks physicians and surgeons who might know that proper cures for such diseases, as well as pharmacies and drugs to make them better. And for this reason many of those who have been already confirmed and instructed in the things of the holy faith of Our Lord Jesus Christ perish and die. And the rest of the people for the most part cure themselves with herbs and sticks and other ancient methods, so that they live putting all their faith in these herbs and ceremonies, and die believing that they are saved; and this serves God poorly.

And to avoid such a great error, I think, and inconvenience, since it is from God and from your highness that all the good and the drugs and medicines have come to us for our salvation, we ask your merciful highness to send us two physicians and two pharmacists and one surgeon, so that they man come with their pharmacies and necessary things to be in our kingdoms, for we have extreme need of each and every one of them. We will be very good and merciful to them, since send by your highness, their work and coming should be for good. We ask your highness as a great favor to do this for us, because besides being good in itself it is in the service of God as we have said above.

Moreover, sir, in our kingdoms there is another great inconvenience which is of little service to God, and this is that many of our people, out of great desire for the wares and things of your kingdoms, which are brought here by your people, and in order to satisfy their disordered appetite, seize many of our people, freed and exempt men. And many times noblemen and the sons of noblemen, and our relatives are stolen, and they take them to be sold to the white men who are in our kingdoms and take them hidden or by night, so that they are not recognized. And as soon as they are taken by the white men, they are immediately ironed and branded with fire. And when they are carried off to be embarked, if they are caught by our guards, the whites allege that they have bought them and cannot say from whom, so that it is our duty to do justice and to restore to the free their freedom. And so they went away offended.

And to avoid such a great evil we passed a law so that every white man living in our kingdoms and wanting to purchase slaves by whatever means should first inform three of our noblemen and officials of our court on whom we rely in this matter, namely Dom Pedro Manipunzo and Dom Manuel Manissaba, our head bailiff, and Gonçalo Pires, our chief supplier, who should investigate if the said slaves are captives or free men, and, if cleared with them, there will be no further doubt nor embargo and they can be taken and embarked. And if they reach the opposite conclusion, they will lose the aforementioned slaves. Whatever favor and license we give them [the white men] for the sake of your highness in this case is because we know that it is in your service too that these slaves are taken from our kingdom; otherwise we should not consent to this for the reasons stated above that we make known completely to your highness so that no one could say the contrary, as they said in many other cases to your highness, so that the care and remembrance that we and this kingdom have should not be withdrawn....

We kiss your hands of your highness many times.

From our city of Kongo, the 18th day of October.

The King, Dom Afonso

Andrew Ure: The Philosophy of Manufactures

1835

Document Text

This island is pre-eminent among civilized nations for the prodigious development of its factory wealth, and has been therefore long viewed with a jealous admiration by foreign powers. This very pre-eminence, however, has been contemplated in a very different light by many influential members of our own community, and has been even denounced by them as the certain origin of innumerable evils to the people, and of revolutionary convulsions to the state. If the affairs of the kingdom be wisely administered, I believe such allegations and fears will prove to be groundless, and to proceed more from the envy of one ancient and powerful order of the commonwealth, towards another suddenly grown into political importance, than from the nature of things.

In the recent discussions concerning our factories, no circumstance is so deserving of remark, as the gross ignorance evinced by our leading legislators and economists, gentlemen well informed in other respects, relative to the nature of those stupendous manufactures which have so long provided the rulers of the kingdom with the resources of war, and a great body of the people with comfortable subsistence; which have, in fact, made this island the arbiter of many nations, and the benefactor of the globe itself. Till this ignorance be dispelled, no sound legislation need be expected on manufacturing subjects....

The blessings which physio-mechanical science has bestowed on society, and the means it has still in store for ameliorating the lot of mankind, have been too little dwelt upon; while, on the other hand, it has been accused of lending itself to the rich capitalists as an instrument for harassing the poor, and of exacting from the operative an accelerated rate of work. It has been said, for example, that the steam-engine now drives the power-looms with such velocity as to urge on their attendant weavers at the same rapid pace; but that the hand-weaver, not being subjected to this restless agent, can throw his shuttle and move his treddles at his convenience. There is, however, this difference in the two cases, that in the factory, every member of the loom is so adjusted, that the driving force leaves the attendant nearly nothing at all to do, certainly no muscular fatigue to sustain, while it procures for him good, unfailing wages, besides a healthy workshop gratis: whereas the non-factory weaver, having everything to execute by muscular exertion, finds the labour irksome, makes in consequence innumerable short pauses, separately of little account, but great when added together; earns therefore proportionally low wages, while he loses his health by poor diet and the dampness of his hovel....

The constant aim and effect of scientific improvement in manufactures are philanthropic, as they tend to relieve the workmen either from niceties of adjustment which exhaust his mind and fatigue his eyes, or from painful repetition of efforts which distort or wear out his frame. At every step of each manufacturing process described in this volume the humanity of science will be manifest. . . .

The term *Factory*, in technology, designates the combined operation of many orders of work-people, adult and young, in tending with assiduous skill a system of productive machines continuously impelled by a central power. This definition in eludes such organizations as cotton-mills, flax-mills, silk-mills, woolen-mills, and certain engineering works; but it excludes those in which the mechanisms do not form a connected series, nor are dependent on one prime mover. Of the latter class, examples occur in iron-works, dye-works, soap-works, brass-foundries, &c. Some authors, indeed have comprehended under the title *factory*, all extensive establishments wherein a number of people co-operate towards a common purpose of art; and would therefore rank breweries, distilleries as well as the workshops of carpenters, turners, coopers, &c. under the factory system. But I conceive that this title, in its strictest sense, involves the idea of a vast automaton, composed of various mechanical and intellectual organs, acting in uninterrupted concert for the production of a common object, all of them being subordinated to a self regulated moving force. If the marshalling of human beings in systematic order for the execution of any technical enterprise were allowed to constitute a factory, this term might embrace every department of civil and military engineering; a latitude of application quite inadmissable.

In its precise acceptation, the Factory system is of recent origin, and may claim England for its birthplace. The mills for throwing silk, or making organzine, which were mounted centuries ago in several of the Italian states, and furtively transferred to this country by Sir Thomas Lombe in 1718, contained indeed certain elements of a factory, and probably suggested some hints of those grander and more complex combinations of self-acting machines, which were first embodied half a century later in our cotton manufacture by Richard Arkwright, assisted by gentlemen of Derby, well acquainted with its celebrated silk establishment. But the spinning of an entangled flock of fibres into a smooth thread, which constitutes the main operation with cotton, is in silk superfluous; being already performed by the unerring instinct of a worm, which leaves to human art the simple task of doubling and twisting its regular filaments. The apparatus requisite for this purpose is more elementary, and calls for few of those gradations of machinery which are needed in the carding, drawing, roving, and spinning processes of a cotton-mill.

When the first water-frames for spinning cotton were erected at Cromford, in the romantic valley of the Derwent, about sixty years ago, mankind were little aware of the mighty revolution which the new system of labour was destined by Providence to achieve, not only in the structure of British society, but in the fortunes of the world at large. Arkwright alone had the sagacity to discern, and the boldness to predict in glowing language, how vastly productive human industry would become, when no longer proportioned in its results to muscular effort, which is by its nature fitful and capricious, but when made to consist in the task of guiding the work of mechanical fingers and arms, regularly impelled with great velocity by some indefatigable physical power. What his judgment so clearly led him to perceive, his energy of will enabled him to realize with such rapidity and success, as would have done honour to the most influential individuals, but were truly wonderful in that obscure and indigent artisan. . . .

The principle of the factory system then is, to substitute mechanical science for hand skill, and the partition of a process into its essential constituents, for the division or graduation of labour among artisans. On the handicraft plan, labour more or less skilled was usually the most expensive element of production . . . but on the automatic plan, skilled labour gets progressively superseded, and will, eventually, be replaced by mere overlookers of machines.

By the infirmity of human nature it happens, that the more skilful the workman, the more self-willed and intractable he is apt to become, and, of course, the less fit a component of a mechanical system, in which, by occasional irregularities, he may do great damage to the whole. The grand object therefore of the modern manufacturer is, through the union of capital and science, to reduce the task of his work-people to the exercise of vigilance and dexterity,— faculties, when concentred [sic] to one process, speedily brought to perfection in the young. In the infancy of mechanical engineering, a machine-factory displayed the division of labour in manifold gradations—the file, the drill, the lathe, having each its different workmen in the order of skill: but the dextrous hands of the filer and driller are now superseded by the planing, the key groove cutting, and the drilling-machines; and those of the iron and brass turners, by the self-acting slide-lathe. . . .

It is, in fact, the constant aim and tendency of every improvement in machinery to supersede human labour altogether, or to diminish its cost, by substituting the industry of women and children for that of men; or that of ordinary labourers for trained artisans. In most of the water-twist, or throstle cotton-mills, the spinning is entirely managed by females of sixteen years and upwards. The effect of substituting the self-acting mule for the common mule, is to discharge the greater part of the men spinners, and to retain adolescents and children. The proprietor of a factory near Stockport states, in evidence to the commissioners, that, by such substitution, he would save 50l£ a week in wages in consequence of dispensing with nearly forty male spinners, at about 25s of wages each. This tendency to employ merely children with watchful eyes and nimble fingers, instead of journeymen of long experience, shows how the scholastic dogma of the division of labor into degrees of skill has been exploded by our enlightened manufacturers. . . .

Machines are of three kinds:—

1. Machines concerned in the production of power.

2. Machines concerned in the transmission and regulation of power.

3. Machines concerned in the application of power to modify the various forms of matter into objects of commerce....

The philosophy of manufactures is well displayed in the economy of power. The value of steam-impelled labour may be inferred from the following statement of facts, communicated to me by an eminent engineer, educated in the school of Bolton and Watt:—A manufacturer in Manchester works a 60-horse Bolton and Watt's steam-engine, at a power of 120 horses during the day, and 60 horses during the night; thus extorting from it an impelling force three times greater than he contracted or paid for. One *steam* horse-power is equivalent to 33,000 pounds avoirdupois, raised one foot high per minute; but an *animal* horse-power is equivalent to only 22,000 pounds raised one foot high per minute, or, in other terms, to drag a canal boat 220 feet per minute, with a force of 100 pounds acting on a spring: therefore a steam horse-power is equivalent in working efficiency to one living horse, and one-half the labour of another. But a horse can work at its full efficiency only eight hours out of the twenty-four, whereas a steam-engine needs no period of repose; and therefore, to make the animal power equal to the physical power, a relay of 1½ fresh horses must be found three times in the twenty-four hours, which amounts to 4½ horses daily. Hence, a common 60-horse steam-engine does the work of 4½ times 60 horses, or of 270 horses. But the above 60-horse steam-engine does one-half more work in 24 hours, or that of 405 living horses!...As to prime cost and superintendence, the animal power would be greatly more expensive than the steam power. There are many engines made by Bolton and Watt, forty years ago, which have continued in constant work all that time with very slight repairs. What a multitude of valuable horses would have been worn out in doing the service of these machines! and what a vast quantity of grain would they have consumed! Had British industry not been aided by Watt's invention, it must have gone on with a retarding pace, in consequence of the increasing cost of motive power, and would, long ere now, have experienced, in the price of horses, and scarcity of waterfalls, an insurmountable barrier to further advancement, could horses, even at the low prices to which their rival, steam, has kept them, be employed to drive a cotton mill at the present day, they would devour all the profits of the manufacturer.

Steam-engines furnish the means not only of their support but of their multiplication. They create a vast demand for fuel; and, while they lend their powerful arms to drain the pits and to raise the coals, they call into employment multitudes of miners, engineers, shipbuilders, and sailors, and cause the construction of canals and railways. Thus therefore, in enabling these rich fields of industry to be cultivated to the utmost, they leave thousands of fine arable fields free for the production of food to man, which must have been otherwise allotted to the food of horses. Steam-engines moreover, by the cheapness and steadiness of their action, fabricate cheap goods, and procure in their exchange a liberal supply of the necessaries and comforts of life produced in foreign lands.

Improvements in the machinery have a three-fold bearing:

1st. They make it possible to fabricate some articles which, but for them, could not be fabricated at all.

2nd. They enable an operative to turn out a greater quantity of work than he could before,—time, labour, and quality of work remaining constant.

3rd. They effect a substitution of labour comparatively unskilled, for that which is more skilled.

Yukichi Fukuzawa: "Good-bye Asia"

1885

Document Text

Transportation has become so convenient these days that once the wind of Western civilization blows to the East, every blade of grass and every tree in the East follow what the Western wind brings. Ancient Westerners and present-day Westerners are from the same stock and are not much different from one another. The ancient ones moved slowly, but their contemporary counterparts more vivaciously at a fast pace. This is possible because present-day Westerners take advantage of the means of transportation available to them. For those of us who live in the Orient, unless we want to prevent the coming of Western civilization with a firm resolve, it is best that we cast our lot with them. If one observes carefully what is going on in today's world, one knows the futility of trying to prevent the onslaught of Western civilization. Why not float with them in the same ocean of civilization, sail the same waves, and enjoy the fruits and endeavors of civilization?

The movement of a civilization is like the spread of measles. Measles in Tokyo start in Nagasaki and come eastward with the spring thaw. We may hate the spread of this communicable disease, but is there any effective way of preventing it? I can prove that it is not possible. In a communicable disease, people receive only damages. In a civilization, damages may accompany benefits, but benefits always far outweigh them, and their force cannot be stopped. This being the case, there is no point in trying to prevent their spread. A wise man encourages the spread and allows our people to get used to its ways.

The opening to the modern civilization of the West began in the reign of Kaei (1848-58). Our people began to discover its utility and gradually and yet actively moved toward its acceptance. However, there was an old-fashioned and bloated government that stood in the way of progress. It was a problem impossible to solve. If the government were allowed to continue, the new civilization could not enter. The modern civilization and Japan's old conventions were mutually exclusive. If we were to discard our old conventions, that government also had to be abolished. We could have prevented the entry of this civilization, but it would have meant loss of our national independence. The struggles taking place in the world civilization were such that they would not allow an Eastern island nation to slumber in isolation. At that point, dedicated men (*shijin*) recognized the principle of "the country is more important than the government," relied on the dignity of the Imperial Household, and toppled the old government to establish a new one. With this, public and the private sectors alike, everyone in our country accepted the modern Western civilization. Not only were we able to cast aside Japan's old conventions, but we also succeeded in creating a new axle toward progress in Asia. Our basic assumptions could be summarized in two words: "Good-bye Asia (*Datsu-a*)."

Japan is located in the eastern extremities of Asia, but the spirit of her people has already moved away from the old conventions of Asia to the Western civilization. Unfortunately for Japan, there are two neighboring countries. One is called China and another Korea. These two peoples, like the Japanese people, have been nurtured by Asiatic political thoughts and mores. It may be that we are different races of people, or it may be due to the differences in our heredity or education; significant differences mark the three peoples. The Chinese and Koreans are more like each other and together they do not show as much similarity to the Japanese. These two peoples do not know how to progress either personally or as a nation. In this day and age with transportation becoming so convenient, they cannot be blind to the manifestations of Western civilization. But they say that what is seen or heard cannot influence the disposition of their minds. Their love affairs with ancient ways and old customs remain as strong as they were centuries ago. In this new and vibrant theater of civilization when we speak of education, they only refer back to Confucianism. As for school education, they can only cite [Mencius's] precepts of humanity, righteousness, decorum, and knowledge. While professing their abhorrence to ostentation, in reality they show their ignorance of truth and principles. As for their morality, one only has to observe their unspeakable acts of cruelty and shamelessness. Yet they remain arrogant and show no sign of self-examination.

In my view, these two countries cannot survive as independent nations with the onslaught of Western civilization to the East. Their concerned citizens might yet find a way to engage in a massive reform, on the scale of our Meiji Restoration, and they could change their governments and bring about a renewal of spirit among their peoples. If that could happen they would indeed be fortunate. However, it is more likely that would never happen, and within a few short years they will be wiped out from the world with their lands divided among the civilized nations. Why is this so? Simply at a time when the spread of civilization and enlightenment (*bummei kaika*) has a force akin to that of measles, China and Korea violate the natural law of its spread. They forcibly try to avoid it by shutting off air from their rooms. Without air, they suffocate to death. It is said that neighbors must extend helping hands to one another because their relations are inseparable. Today's China and Korea have not done a thing for Japan. From the perspectives of civilized Westerners, they may see what is happening in China and Korea and judge Japan accordingly, because of the three countries' geographical proximity. The governments of China and Korea still retain their autocratic manners and do not abide by the rule of law. Westerners may consider Japan likewise as lawless society. Natives of China and Korea are deep in their hocus pocus of nonscientific behavior. Western scholars may think that Japan still remains a country dedicated to the *yin* and *yang* and five elements. Chinese are mean-spirited and shameless, and the chivalry of the Japanese people is lost to the Westerners. Koreans punish their convicts in an atrocious manner, and that is imputed to the Japanese as heartless people. There are many more examples I can cite. It is not different from the case of a righteous man living in a neighborhood of a town known for foolishness, lawlessness, atrocity, and heartlessness. His action is so rare that it is always buried under the ugliness of his neighbors' activities. When these incidents are multiplied, that can affect our normal conduct of diplomatic affairs. How unfortunate it is for Japan.

What must we do today? We do not have time to wait for the enlightenment of our neighbors so that we can work together towards the development of Asia. It is better for us to leave the ranks of Asian nations and cast our lot with civilized nations of the West. As for the way of dealing with China and Korea, no special treatment is necessary just because they happen to be our neighbors. We simply follow the manner of the Westerners in knowing how to treat them. Any person who cherishes a bad friend cannot escape his bad notoriety. We simply erase from our minds our bad friends in Asia.

Yukichi Fukuzawa: Western Civilization as Our Goal

1875

Document Text

In the preceding chapter I argued that such designations as light and good and bad are relative. Now, the concept of "civilization and enlightenment" (*bunmei kaika*) is also a relative one. When we are talking about civilization in the world today, the nations of Europe and the United States of America are the most highly civilized, while the Asian countries, such as Turkey, China, and Japan, may be called semi-developed countries, and Africa and Australia are to be counted as still primitive lands. These designations are common currency all over the world. While the citizens of the nations of the West are the only ones to boast of civilization, the citizens of the semi-developed and primitive lands submit to being designated as such. They rest content with being branded semi-developed or primitive, and there is not one who would take pride in his own country or consider it on a par with nations of the West. This attitude is bad enough. Not only this: The more those with some intelligence become aware of this situation, the more convinced they become of the situation of their own countries; the more convinced they become of the situation of their own countries, the more they awaken to the distance separating them from the nations of the West. They groan, they grieve; some are for learning from the West and imitating it, others are for going it alone and opposing the West. The overriding anxiety of Asian intellectuals today is this one problem to the exclusion of all others. At any rate, the designations "civilized," "semi-developed," and "primitive" have been universally accepted by people all over the globe. Why does everybody accept them? Clearly, because the facts are demonstrable and irrefutable. I shall explain this point further below. For there are stages through which mankind must pass. These may be termed the ages of civilization.

First, there is the stage in which neither dwellings nor supplies of food are stable. Men form communal groups as temporary convenience demands; when that convenience ceases, they pull up stakes and scatter to the four winds. Or even if they settle in a certain region and engage in farming and fishing, they may have enough food and clothing, but they do not yet know how to make tools. And though they are not without writing, they produce no book learning. At this stage man is still unable to be master of his own situation; he cowers before the forces of nature and is dependent on the favors of others, or on the chance vagaries of nature. This is called the stage of primitive man. It is still far from civilization.

Secondly, there is the stage of civilization wherein daily necessities are not lacking, since agriculture has been started on a large scale. Men build houses, form communities, and create the outward semblance of a state. But within this façade there remains very many defects. Though book learning flourishes, there are few who devote themselves to practical learning (*jitsugaku*). Though in human relations sentiments of suspicion and envy run deep, when it comes to discussing the nature of things men lack the courage to raise doubts and ask questions. Men are adept at imitative craftsmanship, but there is a dearth of original production. They know how to cultivate the old, but not how to improve it. There are accepted rules governing society, but slaves of custom that they are, they could never form rules in the true sense. This is called the semi-developed stage. It is not yet civilization in the full sense.

Thirdly, there is the stage in which men subsume the things of the universe with a general structure, but the structure does not bind them. Their spirits enjoy free play and are not credulous of old customs. They act autonomously and do not have to depend upon the arbitrary favors of others. They cultivate their own virtue and refine their own knowledge. They neither yearn for the old nor become complacent about the present. Not resting with small gains, they plan great accomplishments for the future and commit themselves wholeheartedly to their realization. Their path of learning is not vacuous; it has, indeed, invented the principle of invention itself. Their industrial and business ventures prosper day by day to increase the sources of human welfare. Today's wisdom overflows to create the plans of tomorrow. This is what is meant by modern civilization. It has been a leap far beyond the primitive or semi-developed stages.

Now, if we make the above threefold distinction, the differences between civilization, semi-development, and the primitive stage should be clear. However, since these designations are essentially relative, there is nothing to prevent someone who has not seen civilization from thinking that semi-development is the summit of man's development. And, while civilization is civilization relative to the semi-developed stage, the latter, in turn, can be called civilization relative to the primitive stage. Thus, for example, present-day China has to be called semi-developed in comparison with Western countries. But if we compare China with countries of South Africa, or, to take an example more at hand, if we compare the people of mainland Japan with the Ainu, then both China and Japan can be called civilized. Moreover, although we call the nations of the West civilized, they can correctly be honored with this designation only in modern history. And many of them, if we were to be more precise, would fall well short of this designation.

For example, there is no greater calamity in the world than war, and yet the nations of the West are always at war. Robbery and murder are the worst of human crimes; but in the West there are robbers and murderers. There are those who form cliques to vie for the reins of power and who, when deprived of that power, decry the injustice of it all. Even worse, international diplomacy is really based on the art of deception. Surveying the situation as a whole, all we can say is that there is a general prevalence of good over bad, but we can hardly call the situation perfect. When, several thousand years hence, the levels of knowledge and virtue of the peoples of the world will have made great progress (to the point of becoming utopian), the present condition of the nations of the West will surely seem a pitifully primitive stage. Seen in this light, civilization is an open-ended process. We cannot be satisfied with the present level of attainment of the West.

Yes, we cannot be satisfied with the level of civilization attained by the West. But shall we therefore conclude that Japan should reject it? If we did, what other criterion would we have? We cannot rest content with the stage of semi-development; even less can the primitive stage suffice. Since these latter alternatives are to be rejected, we must look elsewhere. But to look to some far-off utopian world thousands of years hence is mere daydreaming. Besides, civilization is not a dead thing; it is something vital and advancing. As such, it must pass through sequences and stages; primitive people advance to semi-developed forms, the semi-developed advance to civilization, and civilization itself is even now in the process of advancing forward. Europe also had to pass through these phases in its evolution to the present level. Hence present-day Europe can only be called the highest level that human intelligence has been able to attain at this juncture in history. Since this is true, in all countries of the world, be they primitive or semi-developed, those who are to give thought to their country's progress in civilization must necessarily take European civilization as the criterion in making arguments, and must weigh the pros and cons of the problem in the light of it. My own criterion throughout this book will be that of Western civilization, and it will be in terms of it that I describe something as good or bad, in terms of it that I find things beneficial or harmful. Therefore let scholars make no mistake about my orientation.

Feng Guifen: "On the Adoption of Western Learning"

ca. 1850

Document Text

... Today the world is 90,000 *li* around. There is no place boats and vehicles do not travel or human power does not reach.... According to Westerners' maps, there are at least one hundred countries in the world. Of the books of these hundred countries, only those from Italy from the time of the end of the Ming and from present-day England, numbering in all several tens, have been translated....

Books on mathematics, mechanics, optics, light, chemistry, and others all contain the ultimate principles of understanding things. Most of this information is unavailable to people in China....

I have heard that with their new methods the Westerners have found that the movements of the earth conform closely to those of the heavens. This can be of assistance in fixing the calendar.... I have heard that the Westerners' method of clearing sand from harbors is very effective.... This can be of assistance to keep the water flowing. Also, for agricultural and sericultural tools, and things required for the various crafts, they mostly use mechanical wheels, which require little energy but accomplish much. These can assist the people to earn their living. Other things beneficial to the national economy and the livelihood of the people should also be used....

There are many intelligent people in China. Surely there are some who, having learned from the barbarians, can surpass them....

The principles of government are derived from learning. In discussing good government, [the famous historian] Sima Qian [Ssu-ma Ch'ien] said, "Take the later kings as models," because they were closer to his own time, and customs, having changed, were more alike, so that their ideas were easy to implement because they were plain and simple. In my humble opinion, at the present time it is also appropriate to say "Learn from the various nations," for they are similar to us and hence their ways are easy to implement. What could be better than to take Chinese ethical principles of human relations and Confucian teachings as the foundation (*ti*) and supplement them with the techniques (*yong*) of wealth and power of the various nations?

Hu Shi: "Our Attitude toward Modern Western Civilization"

1926

Document Text

At present the most unfounded and more harmful distortion is to ridicule Western civilization as materialistic and worship Eastern civilization as spiritut The modern civilization of the West, built on the foundation of the search for human happiness, not only has definitely increased material enjoyment to no small degree, but can also satisfy the spiritual needs of mankind. In philosophy it has applied highly refined methods to the search for truth and to investigation into the vast secrets of nature. In religion and ethics, it has overthrown the religion of superstitions and established a rational belief, has destroyed divine power and established a humanistic religion, has discarded the unknowable Heaven or paradise and directed its efforts to building a paradise among men and Heaven on earth. It has cast aside the arbitrarily asserted transcendence of the individual soul, has utilized to the highest degree the power of man's new imagination and new intellect to promote a new religion and new ethics that are fully socialized, and has endeavored to work for the greatest amount of happiness for the greatest number of people.

The most outstanding characteristic of Eastern civilization is to know contentment, whereas that of Western civilization is not to know contentment.

Contented Easterners are satisfied with their simple life and therefore do not seek to increase their material enjoyment. They are satisfied with ignorance and "not understanding and not knowing" and therefore have devoted no attention to the discovery of truth and the invention of techniques and machinery. They are satisfied with their present lot and environment and therefore do not want to conquer nature but merely [to] be at home with nature and at peace with their lot. They do not want to change systems, but rather to mind their own business. They do not want a revolution, but rather to remain obedient subjects.

The civilization under which people are restricted and controlled by a material environment from which they cannot escape, and under which they cannot utilize human thought and intellectual power to change environment and improve conditions, is the civilization of a lazy and nonprogressive people. It is truly a materialistic civilization. Such civilization can only obstruct but cannot satisfy the spiritual demands of mankind.

Osama bin Laden: Declaration of Jihad against Americans

1996

Document Text

Expel the Polytheists from the Arabian peninsula.

A Letter from Sheikh Osama bin Muhammad bin Laden to his Muslim Brothers across the world, and particularly those in the Arabian peninsula.

Praise be to God. We beseech Him for help and forgiveness. We seek refuge in God from the evil of our souls and our bad deeds. He whom God guides will not go astray, and he whom He leads astray can have no guide. I testify that there is no god but God alone, who has no partners. And I testify that Muhammad is His Servant and Prophet.

"You who believe, be mindful of God, as is His due, and make sure you devote yourselves to Him, to your dying moment."

"People, be mindful of your Lord, who created you from a single soul, and from it created its mate, and from the pair of them spread countless men and women far and wide; be mindful of God, in whose name you make requests of one another. Beware of the severing of ties of kinship: God is always watching over you."

"Believers, be mindful of God, speak in a direct fashion and to good purpose, and He will put your deeds right for you and forgive you your sins. Whoever obeys God and His Messenger will truly achieve a great triumph."

Shu'ayb said: "I cannot succeed without God's help: I trust in Him, and always turn to Him."

Thanks be to God, who said: "[Believers], you are the best community singled out for people: you order what is right, forbid what is wrong, and you believe in God."

And blessings and peace upon His Servant and Prophet, who said: "The people are close to an all-encompassing punishment from God if they see the oppressor and fail to restrain him."

It is no secret to you, my brothers, that the people of Islam have been afflicted with oppression, hostility, and injustice by the Judeo-Christian alliance and its supporters. This shows our enemies' belief that Muslims' blood is the cheapest and that their property and wealth is merely loot. Your blood has been spilt in Palestine and Iraq, and the horrific images of the massacre in Qana in Lebanon are still fresh in people's minds. The massacres that have taken place in Tajikistan, Burma, Kashmir, Assam, the Philippines, Fatani, Ogaden, Somalia, Eritrea, Chechnya, and Bosnia-Herzegovina send shivers down our spines and stir up our passions. All this has happened before the eyes and ears of the world, but the blatant imperial arrogance of America, under the cover of the immoral United Nations, has prevented the dispossessed from arming themselves.

So the people of Islam realised that they were the fundamental target of the hostility of the Judeo-Crusader alliance. All the false propaganda about the supposed rights of Islam was abandoned in the face of the attacks and massacres committed against Muslims everywhere, the latest and most serious of which—the greatest disaster to befall the Muslims since the death of the Prophet Muhammad—is the occupation of Saudi Arabia, which is the corner-stone of the Islamic world, place of revelation, source of the Prophetic mission, and home of the Noble Ka'ba where Muslims direct their prayers. Despite this, it was occupied by the armies of the Christians, the Americans, and their allies.

I meet you today in the midst of this gloomy scenario, but also in light of the tremendous, blessed awakening that has swept across the world, and particularly the Islamic world. After the scholars of Islam underwent an enforced absence—enforced due to the oppressive Crusader campaign led by America in the fear that these scholars will incite our Islamic *umma* against its enemies, in the same way as did the pious scholars of old (God bless their souls) such as ibn Taymiyya and al-Izz ibn Abd al-Salam—this Judeo-Crusader alliance undertook to kill and arrest the righteous scholars and hardworking preachers. May God sanctify who He wishes. They killed the *mujahid* Sheikh Abdallah Azzam, they arrested Sheikh Ahmed Yassin in Jerusalem, and they killed the *mujahid* Sheikh Omar Abd al-Rahman in America, as well as arresting—on the advice of America—a large number of scholars, preachers and youth in Saudi Arabia. The most prominent of these were Sheikh Salman al-Auda and Sheikh Safar al-Hawali and their brothers.

This injustice was inflicted on us, too, as we were prevented from talking to Muslims and were hounded out of Saudi Arabia to Pakistan, Sudan, and then Afghanistan. That is what led to this long absence of mine, but by the grace of God there became available a safe base in Khurasan, high in the peaks of the Hindu Kush, the very same peaks upon which were smashed, by the grace of God, the largest infidel military force in the world, and on which the myth of the great powers perished before the cries of the holy warriors: God is greatest!

And today, in the same peaks of Afghanistan, we work to do away with the injustice that has befallen our *umma* at the hands of the Judeo-Crusader alliance, especially after its occupation of Jerusalem and its appropriation of Saudi Arabia. We pray to God that He might bless us with victory—He is our protector and is well capable of doing so.

And so here we are today, working and discussing with each other to find ways of rectifying what has happened to the Islamic world generally and Saudi Arabia in particular. We need to study the appropriate paths to take in order to restore things to good order, and to restore to the people their rights after the considerable damage and harm inflicted on their life and religion. This has afflicted every section of society, whether civilian or military or security personnel, whether employees or merchants, young or old, university students, graduates or the unemployed, who now represent a broad section of society numbering hundreds of thousands. The situation in Saudi Arabia has begun to resemble a huge volcano that is about to explode and destroy unbelief and corruption, wherever it comes from. The two explosions in Riyadh and Khobar are merely warning signs pointing to this destructive torrent which is produced by bitter repression, terrible injustice, and the humiliating poverty that we see today.

People are struggling even with the basics of everyday life, and everyone talks frankly about economic recession, price inflation, mounting debts, and prison overcrowding. Low-income government employees talk to you about their debts in the tens or hundreds of thousands of riyals, whilst complaining that the riyal's value is declining dramatically. Domestic debts owed by the government to its citizens have reached 340 billion riyals, and are rising daily due to usurious interest, let alone all the foreign debt. People are wondering: are we really the biggest source of oil in the world? They feel that God is bringing this torture upon them because they have not spoken out against the regime's injustice and illegitimate behaviour, the most prominent aspects of which are its failure to rule in accordance with God's law, its depriving of legal rights to its servants, its permitting of the American occupiers into Saudi Arabia, and its arresting of righteous scholars—inheritors of the Prophet's legacy—and unjustly throwing them in prison. The regime has desecrated its legitimacy through many of its own actions, the most important being:

1. Its suspension of the rulings of the Islamic law and replacement thereof with man-made laws, and its entering into a bloody confrontation with the righteous scholars and pious youth. May God sanctify whom He pleases.

2. Its inability to protect the land and its allowing the enemies of God to occupy it for years in the form of the American Crusaders, who have become the principal reason for all aspects of our land's disastrous predicament.

The voices of the shadows have spoken up, their eyes uncovering the veil of injustice and their noses smelling the stench of corruption. The voices of reform have spoken up, calling for the situation to be put right: they have sent petitions, testimonies, and requests for reform. In the year 1411 AH, at the time of the Gulf War, a petition was sent to the king with around 400 signatures calling for reform in the country, but he made a mockery of them by completely ignoring their advice, and the situation went from bad to worse.

Brother Muslims in Saudi Arabia, does it make any sense at all that our country is the biggest purchaser of weapons from America in the world and America's biggest trading partner in the region, while at the very same time the Americans are occupying Saudi Arabia and supporting—with money, arms, and manpower—their Jewish brothers in the occupation of Palestine and their murder and expulsion of Muslims there? Depriving these occupiers of the huge returns they receive from their trade with us is a very important way of supporting the *jihad* against them, and we expect you to boycott all American goods. Men of the radiant future of our *umma* of Muhammad, raise the banner of *jihad* up high against the Judeo-American alliance that has occupied the holy places of Islam. God told his Prophet: "He will not let the deeds of those who are killed for His cause come to nothing; He will guide them and put them in a good state; He will admit them into the Garden He has already made known to them." And the Prophet said: "There are one hundred levels in Heaven that God has prepared for the holy warriors who have died for Him, between two levels as between the earth and the sky." And the *al-Jami al-Sahih* notes that the Prophet said: "The best martyrs are those who stay in the battle line and do not turn their faces away until they are killed. They will achieve the highest level of Heaven, and their Lord will look kindly upon them. When your Lord looks kindly upon a slave in the world, He will not hold him to account." And he said: "The martyr has a guarantee from God: He forgives him at the first drop of his blood and shows him his seat in Heaven. He decorates him with the jewels of faith, protects him from the torment of the grave, keeps him safe on the day of judgment, places a crown of dignity on his head with the finest rubies in the world, marries him to seventy-two of the pure virgins of paradise and intercedes on behalf of seventy of his relatives," as related by Ahmad al-Tirmidhi in an authoritative *hadith*.

I say to the youth of Islam who have waged *jihad* in Afghanistan and Bosnia-Herzegovina, with their financial, spiritual, linguistic, and scholarly resources, that the battle is not yet over. I remind them of what Gabriel said to the Prophet, after the battle of Ahzab: "When the Messenger of God, prayers and peace be upon him, departed to Medina and laid down his sword, Gabriel came to him and said: 'You have laid down your sword? By God, the angels have not yet laid down their swords. Get up and go with whoever is with you to the Bani Qorayza, and I will go ahead of you to shake their fortresses and strike fear into them.' So Gabriel went off, accompanied by his pageant of angels, the Prophet, and his holy warriors and helpers." This is as it was told by al-Bukhari.

I say to our Muslim brothers across the world: your brothers in Saudi Arabia and Palestine are calling for your help and asking you to share with them in the *jihad* against the enemies of God, your enemies the Israelis and Americans. They are asking you to defy them in whatever way you possibly can, so as to expel them in defeat and humiliation from the holy places of Islam. God Almighty has said: "If they seek help from you against persecution, it is your duty to assist them."

Cavalry of Islam, be mounted! This is a difficult time, so you yourselves must be tough. You should know that your coming-together and cooperation in order to liberate the holy places of Islam is the right step towards unification of the word of our *umma* under the banner of God's unity. At this point we can only raise our palms humbly to ask God Almighty to provide good fortune and success in this matter.

Lord, bless your slave and messenger Muhammad, and his family and companions. Our final prayer is praise to God, Lord of the worlds.

Your brother in Islam,

Osama bin Muhammad bin Laden